MEANING
—— OVER ——
MEMORY

The University of

North Carolina Press

Chapel Hill & London

MEANING

OVER

MEMORY

Recasting
the Teaching
of Culture
and History

PETER N. STEARNS

Library of Congress

Cataloging-in-Publication Data

Stearns, Peter N.

  Meaning over memory : recasting

the teaching of culture and history /

by Peter N. Stearns.

    p. cm.

  Includes bibliographical references and index.

  ISBN 0-8078-2090-3 (cloth : alk. paper)

    1. Civilization—Historiography—History.

  2. Civilization—Study and teaching—United

States.   3. Humanities—Study and teaching—

United States.   4. Historiography—United

States—History.   I. Title.

CB15.S74   1993

907'.1'073—dc20   92-50815

                                        CIP

This book was published with the assistance of

the H. Eugene and Lillian Lehman Fund of the

University of North Carolina Press.

The paper in this book meets the guidelines for

permanence and durability of the Committee

on Production Guidelines for Book Longevity

of the Council on Library Resources.

97 96 95 94 93   5 4 3 2 1

For Clio and Cordelia,

humanists by nature

and by name

CONTENTS

PREFACE

This book offers a wide-ranging new look at education in the humanities—the disciplines that study people's expressions and social institutions. My goal is to improve student understanding of how cultures operate and how societies function, by using advances in humanistic research and by rethinking some of the purposes of existing humanities training in our schools and colleges.

Humanities programs, particularly in history (in the schools) and English (in the colleges) are hotly contested at present, and the debates have spilled over into the public arena. This book addresses the debates, for they are inescapable and, in certain respects, potentially creative. But it explicitly seeks to establish a different basis for discussing humanities education by focusing primarily on the habits of mind the humanities should be establishing rather than merely the subject matter to which students should be exposed.

In this crucial respect, the book differs from several recent pleas for reason and tolerance that, though otherwise sensible, have not managed to move discussion to the proper plane.[1] It is important to stake out a new balance between traditional coverage of Western culture and our urgent need to understand African and Asian cultures, and the following chapters will venture another statement in this area. It is valid, also, to plead for a new dose of tolerance on both of the principal sides in the current war over the humanities.[2] But, as we will see, the bitter quarrels over whose cultures to teach profoundly misconstrue what should be the fundamental cast of the debate. Despite all the ink that has been spilled, we need a fresh start.

The central purpose of courses in the humanities is the inculcation of essential analytical skills that are not easy to define (because they are less precise than their analogues in science) but are vital for a critically informed citizenry. A discussion of humanities goals must include awareness of the need to widen the factual frame of reference, but it should concentrate on identifying and teaching methods by which we gain understanding, interpretive habits that allow us to move from the inevitably bounded examples of any classroom to other instances in which the role of culture demands assessment or the nature of social change must be grasped.

Such goals are ambitious, but this book argues that they are attainable—or at least open to measurable advancement—if the humanities are understood not primarily as guardians of unchanging truths but as sources of new knowledge. The gains achieved by the humanities outside the classroom need to be conveyed more effectively within it. Sketching the means and purposes of this translation constitutes the quietly radical purpose of the following chapters. Of course, the furor roused by the standoff between conservative canonists and political correctness adepts must be handled as well, but my real aim is different: to recast the debate itself.

These are truly exciting times in the humanities. Advances in knowledge have been accumulating for almost three decades, thanks to movement into new directions of research. The current debates, though frequently misdirected, convey the excitement of the major teaching fields. We are, as a nation, facing substantial problems in redefining our own identity or identities and in relocating our place in the world. We realize, sometimes inchoately, that lessons in history and culture are central to our groping quests. This is why debates in the humanities rouse such passions. This is why a new set of opportunities has arisen: not to retrieve some largely imaginary past attainments, but to place the humanities at the center of a new effort at social understanding.

The challenge is obvious, as is the urgency. A somewhat similar moment existed twenty-five years ago, the last time the nation debated its meanings and recognized the need to redefine humanistic teaching in the process. This mood faded before constructive change could result, and humanities teaching largely returned to the slightly shopworn formulas of the past.

Opportunities are greater now, if we can place partisan quarrels in the proper perspective. The national search for an understanding of our past and of the cultures around us is even more intense than in the troubled 1960s. Equally important, the resources made available by advances in humanistic scholarship are immensely richer than they were a generation ago. Using them, we can derive more from the lessons about cultural meanings and social change. This book, in joining a number of practical efforts that already point the way, seeks to extend this educational horizon.

ACKNOWLEDGMENTS

The number of people who have contributed to my sense of what humanities teaching is all about is far too great for me to mention them all here. A variety of teachers have responded to earlier writings of mine in this area and have clarified my thinking in the process. I am grateful to them and to the many creative teachers I've encountered in workshops over the past decade. Experiences with the College Board and the Educational Testing Service have been important to me, and I'm grateful to the officials and teachers involved with projects there, including Larry Beaber, James Herbert, Robert Orrill, and Robert Blackey. Two teachers associated with Board programs helped show me what an imaginative classroom could be like (Millie Alpern) and why world history was the way to go (Vivian Tom). Alan Kennedy of Carnegie Mellon's English Department has assisted me greatly in the cultural studies area. For suggestions and comments on the manuscript, my thanks go also to Carol Stearns, Joel Tarr, and John Modell. Steve Beaudoin and Gail Dickey aided greatly in the manuscript preparation. Judith Modell made a number of inquiries, for which I am grateful. Pamela Upton and others at the University of North Carolina Press managed editorial work with unusual skill. My biggest debt, overall, goes to the students whose responses, comments, and enthusiasms continue to help me define a constructive path, at least for my own efforts.

MEANING
—— OVER ——
MEMORY

INTRODUCTION

Battles swirl around American education in the early 1990s. This conflict over schooling is hardly unprecedented, for the United States has long maintained something of a love/hate relationship with teaching, but there is no question that some of the recent controversies have reached significant, perhaps troubling, intensity. Many college campuses are newly politicized after a decade or more of relative tranquility following the end of active student protests in 1973. New demands from minority students, international students, women, and gays are supported by certain faculty members for whom political agendas coincide with new scholarly approaches that emphasize diversity and relativity over the presumably less mutable verities of a white, male, heterosexual establishment. Many university administrators, eager for calm, anxious to appeal to new sources of students in a demographic trough period, and sincerely convinced of the justice of many minority claims, contribute to an intellectual climate that can range from foolishness to oppression. In late 1990, *Newsweek* wrote of a new canon of "political correctness" that insisted on banning even somewhat humorous sallies against any of the protected campus groups. A law school was prevented from discussing a case involving custody rights of a lesbian mother, because students thought that even imagining arguments against the mother's claims might be "hurtful" to the group in question. Several colleges urged a new spelling, *womyn*, to make the separateness and equality of the genders crystal clear.[1]

But it takes two sides to politicize an issue, and although the demands for reform won the greatest attention, they followed, in part, from new conservative strictures on academic life that generated additional expressions simply in response. In their zeal to make capital out of politically correct campus excesses, too many journalists neglected this context. During the 1980s, a growing percentage of

I

scientific funding, even into such areas as psychiatry and psychology, came from the Department of Defense. DOD projects were by no means necessarily tainted or restricted, but they cast at least potential shadows on free scientific inquiry. More direct was the goals redefinition of the National Endowment for the Humanities, begun under William Bennett and substantially maintained by his successor, Lynne Cheney. The NEH frowned on innovations in key disciplines such as history and English, arguing that new scholarly interests like social history should be jettisoned or at least downgraded in favor of reexaminations of the great traditions of American and Western society, primarily meaning official political experience and "great ideas." Bennett, for example, specifically condemned projects that studied the working-class experience as irrelevant to the real past.[2] By the mid-1980s, several individual scholars had joined the crusade, lamenting the dilution of attention to the great classics of Western philosophy and literature or the great men of American democracy and producing lists of facts, derived mainly from these areas, that every educated person should know.[3]

The gauntlet thrown down, it was hardly surprising that, toward 1990, revived academic radicalism generated additional conservative efforts to define a humanistic canon that could resist change and challenge. The American Association of Colleges won NEH support for a Cultural Legacies project that, although not entirely monochrome, focused largely on disseminating core curricula that touted classical great works and the values they presumably represented. Dissident groups and other traditions need not apply. A conservative historian at the University of Wisconsin founded the National Association of Scholars to defend university traditions, criticizing special efforts at minority hiring and urging colleges to instill a solid knowledge of American history and culture "before" turning to such specialties as Afro-American history—thereby implying, of course, that a standard American history could be defined apart from the latter themes.

Thus have the lines seemingly been drawn, focusing on basic questions about how education and scholarship are to be defined. Humanistic disciplines in particular are engaged in this debate because their research methods are harder to pinpoint than those of the sciences and some social sciences and because they deal most directly with "values." Innovations in humanities scholarship, dating back to the 1960s, have also provoked concern and uncertainty, leading some conservatives to advocate a return to teaching with no specific scholarly agenda at all.

Controversies also engulfed primary and secondary school education. Though these battles had receded somewhat from public view by the 1990s following a series of dire reports in the mid-1980s, they were still of considerable potential importance, and they related—as too few observers noted—to the more public arguments at the university level.

Thus, if colleges owed their students a prolonged exposure to the great canons of Western literature and history, so too the high schools had a primary responsibility—along with their duty to inculcate the skills necessary to redeem us against the Japanese economic challenge—to civilize the savages by introducing them to Western and democratic values. History, wrote one critic of recent scholarship, must provide students with examples of heroic behavior, so that students could in turn model their lives appropriately; other information about the past was irrelevant to this high purpose and might even dilute it.[4] To the civilizing argument was joined a more familiar but unquestionably anguished lament about how few of the necessary facts of educated life students seemed to know. Not only were they unfamiliar with most of the items on the new pedagogical knowledge lists; if the lists were located in Florida these students would apparently, given their poor map skills, be unable to find them in the first place. (Over 40 percent of American high school students could not find Florida on an unlabeled map, according to one survey.) Clearly, students needed to be drilled extensively in basic skills and data and tested carefully on their level of mastery. Teachers' latitude must be curtailed lest they stray from the essential education diet, and increasingly detailed curricula, tied to the omnipresent tests, ruled the classroom agenda.

By the early 1990s many of these developments, it must be noted, had passed from controversy to virtually established wisdom at the precollege level. Lively discussion still surrounded such issues as how much minority history to teach in a mainstream U.S. survey course, or how to introduce students to data about the wider world without losing an essential Western flavor. Despite these gray areas, however, precollege teaching increasingly emphasized drills, factual retention, and centrally prepared, machine-gradable tests that were, in the humanities and social studies areas, primarily focused on conventional literary and historical themes. Textbooks both reflected and reified the process; in so-called world history, for example, the most venturesome basic high school text risked devoting only 25 percent of its total space to distinctly non-Western areas, while U.S. surveys made some gingerly bows to women and African Americans—usually in feature sections unrelated to the central, testable text coverage.

As far as many students were concerned, the battles that radicals of various stripes purported to wage over college curricula had already been largely lost during the "preparation" of the middle school and high school years, before college was more than a glimmer in a loan officer's eye. These students already knew, when they got to college, that U.S. history equaled democracy, equal opportunity, and unprecedented social mobility, and that literary study consisted of memorizing character names and plot lines. They certainly knew that history consisted almost exclusively of "one damned thing after another"—though they did not know that it was Woodrow Wilson who first said this. They might not like what they knew—indeed, they commonly professed active hatred of history memorization—and they might well find what they knew inapplicable to their own life experiences, but it would be hard to wean them from their machine-gradable molds. They certainly, as one scholar put it, possessed a "massive, uniform subsurface reef of cultural memory" that severely constrained further learning.[5] Knowing that history consists of names and dates, they would be extremely skeptical of claims to the contrary.

All sorts of educational issues properly concern both policymakers and the interested public, and what follows by no means delves into all of these areas, though many are evoked at various points. Options for school organization, including tracking, or problems of teacher rewards and training are vital concerns that are not entirely unrelated to my subject, but I do not directly explore them. The same holds true for the ongoing problems of racial balance and integration. The focus of this essay is on the curriculum and curricular goals. Even that coverage is limited, with my primary attention going to a broadly construed definition of the humanities: the disciplines of literary study, philosophy, history, and some of the kindred social sciences such as anthropology and sociology. Educational problems in science have more to do with teaching techniques than with curricular goals per se. This was not always the case, of course. In the nineteenth century, battles were fought simply to establish the place of science in the curriculum, and then the conflict between evolution and creationism propelled science to the center of major debates about the relationship between education and values. While echoes of these discussions linger, unquestionably, the main arguments have faded, though an important discussion of general education science teaching—including its cultural assumptions—is beginning to gain ground. It is in the humanities area that we now confront the most agonizing issues about the purposes and directions of the appropriate curriculum, and though the resultant contests are less stark, they evoke some parallels with the earlier creationist controversies. It is vital to improve our understanding of the debates now raging, sometimes out of the public eye, and in my judgment it is vital to resolve some of the major debates decisively and imaginatively lest other efforts at educational improvement, even in organizational and training areas, bear stunted fruit.

The humanities embraces a broad spectrum of disciplines that form the core of much research and most teaching about the nature of society and cultures—the principal relationships among people that go beyond the strictly biological or economic. History and English constitute the core of the teaching humanities, but foreign languages and philosophy also enter in, particularly beyond the basic skill levels. Foreign language study logically flows into the teaching of literature and, once some fluency is acquired, into history and anthropology as well, and in what follows *cultural study* is not meant to be confined to works written in English or to students reading in English; we will return to the confusion with the first stages of language training in a later chapter. Also included here, though not usually labeled as humanistic disciplines, are cultural anthropology and many branches of sociology that rely wholly or in part on impressionistic data for generalizations about human social relationships.[6] Humanities, then, includes important parts of the social sciences, and interdisciplinary connections in research methods and in theory will play an important role in my assessments. The disciplines share the task of finding newly solid bases on which to build their educational programs.

Because my focus is on the humanities generally and broadly defined, I do not spend a great deal of time worrying about how much of which discipline should appear at what level. Educators concerned with the high schools have recurrently fulminated (since the late 1930s) about the dilution of history amid a more general social studies amalgam. The issues involved are important, but they have been widely discussed elsewhere.[7] A variety of sensible recent statements has boosted the historical core once again. The debate is particularly relevant to this essay when the dilution involves not just including some sociology along with history but also moving away from the serious study of society entirely (through whatever disciplinary combination) by injecting training in "social skills" such as checkbook writing or the other embellishments of "commercial economics." The inadequacy of most of our foreign language education, which far too often compels numbingly basic training at the college level, is another perennial controversy relevant to this discussion but not elaborately explored. In order to focus on the main thrusts of humanistic analysis in relation to educational goals, I have relegated important subsidiary problems to one side, though they can be integrated into my the central argument without great difficulty.

This is a book, then, about defining teaching goals and appropriate strategies in American education at various levels, with major emphasis on the disciplines that study human and social values and behaviors. It argues against the extreme positions currently available, in part espousing a middle way but primarily searching for a distinctive alternative not adequately explored in the extensive and often challenging recent literature on similar topics. The humanities, particularly, have been badly represented in discussions of educational goals and implementations; agendas have been needlessly polarized, while—still more important—the implications of new humanistic research have been unduly ignored in the educational realm.

I need to call attention briefly to the complex combination of compromise and radicalism in my treatment. In dealing with the current furor over conventional humanistic coverage versus multiculturalism, I join a few other recent observers in offering intermediate positions and certainly in rejecting the extremes urged from both sides. A purely white, elitist cultural diet is no longer tenable or desirable, but neither is Afrocentrism the only valid alternative. Other issues, too, will find degrees of compromise in the following pages, and on some points I'm quite content to be seen as a reconciling voice eager to combine genuine elements of both the polarized approaches. My mugwumpery is not, I hope, cosmetic. I share skepticism about some recent attempts by conservative educators to acknowledge the "inevitability" of multiculturalism while urging that it be "done right." Without concrete demonstrations of real commitment to cultural diversity, these gestures may be, whether intentionally or not, fraudulent; where I deal with compromise, I try to offer substance along with honeyed words.

At the same time, I insist that my intentions go far beyond peace-making. My goals are more radical than the radicals' in that I seek to reshape the discussion of the humanities by moving away from debates about which groups it would privilege—essentially a turf fight, however recondite its phrasing—and toward a determination of what kinds of analyses it should further. I aim for a real transformation of humanities education in light of the kinds of analytical perspectives—the habits of mind—it should inculcate. Teaching in the humanities should above all foster a critical imagination—and this point is not recognized in most of the current debates.

The middle course steered through this book is easy enough to state using a specific case in point. Although trained to teach Western civilization courses, and having benefited greatly from such a course in my own collegiate past, I was converted some years ago to a world history approach. The international context in which Americans now operate, as well as the increasingly international sources of American immigration, call for knowledge of traditions and processes beyond those of Western Europe. Happily, after considerable self-education, I discovered that world history offers not only vital information about diverse historical trajectories, but also a host of challenging analytical themes; I also discovered that it can be presented in manageable form, albeit with massive departures not only from the subject matter but also from the detailed national coverage instilled in the Western civilization teaching tradition. While granting that it is difficult to convey, in world history, some of the rich flavor of the specifically Western past, I remain convinced—against the partisans of a more traditional insistence on teaching respect for our own presumed values above all others—that the larger canvas is essential. Indeed, it was the lack of an adequate "non-Western" perspective that drove me to my self-improvement project in the first place. My evolution parallels that of a growing number of other historians who are persuaded that studies of single major areas, and particularly of the West, must yield to a more genuinely international context. The resulting world history is measurably different from Western history in concept as well as coverage, and it must not be misrepresented by simply relabeling as "global" a course or a textbook that still maintains a primarily Western focus—an impulse all too prevalent in American education at several levels.

Yet—consistent with this middle way—I dissent also from those radicals who want to leave Western civilization out of history requirements entirely, so that students can be properly socialized to, say, the African experience. And I dissent from world history scholars, not necessarily radical in other respects, who seek to downgrade essential Western coverage in their eagerness to convey alternative values and to combat the undeniable tendency to emerge from history studies with a "West is best" outlook. Western history, particularly from the fifteenth century onward, is a vital part of the world experience—at times even a predominant part, though never to the exclusion of other important areas. The need for balance, quite apart from questions of showing due regard for the traditions of a civilization particularly important to our own institutions, requires integration of Western history into the world panorama in approximate proportion to its international role.

The middle way in today's educational thicket has too rarely been spelled out, partly because it is less dramatic and more complex than either/or alternatives. In survey history teaching, one is either for Western civilization or for a somewhat de-Westernized world history, with scant in-between. Efforts to spell out compromise positions do exist. A recent report by the Bradley Commission on History in the Schools seeks to emphasize both standard political experience and the new social history (though it tends to push the latter more at the grade school than at the high school level), and it makes appropriate noises about both the West and the world.[8] Yet the report does not fully face the hard question of how to cover all these issues manageably and coherently, and thus it can be read as a fuller endorsement of present curricular emphases than its authors intend. A good section on world history follows a previous Western civ framework, with no discussion of the hard stuff of integrating, relegating, and establishing priorities. And the report obscures its interest in a middle way by adopting titles such as "historical literacy," designed to appeal to those authorities who view history as a parade of mostly conventional, testable facts. In an educational environment that is heavily polarized—though with most of the chips on conservative tables—establishing a viable set of compromises remains a useful task, and a portion of my work is targeted to this end.

As a middle-way statement, then, this book shares the "radical" contention that the Allan Bloom–NEH insistence on conventional humanities coverage closes American minds and neglects the growing pluralism of American society and its student bodies.[9] But it rejects the most simplistic alternative, which is to produce curricula that list the achievements of minority groups and other cultures simply for their own sakes, for this approach can lack coherence and fails to rethink educational goals at sufficient depth. It can also, as insightful critics have already noted, lead to some dangerously mindless uses of culture to celebrate particular groups and to generate "feel-goodness" without generating any understanding of what society is all about.[10]

But middle-way mugwumpery, even translated into doable educational agendas, is not the main point. What both conservatives and many radical critics have missed, in my judgment, is an appropriate emphasis on education as a process of discovery and debate. They have missed the implications of much of the most insightful scholarship in various humanistic fields. Thus, while conservative educators emphasize their desire to concentrate on Western and American traditions, their opponents (particularly when discussing high school or entry-level college courses) tend to urge greater coverage of alternatives. Don't give us American great men, but make sure students know about some great women, or at least key aspects of women's experience. Do less on the West, more on Africa. These appeals are correct to a degree, in that they redress the misleading narrowness of the conventional agenda, but they still view education as consisting primarily of a series of datapoints. It would be possible, following this view (and I confess to being tempted in this direction for a time), to prepare a "better" list of facts that everyone should know, using demography as well as demagogues, classes and ethnics as well as classical ethics—without thinking through the implications of the list concept in the first place.

Better lists would still mislead, and it is best not to play this game at all. The purpose of education is to provide understanding—a pious sentiment with which most people would doubtless agree. It is increasingly possible, based in part on new discoveries but also in part on old principles, to envisage curricula that would promote understanding rather than overwhelming critical thought with memorization, whether old or new. Exploring this goal, which has been downplayed in the zealous discussion of whose coverage is best, is the purpose of this book.

This is hardly a solo flight. Various historians, including three senior figures who contributed to the Bradley Commission report, have urged the salience of their discipline primarily in terms of the insights it provides, not the data it amasses. During the 1990s a new project, funded by two prestigious foundations, seeks to review high school testing procedures, to wean them away from machine-gradable, factual coverage and toward more reliance on special projects, written reports, and other performances that will better demonstrate the capacities to think and to organize rather than simply to regurgitate.[11] Also, a wealth of commentary on educational issues by historians and other humanists points firmly in the appropriate direction. David Bromwich, for example, emphasizes the folly of siding fully with either elitists or radicals in the hot debate over teaching literature. On the history side, Elizabeth Fox-Genovese similarly criticizes feminists who seek to throw out the canon in favor of teaching only about minorities and women, on the sensible grounds that: "If you do not include a heavy dose of the history of elite white males, how do you explain why women and members of minorities are not running the world? How do we explain thousands of years of submission by those we claim to honor and respect?"[12] Other scholars and teachers also offer insights of great strength. Signs of this sort are immensely cheering. They do go against the current grain, however, and they can only benefit from some further comment on wider educational purposes. The full statement, in my judgment, has yet to be made.

For although an encouraging number of innovative efforts are being developed, they are not clearly winning the high ground, and they are not always coherently defined. For example, the portfolio evaluation schemes that are gaining popularity as alternatives to machine-graded testing can become mired in enthusiasm for technique and style over analytical content; students capable of presenting a vivid reenactment may not always be judged in terms of their grasp of the meaning of a past culture. Eloquence—surely to be rewarded as a general rule—may overshadow real perceptiveness. The portfolio plans, in other words, move in the right direction, but they need to be connected with a wider definition of the substantive fields involved.

A number of high school and grade school history projects have been undertaken in various parts of the country, some of them linked to a general project called CHART (Collaboratives for Humanities and Arts Teaching). Many of these projects are founded on a goal of encouraging students "to think and act like historians." The projects have accomplished all sorts of good things, including eliciting an impressive fund of enthusiasm and intelligence from the teachers involved. Beyond these individual projects, there are larger ventures as well that hold considerable promise. The recasting of California's school curriculum in the social studies, for example, makes (or intends to make) grade school work more serious, builds real sequences of learning in a field too often treated as a scattered collection of individual courses, and attempts (though inadequately, I believe) some integration of multiculturalism and mainstream cultural interests. The College Board is developing "Pacesetter" models for achieving more analytical goals in high school English and world history courses (as well as in other areas), and the planning efforts have stirred great interest. Initiatives of this sort directly inspire many of my own proposals. But they also signal the twin difficulties of innovation in the present educational climate. First, they are hemmed in by the inescapable constraints of standardized, machine-graded testing; a South Carolina CHART project, for example, grinds to a halt every six weeks to give students time to memorize dates and names. Second, they are often based on an unduly limited understanding of what the proper analytical goals of the humanities should be and thus, although reaching bravely for higher attainment, they fail to reach far enough. Teachers' conceptions of how to "think like a historian," for example (apart from the phrase's suggestion of a misleadingly professional goal), sometimes turn out to be inadequate, as we will discuss later on. The intentions are exciting, and the CHART projects and other brave experiments are definitely worth pursuing, but the terrain is not adequately mapped. Even for many innovators, the humanities need a fuller statement of purpose.

Ventures in humanities education must and will be diverse. No single plan will suffice. Exciting innovations are already occurring; no reform approach should imply a virgin discovery, and certainly what follows is heavily dependent on ideals and practical classroom experiences in which many teachers are already involved. The desirability of a systematic statement, however, is clear.

One of the more pressing needs in this area is demonstrated by the relative obscurity of some of the most exciting new teaching in the humanities, compared to the trumpet blasts of public argument between radicals and conservatives. It is easy to ignore constructive change amid the furor of the more dramatic debate, and for every member of the interested public aware of humanities reforms, there are five who know only the real or imagined problems of political correctness. Both sides attack not only each other but also real or (often) imagined realities in the present educational system. The recent conflicts thus make it easier to criticize than to project consistent and substantive alternatives. Some commentators have indeed made something of a career out of blasting first conventional textbooks, then radical alternatives, then compromise proposals—all with great intelligence and with some suggestions of positive principles, but without risking a real plan. This book spends some time pecking away at other positions but seeks primarily to construct a feasible alternative to what now exists and to the major options currently at loggerheads.

In the following pages, then, my goal is to provide fuller information on the relationship between teaching and discovery, and between teaching and scholarship. My path skirts between current stridencies, seeking both some conciliation and some real alternatives to the diverse, often belligerent statements currently available. I deal with some basic principles but also with some curricular practicalities. This book is not a formal study of education or of the learning process, though it will at points comment on such studies. Emphasizing mainly the humanities and "softer" social sciences, and history in particular, it will also venture some remarks on other disciplines and on various methodologies. The disciplinary focus derives, obviously, from my own experience, but also from the central position of humanities in the current educational debates. The questions to be explored seem, to me, fundamental: If American education, aside from training in obvious skills, is not primarily devoted to the explicit defense of Western civilization and American democracy, then what might its purpose be? If we don't measure what facts students are mastering, how do we evaluate them, and what are teachers to teach? And can general sentiments about promoting understanding translate into feasible curricula of any sort?

Amid such murky waters, the central arguments of this book must be kept in mind. It attacks some of the dominant beliefs about humanities teaching, chiefly—though not exclusively—those emanating from conservative academics and the Reaganite establishment and its successors. It points, however, to areas of substantial (if sometimes unrecognized) agreement and, above all, to the need to consider basic approaches in a framework different from those currently emphasized by several opposing camps.

One other radical departure: This discussion does not depend on an argument that American students' grasp of the humanities has deteriorated. Such may be the case, but the facts are not clear. Educational critics, most of them conservative, have made much of their claims of declination. Their purpose, of course, is to argue that we have already moved too far toward innovation and must pull back in order to regain the ground lost since the good old days. These arguments are suspect. Applied to literacy, they are often demonstrably incorrect.[13] What is obvious, instead, is that we should not simply be doing better than we now are, but better than we ever managed in the past. Doing better surely includes retaining some current and past goals, but it must involve substantial change. It is not only misleading but factually incorrect to constrain discussion by pretending that, at some unspecified time in the past, students once gained more from the humanities than they now do. The goal—a challenging one—is to determine what we can do better, not to indulge in misguided nostalgia.

As a book of opinion—for I make no pretense of presenting yet another set of formal findings about the educational process—what follows depends on some brief acquaintance with my own credentials as an author. This study falls outside my usual genre; for the most part my work has focused on historical research and history writing for teaching purposes (which often means textbooks). I have taught college-level history for more than twenty-five years. I have also worked with high school history programs in various ways, though since my own graduation I have actually entered high schools only to observe my children's progress. Work with the College Board, particularly the Advanced Placement program, acquainted me with many high school teaching issues, and I have also participated in a number of summer workshops on various aspects of social history designed for secondary school teachers—most of these, in fairness, funded by the NEH, though largely in its pre-Bennett days. Further, I have been involved with a number of school curriculum projects, including an effort to relate examinations to revised history coverage in the Pittsburgh school system. None of this makes me a certified expert on educational settings, particularly those below the college level. My work has also involved me in some projects, including the compilation of a massive high school text, of the sort that I will criticize in these pages; one learns from experience, even at the expense of lifelong consistency.

Finally, I have and have had children in the school system, a situation that has contributed to my sense of what education should be about and of how often we currently fall short. When my seventh grader reported that, in a relatively well-taught social studies course, one unit emphasized burial practices and the pyramids as the core of our understanding of ancient Egypt, to the exclusion of other subjects—an approach that seemed to translate the classroom experience into an American Express tour of famous sights—I had to ponder a bit about what kind of thinking went into justifying topic selection, or whether much thinking was involved at all. That there were questions to be asked about ancient Egypt (beyond how tall the pyramids were) that might shed some light on how societies function was not acknowledged: hit the monuments and move along.

The context for the following discussion is broader than the current debates over ideological direction on college campuses, encompassing more than impressionistic potshots at the earlier levels of schooling. There is widespread agreement that American educational standards must become more rigorous, with greater attention being paid to basic subjects, less watering down of the curriculum, and possibly longer school years. Educational clients should not be content with the status quo, as observers of many stripes agree, and I certainly share that judgment.[14] But they should also rebel against some of the reform scenarios being sketched. The danger is that rigor may be misdefined, that more education may turn out to mean more passive learning, that zealous testing will generate misleading, even destructive, measurements of accountability. Some of these trends, indeed, have already been launched. Despite the voluminous literature on educational goals already available, there is need for further debate and for fundamental clarifications based on a better understanding of the extent to which knowledge itself has changed. Quite possibly, more zealous instruction in traditional learning would be preferable to the current educational drift, but such instruction would fall tragically short of what *might* be attained.

Discussion of humanities education also involves politics, and any sketch of alternatives to traditional emphases must squarely face the issue of socialization for a democracy. This subject will not be my starting point, for some substantive educational agendas must be established before one rushes into a defense of presumably essential values, but I will not evade the challenge.

When I began my own scholarly career in the humanities, I did not feel engaged in an overtly political agenda. (Radicals and some conservatives might easily point out that I was wrong, or at least naive.) I was interested in modestly expanding knowledge about the past, and although some kindred historians were attaching the same goal to more partisan arguments about working-class or minority causes, I did not find the linkage essential. In the past decade, radical uses of new knowledge have been more than matched by conservative attempts to appropriate an educational agenda for their defense of the status quo—an appropriation all the more influential because it is often masked by claims of neutrality, as opposed to the frankly political arguments of multiculturalists and other reform advocates. Thus Lynne Cheney of the NEH combined warnings against radicalism (which she saw as the chief problem facing universities—an empirically dubious claim) with active promotion of a fairly traditional, coverage-dominated educational agenda that included national standards for secondary schools; the combination inevitably injected politics into the curricular proposals—whatever their potential independent merits—because attacks on radicalism proved central to their defense.

In a grant application issued in the fall of 1992, the Department of Education's often-innovative Fund for the Improvement of Postsecondary Education claimed that "most colleges seem to have reached a local agreement on the proper content of general education" and went on to argue that implementation, not goals, should at least for the moment command our creative attention. This claim was factually inaccurate, expunging huge debates that even Lynne Cheney admitted; it was hard not to see a political motivation in the attempt to convince us that a standpat approach was best while diverting our attention to what computer programs could best be adapted to humanities classes. A decline of the neoconservative hold on our federal educational establishment may permit a more open, less deeply politicized curricular atmosphere. One of the real challenges for a Clinton-era NEH is to promote humanities innovations while also fostering a more tolerant, less partisan humanities climate than the one disingenuously supported during the past twelve years. For the moment, however, political commitments cannot be evaded, and those who claim to rise above the fray are often the most insidiously partisan of all.

The primary focus of this book, however, is not bent on narrowly political goals, despite the effort to beat back conservative claims. Above all else, this book results from my commitment to the marriage of research and teaching in an educational climate that too often opposes the two impulses, at least in the humanities. Knowledge is an evolving process fed by good research, and teaching goals that attack major research trajectories, rather than building on them, must be seriously questioned. Humanistic research, which has been changing greatly over the past twenty-five years, requires an imaginative pedagogical response, not a toes-dug-in insistence on eternal classroom verities. It is true that many humanistic researchers, for their part, have been insufficiently concerned with the teaching implications of their work, or with communicating the results with the clarity and synthesis essential for relating new knowledge to the student experience. We can do better, and my book is intended to further this process. Only because existing approaches have not captured what seems to me the essential teaching-research relationship have I been emboldened to venture a statement of my own.

The book is intended for educators and others seriously interested in the educational process. It systematizes what a good many humanities scholars are already thinking and should interest them accordingly (while benefiting from their thoughts). It also aims at people misled by recent sound and fury into neglecting what humanities scholarship really involves and what it has to do with campus stridency. In this area, particularly, an explanation of the major camps and of the scholarly trends they too often overshadow is essential. My argument does not depend on a claim that we can devise humanities curricula free from political involvement; the same involvement in fact applies to scientific fields, though we too rarely see the politics embedded there. Presenting a viable humanities alternative does depend, however, on showing that the political quotient is not captured accurately by the current canonist-antielitist free-for-all, and that moderates in both camps, plus educable neophytes among the humanities thickets, can embrace a more exciting set of options.

This is a crucial period for humanities education, as the recent outpouring of reports suggests. Our preoccupation with international economic challenge can lead to an overemphasis on educational sectors associated with skills attainment and with science and technology. President Bush, in setting firm competitive goals for science training, said nothing about the desirability of achieving international standing in student grasp of social and cultural patterns—though his administration sponsored a potentially dangerous standard-setting effort in the humanities. Scientific and technical fields do merit attention, but they must not occlude the importance of the humanities. Indeed, mounting an international challenge requires humanistic skills and insights at least as much as technical ones.

At the same time, humanistic controversies, because of their wide publicity, risk reducing the status of the disciplines involved: If humanists are so silly, so extremist, or so obviously unable to put their own house in order, then perhaps we should turn to other agendas or at least reduce the humanities to the most prosaic, least controversial kind of subject matter. Impulses of this sort are understandable, but they are profoundly misplaced. For our educational system also suffers from a narrow kind of scientism that is prone to ignore any intellectual issue if it cannot be subdivided into laboratory-testable or at least quantifiable components; this view omits too much and unduly risks converting the quest for new knowledge into endless minor accretions, with no thought to wider issues or underlying assumptions. For traditional reasons, then, but also to address new needs and issues, and to accommodate a surge in new kinds of research that provide vigorous responses to the varied educational goals, the position of the humanities in schools and colleges needs an imaginative restatement—the kind of restatement that, despite all the recent turbulence, has yet fully to emerge.

ONE

The Question

of Urgency:

The Issues

in Perspective

Amid all the problems that beset American schools and colleges, why bother with another plan for the humanities? The essential answer to this question involves tracing the opportunities a proper humanistic curriculum will offer in improving understanding and even, to some measurable extent, bettering the larger climate of American education. The answer follows from a recognition that, however unintentionally, several current initiatives risk worsening what we already have. Both of these points underlie the chapters that follow. Before we begin, however, a brief justification will help clarify the situation of the humanities within the larger educational setting.

The outpouring of concern about American education in recent years has been so diverse and so vast that it would be easy to overload. Even a fairly casual newspaper reader knows much about what is wrong with our school system. Drugs and violence pervade many high schools. Achievement levels often deteriorate after grade school, so that many high school seniors read at lower levels than they did as sixth graders. Scores on the College Board and similar tests have stagnated for a decade—give or take a few adjustments—after a precipitous decline in the late 1960s and early 1970s.[1] Educational performances in many other countries eclipse our own.

Japanese students go to school more days per year than their American counterparts. They demonstrate a greater ability to focus on educational goals rather than on other stimuli in the classroom. Compared to most urban East Asians and most Europeans, American students do badly on mathematics and science tests. On average, the intellectual capacities of recently recruited American teachers compare unfavorably with those of Americans in the professions or in business (judging by college scores and grades), and the status of the occupation is not highly regarded.

This list of problems is intimidating, because the problems are varied and real. Virtually no type of school and no category of American student is exempt from some serious concern. It is also true that Americans place immense faith in education as a solution to social ills. They see the provision of scholastic opportunities as one of society's crucial obligation to the masses; after the school years, inequalities and outright pathologies become the fault of individuals, not of the nation as a whole.[2] This faith raises expectations to high levels and makes Americans vulnerable to particular dismay when they hear reports of deteriorations or inadequacies in the system. As a nation, we have often praised education for its vital social role while condemning its effectiveness and attacking intellectual values. Several authorities have plausibly argued that this mood is upon us once again.[3]

In this context, various panaceas are periodically ventured. Currently fashionable, and not necessarily a bad idea, is the notion of voluntary national testing that will encourage schools to toe the mark and provide a better means of goading and measuring student performance than the more haphazard instruments now available. Other systemic proposals involve the idea of allowing free choice of schools under some kind of government voucher system, or (slightly passé already) the idea of relying heavily on the testing and retesting of teachers. And there are many ongoing laments about the lack of interest in teaching and about curricular issues at the college level.

Problems of teaching about society and about human behavior and values—the subject matter of the humanities and related social sciences—clearly form only part of a much larger picture. The issues and approaches discussed in this book do not address the full and ominous range of educational challenges currently on the agenda. They do not relate directly to structural proposals about schools. They do not deal with drugs and weapons in the lockers.

They do not deal head on with deficiencies in science and math training and the availability of qualified teachers in these areas. They do not explicitly address the need for fuller competitiveness with the economies of Japan or the new European Community juggernaut. My focus is limited, and certainly this essay is not meant to detract from appropriate attention to many other educational concerns that some may judge more pressing.

Nevertheless, while fully recognizing the number of agonizing dilemmas that can engage Americans concerned about their schools and colleges, I believe that the current problems facing education in the humanities—and the opportunities that we are at risk of passing by—do claim a genuine urgency for several reasons.

First, as I suggested in the previous chapter, the smoke raised by the current name-calling in the humanities arena too readily beclouds any coherent focus. Because Americans value courses in English, history, and related subjects to some degree but also tend to have a somewhat hazy notion of what the disciplines behind them entail, it is hard to sort through the current battles. Clarification is essential if we are to determine more fully what the real issues are and then to move toward constructive solutions. A large amount of time is now being consumed by debates in this area. Universities are being clobbered because of their real or imagined deficiencies in dealing with humanities issues the way many Americans, and many American leaders, wish them to do. Simply as a means of improving the intellectual and educational climate in a vital area, then, the present effort to move discussion to a more fruitful plane is timely.

It is worth noting at this early stage, by way of an initial illustration, that many of the attacks on universities for rigid "political correctness" stances that seek to privilege minorities and limit free expression of criticism in their direction have far more to do with student life decisions than with fundamental curricular issues. Lots of deans have issued rulings about Confederate flags in dorms and drunken epithets directed against women and gays, and their decisions may in some instances go too far in protecting "diversity" from even verbal unpleasantness. Rulings of this sort are not unrelated to curricular issues: colleges that have pushed African history requirements, say, in lieu of Western civilization (the Mount Holyoke pattern at present) do reveal their own views of political correctness at a classroom level. It remains true, however, that overall curricula have changed relatively little, even at avant-garde institutions, during the current political correctness campaign.[4] In many instances, long curricular discussions have yielded very little in the way of novel results. Although non-Western history and literature courses have gained ground, there has been no revolution in subject matter, and stagnation, more than sweeping change, may be our real problem.[5] Conservative efforts to blast universities over these issues predicate an anarchy that does not exist, and one must assume a larger agenda on the conservatives' part in indulging in the recurrent American pastime of intellectual-bashing.

Similarly, humanities in the lower schools also have not changed dramatically. Students encounter a somewhat different selection of literature with the introduction of some nonwhite and non-Western authors in their texts. In history classes, high school seniors have notably increased their ability to identify Harriet Tubman as a major figure in American history—a shift that might be either modestly applauded or lamented, depending on one's point of view. But, with this exception, the major presidents—with George Washington at their head—continue to constitute the most widely known and frequently cited figures in U.S. history for these same seniors. In this, generations of school training persist unchallenged. Thus actual changes in the body of student knowledge largely come about through what is at most a gradual evolution, not the ominous abandonment of the mainstream that some critics evoke.

Humanities curricula, in sum, are not in some crisis phase of heedless experimentalism. Yet the distractions of current editorializing, which may provoke unfounded counterreactions, do lend an immediacy to the curricular issues that should be discussed. On the positive side, this same furor may provide one of those rare moments at which opportunities for constructive change in the humanities, brewing for several decades, can fruitfully be seized—and the urgency is that we not let that moment slip.

To be more specific, the quality of education in humanities and related social science subjects—history, literature, philosophy, languages, and large swathes of anthropology, sociology, and political science—is central to three wider concerns detailed below—all of them pressing, all of them warranting a genuine sense of priority despite the many other claims on educational attention. The current political and international scene calls for analytical abilities too many Americans needlessly lack. These abilities depend on training in areas that may be downgraded because of our fascination with technological lag, and the structural reforms looming on the educational horizon generally may do more harm than good if, along

with their implementation, we fail to gain a clearheaded understanding of the humanities essentials.

1. Various authorities have claimed to be appalled at the ignorance of American students in subjects like history, and I will address this issue at various points. Some of their formulations are
dated at best; some suggest a past level of knowledge for which
there is no evidence, claiming deterioration, then, without a factual
base.[6] Nevertheless, certain kinds of ignorance, whether or not they
are more advanced than in the past, are extremely troubling. President George Bush claimed, in a 1991 commencement address in
Michigan, that the United States had become "the most egalitarian
system in history and one of the most harmonious." The latter
claim could be defended, at least in the brief historical moment of
1973–92, but the first is preposterous, and the notion that such a
statement could be made and credited (and in a university setting)
is staggering. Granted, politicians notoriously exaggerate; granted
that the public has considerable built-in skepticism; granted, finally
(lest we become too narrowly political), that the American system
can be defended on many grounds. Nevertheless, the president's
remarks so clearly echoed widespread student assumptions about
American achievements, so clearly reflected the factual ignorance
and analytical simplicity both of potential audiences and even, perhaps, of political speakers dazzled by their own myths, that doubts
about the quality of our education concerning our own society, its
directions of change, and its comparative standing cannot be put to
rest. As the principal sources of social information and relevant analytical training, the humanities and kindred social sciences (including, in this case, economics and statistics) clearly require a new kind
of attention, freed from some of the present distracting debate and
concentrating on their classic goals—updated in implementation—
of providing an informed and alert citizenry.

The world we live in may be changing more rapidly than ever before.[7] It is certainly becoming more complex in relation to our own
expectations. This complexity demands—urgently demands, in fact
—better understanding of the patterns amid which we live. Regardless of whether the deterioration of humanities learning is real or
imagined, we need to develop a series of humanistic appreciations
more attuned to our changing setting, including the ways in which
this setting clashes with the expectations many Americans maintain. We need a better grasp of what is happening in our own soci-

ety and in societies around it. Using available humanistic tools, we can attain this grasp.

The international framework places the most obvious demands on this component of our education. The United States increasingly operates in an intricate international context, dealing with societies whose cultures are not simple extensions of our own. There is reason to believe that, in the not-too-distant past, improved training in history and related subjects helped the United States to better deal with Europe than it had earlier in the twentieth century. The spread of Western civilization courses, which broke into a more parochial Americanist program leavened, at best, with some ancient history, did provide a better-informed and more analytically sophisticated public and may have contributed to an improved policymaking climate as well, as the United States dealt with Europe after World War II. Now the challenge is to extend education yet again, to encompass the larger global dimension. Even more than in domestic matters, this requires new levels of attention and also outright innovation, both in content and in analytical range. The debates that currently dominate humanities education distract us, on the whole, from sensible discussion of how to meet this goal. The need to take a more constructive direction is pressing.

2. American intellectual and educational life has long been complicated by divisions between scientific and nonscientific—or, broadly speaking, humanistic—approaches. These are the two cultures to which C. P. Snow referred in discussing Western intellectual endeavors more generally.[8] The divisions are by no means complete ones, and later in this discussion we will return to look at the linkages. Nevertheless, scholars focusing on "hard" data—that is, quantifiable and/or laboratory-replicable facts—are often prone to disparage their humanistic colleagues, who deal with impressionistic evidence, who cannot fully "prove" any major claim, and who seem to enjoy dispute and ambiguity. The government, despite a recent desire to promote humanities standards, shares and enhances the disparity in spending only .5 percent of federal research funds in humanities areas.

Science-humanities debates can be fruitful, for both scholars and students. We should have more of them. At this moment, however, the scientists' tendency to disparage the humanities in general, or to acknowledge only those that fulfill traditional culture-conveyance roles without pretending to advance claims of truth or analysis, risks overtipping the desirable balance. The current arguments within the humanities disciplines themselves encourage some scientists—and perhaps even more social scientists who are bent on asserting their own scientific claims without quite possessing the secure prestige of physics or chemistry—to dismiss the humanities more cavalierly than ever. At the same time, our national preoccupation with educational reforms designed to prod us to the level of the Japanese (or whoever) in science and technology moves us in the same direction. Few of our leaders have urged us to match or surpass other nations in our social and cultural knowledge and skills—yet in fact the challenge is reasonable and should be addressed. Indeed, we have a chance to excel in instilling useful analytical methods and cultural understandings (not, for example, a strong point in Japanese education), and we should seize this chance.

The point is obvious. Education in the humanities is at risk of being systematically downgraded because it presents a needless impression of incoherence and internal controversy and because of its failure to advance analytical claims that parallel—though while differing from—those of science. The glory of the humanistic and "soft" social science disciplines is that they allow scholars and students to address vital questions that simply cannot be answered scientifically, in the conventional sense, and yet should not be ignored—questions about human nature, about the ways societies and political systems function, about the ways social change occurs. We urgently need to develop curricula that will display these features of the humanities to better advantage, not to end debate and disagreement—for it is true, and probably useful, that humanists love to quarrel among themselves—but to situate that debate on different grounds. The danger of shrinking the humanities sector and drifting toward an unduly narrow and technical educational base is real, especially if we define education in terms of business competitiveness in the most short-run sense; but the danger is also avoidable.

3. Some of the structural innovations being discussed as ways to deal with problems of educational quality in general have important implications for the humanities. They could easily add to the trivialization of humanistic education if a secure alternative vision of goals is not put forth.

The interest in national testing programs serves as a good example, important in its own right amid current enthusiasms. As I noted in the introduction, a number of sensible testing approaches are under discussion, and it is also true that several projects are study-ing the possibilities for improving those skills that can be examined in machine-gradable formats.[9]

The fact is, however, that widespread testing in the United States has almost invariably meant machine-gradable questions dealing ei-ther with aptitudes or, in substantive fields like physics or literature, with memorized recall.[10] It may be that standardized tests might do somewhat better in future, given innovative procedures, but the lay observer has the right to skepticism. Years of College Board experi-mentation with "new style" multiple-choice questions, imaginative-ly designed to elicit interpretive skills, did not alter the impressions the Board's achievement tests made on history teaching, for exam-ple: teachers continued to stress memorization, leaving analytical skills to the students' own talents. The dominant approach to test-ing in the major disciplines is driven by a fascination with aptitude scoring, an odd but durable American passion. It appeals to econo-my: tests of this sort are by far the cheapest to grade, and though Americans love education they also love to pinch the purse. It ap-peals also to a real suspicion of teachers that goes hand in hand with the love affair, in principle, with schooling. Americans do not trust their teachers to grade generalized tests; their attitudes con-trast notably with most European systems, wherein essay grading or oral examinations are hallowed components of testing programs. Finally, Americans fail to distinguish between subjects in which ma-chine-graded tests are appropriate because they include easily mea-sured skills components, and subjects in which the principal educa-tional objectives lie beyond this testing mode. We tend to equate grammar with literary analysis, or problem sets with a more basic grasp of scientific method.

When discussion turns, then, to new national tests, it requires no paranoia to fear the implications for the humanities. The United States has generated one test that is not simply multiple choice: the Advanced Placement (AP) tests offered by the College Board to give high school students college-level credit (subject to the stipulations of whatever college a student attends). AP tests in all subjects—in-cluding, of course, history, English, and modern languages—have a significant essay component, though the Board has also insisted on a substantial multiple-choice segment because only that format pro-vides statistical, or psychometric, reliability. The tests are not, as a result, analytically equivalent to essay examinations in real courses at many universities. They are too short and too dominated by memorization. Further, the multiple-choice component, combined with larger educational and testing traditions in this country, encourages many high school AP teachers (like their counterparts who prepare students for the strictly multiple-choice Achievement tests) to emphasize memorization and factual coverage, hoping that essay skills will magically emerge from a largely nonanalytical course framework. Discussions of how to revise components other than multiple-choice segments on other discipline tests formulated by the College Board, notably the Achievement tests that are offered in major disciplines like history, English, and languages, have consistently faltered due to cost considerations and the ubiquitous psychometric measurement gurus.

Foreign testing examples in this same area are diverse. British tests encourage writing; whether they consistently encourage analysis is another matter. A sample history question on the certificate examination administered at the end of secondary school presents two illustrations of public punishments during the Tudor period. Short follow-up essay questions ask students to interpret the pictures' meaning in terms of the impressions they convey of Tudor methods of punishment; to discuss why problems of law and order increased in the sixteenth century; and to describe the importance of justices of the peace in enforcing law and order. Of the three questions, only the first calls on interpretive skills, and then only concerning the meaning of two pictures. The other two questions, albeit discursive, are based on factual recall.

Japanese tests are more strictly factual still. One question on the university qualifying examination briefly describes the 1962 Cuban missile crisis and then asks students to identify two correct sentences about the crisis from a list of five; memorization wins out. German, French, and some British tests, on the other hand, do include essay questions that ask students to interpret contradictory or opinionated sources—the significance of a major event such as the French revolution, the coherence of diverse source materials, or (in the French case) the meaning of freedom. Needless to say, scoring these tests costs money: European examinations cost about twice as much per student as the AP examination and almost ten times as much as a purely multiple-choice battery like the College Board's SATs.

All authorities agree that movement toward new testing procedures in the United States will involve many vital policy decisions. It is possible to offer tests that call upon the ability to use and not merely to parrot knowledge. However, the cost factors and the weight of our own testing tradition do not encourage this course. Our frequent inability to distinguish between tests appropriate for skills areas or disciplines that lend themselves to machine-gradable problem sets and those essential in disciplines that deal with vital issues in the social and cultural areas further clouds the picture. Revealingly, and tragically, some humanists have rushed to define their disciplines in terms of testable skills—hence the popularity of references to historical or geographical literacy. These scholars hope that history or geography will be given priority once it becomes easy to reveal the gaps in basic knowledge of those subjects. The tragedy is that success may be worse than failure because it will encourage learning of the least useful, most readily forgotten kinds of history and social science; in some cases, the proponents may not even know what really useful learning in these areas entails, which is tragedy compounded.

My point is obvious: Sensible decisions about testing approaches in the humanities and social sciences and in some sciences are possible only with prior understanding of the real purpose of education in these disciplines—and in the main, the current debates about purposes do not lead in fruitful directions. Again, we can see an urgent need to clarify the goals and opportunities in humanities teaching in relation to fast-moving discussions about shifts in educational administration and assessment.

The same urgent caveats apply to the current movement to define national standards in the schools for subjects like history. Early in the 1990s, the National Endowment for the Humanities and the Department of Education mounted a program to define guidelines for what students should know and be able to do in history by the time they graduate from high school. The project was pushed forward with great speed: a statement initially was expected within a year, and the major professional associations in the field were given literally only a few weeks to prepare suggestions. The idea, seemingly, was to get out a statement as soon as possible so as to combat recent state plans like that of New York, which has been condemned by Lynne Cheney as a poor example of multiculturalism: "New York has often been the leader in doing things badly."

This project went beyond testing, though it was designed to correlate with the national tests also being developed. Like new testing plans, it could have some salutary results. But the haste with which it was done and the dogmatic stance of the project's organizers, including Lynne Cheney, give one pause. The effort risked serving as a thinly veiled partisan statement, a tit for the multiculturalists' tat. To be sure, Cheney intoned: "It's no longer a question of whether we're going to have a multicultural education. The question is whether we're going to do it well or do it badly." But because the NEH under the Reagan and Bush administrations never allowed more than the grudging inclusion of bits of multiculturalism in a largely conventional humanities agenda, and because it has never, since its engagement in educational standards issues, taken a deeper approach to the humanities that might to some degree transcend the current political debate, there is reason for concern.[11]

The urgency of taking a deeper look at the purposes and possibilities of humanities education derives from the accelerating pace, not simply of the debates over history and English, but of potentially far-reaching structural planning. Movements toward national testing programs and national history and literature standards address a real need to provide new stimulus for quality in American education. They will achieve their ends, however, only when combined with constructive educational goals. Without this their attempt at improving quality will misfire and may produce less rather than more enlightenment. Standardized tests, for example, can easily worsen educational quality. State-based testing programs introduced in the 1970s amid furor about the lack of school accountability almost certainly led to deterioration in history and English teaching as teachers tried to prepare their students for batteries of multiple-choice tests directed toward either rudimentary skills acquisition or subject matter memorization. The danger of new miscalculations is quite real at the present time. Before we rush to refine the mechanisms, we must comprehend what we want and what we can reasonably expect from the major subject areas to which students are exposed.

The note of urgency is not misplaced. A new look at the humanities addresses a series of pressing issues, beginning with the current confusion in the disciplines themselves—and in the public spillover from the bitter debates—and moving to the public usefulness of social and cultural analysis, the importance of moderating understandable enthusiasms for scientific and technical training so that other vital areas are not omitted, and the implications of current policy moves in the revision of educational techniques. Discussion of humanities goals may even overlap with other school concerns. Courses in history or English that engage students' interests—as conventional offerings geared toward memorizing the names of Shakespearean characters or historical dates demonstrably fail to do—will not resolve the issues of student motivation and dropout rates, but they can contribute to such a resolution in a positive way. Opportunities of this kind are largely being neglected in the most familiar recent arguments about what kind of cultural heritage humanities courses are meant to inculcate.

Good humanities teaching will not produce an educational utopia, just as good education will not solve all of the national problems that are sometimes brought to its door. But amid all the issues that bedevil the school system, the need properly to direct the way in which our students learn about society and culture is by no means trivial. Right now, despite many available examples of imaginative teaching and constructive currents of thought, we are not giving ourselves a decent chance.

TWO

Innovations in

the Humanities:

Before the Crisis

Long-standing emphases in humanities education, deriving ultimately from the Renaissance, have in the past two or three decades become definitively outmoded—even though many educators have yet to catch up to this fact. Two major developments have displaced Renaissance certainties. The first involves changing American demography—including the rise of women and Americans of African, Hispanic, and Asian descent to a strong majority enrollment on college campuses—and the increasingly international context in which we operate. The new demography and the advance of the non-European world inevitably challenge educational traditions focused squarely on the primacy of Western culture. When Stanford students noted in 1987, in opposing an exclusive Western civilization course requirement, "It is time for Stanford to recognize that people of color outside Europe have made intellectual and artistic contributions to the world we live in," they were admittedly making a political point, but they—and their colleagues across the nation—were also stating a simple truth. The world we live in has changed, and education must reflect this change in more than cosmetic fashion.

The second reason for the displacement of Renaissance humanistic traditions involves the explosion of knowledge, both within the humanities and without. This explosion increasingly fragments research operations and makes it difficult for us to agree on single standards of factual coverage in any general education program that goes beyond nineteenth-century truisms. Yet this same knowledge explosion is also a precious resource, increasing the information available about how societies and cultures work (as well as about the physical universe), but also highlighting certain analytical skills that can serve as the new center of humanities training. As a result, we are forced to reconsider the traditional staples of the curriculum—an inherently agonizing process, but also one that provides the fundamental directions for reform.

Anyone familiar with debates about college education knows the weary but eternal teaching/research dichotomy. Too many university professors shortchange teaching in favor of research. Reward structures, even at relatively modest institutions, often privilege research (though there are places where the reverse is true, where an active researcher is feared and discriminated against by colleagues).

The results of this pressure to do research, so the argument continues, include not only a tendency to slight the classroom, but also the production of many turgid, insignificant monographs on silly subjects, killing trees and wasting paper to no good purpose. In contrast, the diligent teacher who is devoted to class preparation and contact time with students is not singled out, because the results of that person's work are less tangible than published articles and because it brings the teacher's institution less obvious prestige in the outside world.

Teaching and research do not always mix. There are structural problems inherent in finding ways to identify and then reward good teaching. Much research is petty. A real tension exists, without question, in institutions that proclaim their interest in advancing new knowledge while also serving hordes of undergraduates.

Yet, in the humanities at least, the laments are usually overdone. This book does not pretend to talk about all the structural issues attached to teaching and its rewards, though their importance is real. Rather, it depends on the basic proposition that, more often than not, teaching and research supplement each other. It depends further on the argument that, in the humanities, research gains during the past twenty-five years form a vital basis for redefining the teaching curriculum. Hence, instead of succumbing to the characteristic temptation to dive into the political correctness thickets, like most authors of recent works on humanities education have done, I deliberately emphasize a different base. This chapter will sketch leading research developments, providing a context for the subsequent discussion of the brawls between canonists and multiculturalists and, more significant still, laying a foundation for the delineation of the humanistic alternative: an education predicated on new knowledge and new analytical approaches.

Many excellent teachers do not themselves do research. They must, however, keep up with the findings of leading researchers lest their teaching stagnate. Many, even in institutions whose stringent teaching demands preclude original research, can participate in active synthesis, helping to connect specific research points and blending the whole into a coherent presentation. A few excellent researchers are rotten teachers, by genes or by choice. Most professors in the humanities, however, contrary to academic stereotype, like to teach and to teach well. They view their classroom activities as a stimulus to at least part of their research, encouraging wider formulations and allowing appropriate communication of results. And they view teaching, in part, as a way to convey new learning in combination with established findings.

There is no need to claim that the teaching/research symbiosis is always smooth or fruitful. It often works, however. Furthermore, the advances in knowledge—too often neglected in humanities fields that are viewed as memorialist rather than dynamic—call for even greater integration with teaching in years to come. It is in this integration that the future lies. First, however, we must establish the vigor of humanities scholarship and explain the specific directions taken by the most exciting research. Only with these starting points in mind can the remainder of the task be accomplished.

For the basic division in the humanities today is not found in the vicious but often petty debate between canonists and multiculturalists, but in the more fundamental distinctions between the humanistic disciplines as erudite preservers of past values or as dynamic participants in a generation of new and significant knowledge. The record of innovative scholarship points to the latter direction, even as many people seek to use humanistic instruction to maintain reverence for the same monuments cherished in principle a generation ago. The tension is understandable, for the new thrusts of scholarship are still relatively recent and the departures from conventional perspectives have been great. As innovation matures into wider visions of social and cultural patterns, however, any attempt to turn school humanities programs into museum exhibits becomes less and less viable. For all its admitted vagaries, the new scholarship makes a brash claim: We know more about the way societies and cultures work than we did thirty years ago. As understanding of the dynamism of the humanities gains ground, the challenge, for scholar-teachers but also for their audiences, is to put this claim to use to improve learning.

I n the eighteenth century, imperial China, redefining its longstanding belief in policies of "change within tradition" that had allowed the empire to accept impressive innovations while maintaining vital continuities with beliefs and institutions inherited from Confucian times, began to experience a new kind of cultural stagnation. The emperors themselves, somewhat on the defensive, began to stress unadulterated cultural traditionalism as a means of legitimizing their position, thus heightening the emphasis on the classics of Chinese literature and philosophy. Intellectual life increasingly revolved around collecting prior examples of art and expounding literary comment on older works rather than seeking to create new styles or even to adapt previous ones in significant ways. On the surface, intellectual life remained lively, marked by government patronage and extensive upper-class dabbling in painting, calligraphy, and poetry writing. But rigid traditionalism focused attention on repetition of past principles; creativity, long a hallmark of Chinese culture, was largely stifled, which contributed, in turn, to a sluggishness in Chinese responses to new challenges, most notably the one posed by the increasingly intrusive West.

American intellectual life is hardly comparable to that of eighteenth-century China. Industrialized societies cannot readily be juxtaposed to preindustrial settings. Even as many authorities recommend a return to humanistic traditionalism, scientific innovation continues; and humanistic traditionalism is itself fundamentally challenged. The flaws in an analogy of this sort illustrate some of the complex historical thinking—informed by knowledge of diverse cases from the past but also by an ability to compare in terms more subtle than identity versus contrast—that a good teaching program will work to instill. The example reminds us, however, that a desire to promote tradition as the mainspring of cultural identity can go too far.

And this in turn leads to the central issue in humanities teaching today: whether the defense of cultural tradition is the main goal. The publication in 1987 of the late Allan Bloom's book, *The Clos-*

ing of the American Mind: How Higher Education Has Failed Democracy and Impoverished the Souls of Today's Students, signaled the acceleration of a campaign already launched to define the purposes of humanistic education in terms of the established canon: great books, great minds, great political leaders. Arguments about this canonical approach, in turn, illuminate the most obvious problems of defining educational purpose and the relationships between teaching and research. It is important, for this reason, to investigate the scholarly context in which impassioned defenses of the canon emerged, because only through this context is some perspective possible against the barbarians-at-the-gates tenor of Bloom's title and treatise.

The amazing popularity of Bloom's book—over half a year at the top of the *New York Times*'s best-seller list—testifies to the extent educated American readers are unaware of the issues that Bloom's canonism attempted to sweep under the rug. It is possible, of course, that the book's popularity resulted from rooted convictions that traditionalism constitutes the only appropriate humanistic route, honed by explicit rejection of the claims of new scholarship. If this is so, my arguments herein face heavy going indeed. The sources of canonical popularity are, unquestionably, both complex and significant and must be further assessed. It is my belief, however, that the acclaim for Bloom's work stemmed more from widespread ignorance of humanistic innovation (compounded by the obscurantism of some innovators) than from well-considered rejection. Even research scientists, vitally committed to innovation in their own disciplines, often see the humanities as museum pieces to be treasured only for their familiarities. Two decades of change have passed them by, rooted as they have been in an older approach that touted the humanities as repositories of timeless verities. Understanding educational alternatives and the dangers of overdoing a defense of the canon involves some acquaintance with what noncanonical humanists have been up to and why they have inspired such hatred among educational conservatives.

Humanities research has been changing fundamentally over the past twenty-five years. The major constituent disciplines are fertile sources of expanded knowledge, challenging theories, and fundamental new insights. Not all the new work is good. Some of it explores trivial byways or puffs itself up with unbecoming pomposity. Some panders to whims of the moment. My purpose in this chapter is not to praise the whole current of innovation or to claim that it has entirely swept away the disciplinary pasts. One precondition of further argument about the curriculum is, however, an understanding of those new directions that have won substantial commitment (despite debates over specifics) from scholars in the field. Only then can we turn to the real challenge: exploring how these new trains of thought can revivify teaching. Even most canonists have focused on keeping the results of scholarly dynamism out of the classroom rather than on contesting the research terrain directly. For the most part, the innovations in humanistic research are sufficiently recent—and in some cases their presentations have aimed so exclusively at a scholarly audience—that they need to be briefly sketched in here before the positive curricular implications can begin to emerge.

In other words, before exploring the deficiencies of canonical rigidity—and certainly before venturing curricular alternatives—we should emphasize the positive, which means the scholarly fundamentals. Canonists, obviously incensed by the innovative approaches delineated in this chapter, have tended to conflate basic changes in the humanities with other educational issues, such as wasted time in classrooms or mindless testing, as if there were a coherent package of problems that only revivified traditionalism could correct. Lynne Cheney thus can accurately inveigh against undue reliance on textbooks and a deplorable neglect of teaching while producing curricular recommendations that are riveted on older learning and that distort the research-teaching relationship.[1] The rhetorical strategy is understandable: The canonists don't like the new scholarship, and they correctly attack many other features of the educational system, so they merge and thus simplify their targets.

What is lost in this process is the vitality of new-style humanistic learning, informed by social-science contributions from such sources as anthropology and sociology. Translating that vitality into the classroom, not obscuring it through narrower coverage issues, should be our chief curricular task. Why it is not already pedagogically triumphant requires an explanation—the task of the following chapter—but first the fundamental revision of cultural inquiry must be established.

Humanistic disciplines have been redefined at several points in the twentieth century under the general spur of finding appropriate channels toward understanding how people and societies function. Early in the century, for example, philosophy turned away from sweeping syntheses at the research level in favor of more rigorous inquiries in logic, epistemology, and semantics; more recently, research in the field of applied ethics has been added to the agenda. Philosophical scholars, in other words, without forsaking basic traditional goals, increasingly inquire into how people think and express themselves, the assumptions of other academic disciplines, and the interrelationship between ethical dilemmas and immediate practical and policy decisions in such areas as abortion or the mechanical generation or prolongation of life. Today's research philosophy departments embrace few active political theorists of the nineteenth-century stripe and few general inquirers into the nature of man and the universe, a still-earlier stripe. The result, unquestionably, has been tension between philosophers as active scholars and the pedagogical expectations for college philosophy programs; this tension is often dealt with by offering courses in the history of great philosophers, or in logic and ethics, that differ from the principal research thrusts of the department.

More recently, in another humanistic area, traditional relationships between research and teaching are being reassessed. Modern languages programs have long suffered a gap between the primary teaching mission—instruction in basic languages—and research goals that centered on the exploration of foreign-language literatures. As languages rise once again as a teaching priority, the traditional solution of having graduate students do the drudge work of preliminary language instruction becomes less viable. Language programs, in consequence, are struggling to define relevant research agendas closer to their teaching mission, which involves them in linguistic research, in computer applications relevant to language learning, and in language-acquisition study; the latter, in turn, is linked to cognitive and developmental psychology. Literature has not been abandoned in teaching or in research, but it must now share space with other pressing interests. Language program adjustments are by no means complete, and they differ from the common pattern in that they were driven initially by pedagogical concerns. They suggest, nevertheless, that a review of traditional approaches is essential to keep humanities teaching and research, and the linkage between them, abreast of new demands and developments.

English and history are the humanities disciplines in which the change in research agendas has been most systematic and sweeping over the past generation (since the late 1960s).* These are the disciplines, moreover, whose central place in the curriculum, at both school and college level, prompts the greatest attention. Because most high schools require three or four English courses and usually two history courses, and most college programs specify at least one of each, research innovations have inevitably challenged the classroom agenda. In both disciplines, crucial gaps have opened between what most people expect from teaching (and what most teachers, indeed, have been trained to do) and what the most imaginative scholars have increasingly defined as their turf. Such gaps could not safely persist—in contrast, perhaps, to philosophy, where the tension has been sustained, though at some cost to teaching range. They are now being addressed, but at best chaotically and at worst, through the preachments of unreconstructed traditionalists, with outright ineptitude.

The New Humanities

In English, the conventional central focus on literary studies has undergone a striking reevaluation during the past quarter-century. Several theoretical schools, including deconstructionism and post-structuralism, have rebelled against the traditional emphasis on literary canons—a particular range of literary works defined as sources of enduring values—as the primary research texts. Researchers argue (without entirely agreeing among themselves) that a variety of representations, and not simply the standard great literary works of the past, must be studied in order to interpret a society's culture or cultures. Serious analysis can be applied to potboilers and other literary products, some of them interesting as statements despite what, by conventional standards, is their ques-

*Deconstructionism and post-structuralism and social and world history are not, of course, the first scholarly innovations to hit the bellwether disciplines in the twentieth century. The earlier rise of intellectual history and other kinds of "new" history, and the surge of "new criticism," contributed significantly on their own and in some ways helped lay the foundation for the more basic reformulations discussed here. Despite the importance of such developments, and despite the risk of oversimplification in pointing so heavily to innovations within the past twenty-five years alone, it remains true that the most challenging and fundamental reorientations are the more recent ones. Readers interested in the longer pedigree of change can always consult more extensive histories of individual disciplines.

tionable literary quality, some of them quite worthy but simply ignored by posterity; an example of the latter would be the first American novel by a woman, written in the 1790s but never accorded prime recognition.[2]

Media other than formal literature are now embraced as well. The new cultural scholars argue that all literary works must be assessed according to word meanings and beneath-the-surface symbolism, and that theories of meaning are essential building blocks in this process of understanding. Post-structuralists or "new historicists," in particular, contend that literary productions should be interpreted according to both the interests of the time and the identity and purposes of the valuer. Literary discourse, according to this vision, is historically "produced" by its readers as well as by its writers. Writers, in turn, serve more as agents than as independent shapers of culture and must be interpreted for what they reveal about their cultures rather than as generators of timeless truths.[3]

The purpose of literary inquiry thus shifts from a focus on particular great works to an examination of the process of mutual interaction among authors, ideas, styles, and audiences; the goal is to understand the culture and to discover what a given work says about cultural constraints and opportunities rather than to reiterate the central themes of a particular literary opus. The generation of interpretive theories correspondingly replaces authoritative definitions of great works and assertions of related aesthetic standards as scholarly goals. Whereas, previously, literary scholars in the tradition of F. W. Leavis considered it their primary purpose to state that Shakespeare offered a beautiful representation of the world and to insist that their readers join them in appreciation of this beauty, the new researchers ask questions about the nature of beauty and the nature of representation. Similarly, instead of simply saying that one narrative is better constructed than another (indeed, instead of endorsing this hierarchy at all in some cases), the new theorists try to determine the social effect of narrative. They aim to generalize and contextualize the study of literature in order to make it richer and more rewarding and to decode the larger points it makes about the roles and constraints of culture, rather than evaluating it simply for its own sake. The research canvas, in other words, has substantially expanded, and the analytical purposes have altered and deepened.

The challenges that these innovative approaches pose to the conventional teaching of literature are obvious, for even as the new methods of interpretation have gained ground, most courses on literature have continued to emphasize exposure to the "greats" with desk-thumping insistence on their greatness. The gap has also been compounded, it must be granted, by more than a little deliberate obscurantism on the part of some innovators, who seem bent on introducing new jargon compounded with such dense theoretical references that only the most intrepid explorers venture in. The existence of this gap between teaching and scholarship does not, of course, demonstrate that novelty is a virtue, even if the findings are rendered more consistently intelligible. It does set up a challenge, however, and points to potential new directions for teaching; and although some of these directions take the form of widely publicized efforts to introduce literary materials by authors outside the white male elite, they are not limited to such efforts. Overall, they provide a more general framework for recasting the teaching of literature than the turf battles imply. These are the points to which we will return, drawing on the educational implications of the new cultural studies.

Some scholars in English go on to argue that research into literary and other media representations, even redefined, is not the only point of their discipline. They also want to study the processes of writing and speech, joining forces with cognitive psychologists and making rhetoric and composition central research targets rather than perennial butts of the pedagogical pecking order. In this area, too, the generation of theories of cultural activity—here even more directly related to an end product—becomes central to the research process.

Rhetorical study combined with literary analysis focuses on examining the construction of argument. In this context, writing is a process in which problems are solved in such construction; reading literature is a process in which the arguments embedded in representation can be identified in large part through fuller understanding of the dominant interpretive repertoires already established in the reader's mind. Attention to the social construction of argument becomes the unifying thread both in the study of literature and in developing an informed approach to writing.

Sea changes in the field of English have been paralleled by redefinitions of historical research. The trajectories have been largely independent, and one initial result of innovation was long to preclude any direct dialogue between historians and students of literature. In fact, however, some common processes were at work, challenging older ideas of value and causation and fundamentally altering the roster of subjects for study. In both disciplines, the generation of theory or analysis came to occupy a newly prominent place. Although not necessarily more important than corresponding developments in English, the transformation of historical scholarship can be taken as paradigmatic of the recent and sweeping changes in humanities research approaches and their implications, in turn, for teaching.

The strongest force for change in historical research has been the "new social history" that began to take shape among younger scholars in the late 1960s. Social historians turned their attention to the records of the less powerful and articulate people in past societies—workers, women, racial and ethnic minorities, even children—and to aspects of those societies not directly encompassed by the doings of statesmen and intellectuals—population behavior, class relations, family structure, beliefs and rituals, even leisure.[4]

The shifts in subject matter became obvious by 1970, when social historians began to generate research results. The history of slavery became a major agenda item after decades in which, with few exceptions, conventional American histories had skipped lightly over the topic. (Even today, popular representations of American history such as the displays at Disney World introduce slavery only in time to have it abolished; the implication is that it was an undeniable wart on the American visage but notable mainly for the national triumph of abolition.) Journals were founded not only for social history as a general field, but on special topics such as the family, sports, popular culture, and the working class. The introduction of essentially new topics persisted through the 1980s, partly in response to new political demands, partly in response to the social historians' self-assigned mission of amplifying our understanding of what constituted a society, and therefore a society's past. Thus to the histories of key groups were added studies of men's gender identities (as well as women's), the elderly and adolescents (and, in one essay at least, the middle-aged), Asian Americans as well as African Americans and European ethnic groups, ordinary soldiers, and diverse sexual cultures. Serious research on patterns of drinking, emotional standards, childrearing practices, insanity, physical health, and consumerism joined earlier social history staples such as experiences of mobility and popular protest.

One immediate payoff of the new topical outreach was the correction or emendation of numerous common misimpressions about historical trajectories. For example, we now know that in Western culture, nuclear families did not tidily replace extended families as part of the process of modernization, for an unusual nuclear emphasis developed much earlier. This means that widespread beliefs, current among scholars as well as the general public, that well-structured extended families prevailed until "modern" conditions began to unravel family solidarity are simply incorrect. Western family tradition does not contrast so neatly with modern life. On another front, and again against common assumptions, research has shown that crime rates do not regularly increase with ongoing urbanization, and *perceptions* of these rates must be carefully distinguished from reality. In modern America, it is middle-class people who worry most about divorce rates, but, contrary to their common beliefs, they experience fewer divorces than workers. Historical rates of social mobility, particularly during the twentieth century, have differed relatively little between the United States and Western Europe, though beliefs about social mobility (and political expressions linked to these beliefs) have varied considerably. Not surprisingly, in sum: One of the strengths of social history's topical redefinitions has been to subject to careful scrutiny a number of important subjects about which vivid historical impressions, or rather misimpressions, already existed.

This expansion of the past has inevitably focused attention on new kinds of sources and methods beyond the formal pronouncements of statesmen and intellectuals or the treaties, constitutions, and legal structures that dominated the historical horizon for so long. Social historians use records of crimes and courts; they have discovered long-neglected popular newspapers and diaries; they pour over census returns and the earlier demographic records of parish churches. Quantification, as a means of determining large trends in such areas as demography and crime, has assumed new importance, though by the 1970s it was also joined by anthropologically inspired attention to descriptions of rituals and other ethnographic approaches.

New subject matter has also generated some redefinitions of historical focus and related styles of presentation. Individual "great men" and events no longer organize the past, as social historians see it. Key individuals are still recognized as playing a role in shaping society, but their contributions—the writing of seminal books or the formulation of new laws—are usually fitted into a framework created by larger forces such as economic trends, new technologies, or new patterns of belief. In this view, most presidential administrations do not matter much, as set against the underlying social trends that *really* define American society. The European wars of the mid-eighteenth century, though by no means insignificant, pale in importance when compared with the huge growth in population, its roots in new nutritional sources and new sexual behavior, and its consequences in spurring economic change; the essential reasons for studying the eighteenth century in European history have been substantially redefined.

Major laws are still covered in the historical account, but now they are described not primarily as the results of the activities of individual legislators, but rather as responses to pressure from wider social groups, sometimes even those outside the formal political process; these laws are assessed, not literally, but in terms of unstated as well as stated motives, usually unintended effects, and often incomplete enforcement. Thus, legislation limiting the hours that women could work, a nineteenth-century "humanitarian" staple, is seen now in terms of larger gender shifts (not totally incompatible with some allowance for humanitarianism) and, above all, in terms of its consequences in furthering a redefinition of the relationship between women and work. The institutionalization of jails and asylums is no longer seen simply as the product of Enlightenment-inspired reformers but of wider changes in the perception of deviance and more rigorous definitions of normalcy.

The key focus for social historians has become processes, not events or individuals. In their judgment, single events like an election or a battle rarely cause or instigate major or durable changes in the behavior of ordinary people, in the ordinary activities of life, or even—the boldest assertion, though qualified by some significant exceptions—in the basic functioning of societies. An event that does signal major changes, such as World War II's role in altering women's work patterns, must of course be given due place in the historical account. But social historians are not usually interested in exploring events for their own sake. They rarely adopt a conventional narrative strategy in presentation, because they do not primarily chart one event or one biographical phase after another. Instead, they work to find ways to convey processes such as changes in birth rates or the spacing of children, or shifts in the goals or tactics of labor strikes; these processes are the culmination of many individual events, such as decisions about how many children to have, but they cannot realistically be traced through events alone.

As a result of their distinctive interests, social historians have developed their own approach to time. As historians, they are centrally concerned with change and therefore with exploring chronology; but they normally proceed in terms of fairly large sweeps rather than year-by-year analysis. Major changes are identified in reference to a decade or two, not a specific year.

The attention to processes rather than events and the related alterations in the lengths of time considered have led social historians to gradually refashion some of the labels that long bedecked the past. They have dropped some conventional demarcations as being too narrowly conceived and too event-based—Europe's mid-eighteenth century is rarely, now, described in terms of the category "enlightened despotism" alone. Or they have redefined the subjects covered by some standard terms. Social historians do see the utility of such concepts as the Renaissance or the Enlightenment, but they have greatly expanded (and complicated) the groups and relationships embraced by these phenomena—so that they are no longer seen simply as periods in which imaginative elites issued new standards—and also the range of behaviors covered. A few standard period labels, such as the Reformation and Catholic Reformation, have actually been enhanced in the process because they now take into account the involvement of ordinary people as well as elites and the impact of these movements in areas such as family life and leisure as well as religion per se. Even with the familiar markers still visible, however, the extent of redefinition has significantly altered the landscape of the past.

The major impact of social history, however, goes beyond the topics it emphasizes, the sources and methods it uses, even the ways in which it organizes and presents the past. Social historians argue for an extensive revision of conventional assessments of causation—the factors that shape societies and prompt significant change. As part of this revision, they advocate a greater willingness to look beneath the surface in historical analysis. Emphasis on ordinary people thus follows in part from a desire to provide key groups with an understanding of their own history and a valid sense of their own past identity and importance. It follows also, however, from a firm belief that ordinary people count in shaping society as a whole. They are not merely acted upon, and they do not surface only occasionally, as in a literal revolutionary outburst; their presence is a constant force. The decisions that ordinary people make about family goals, self-expression, or work standards play active roles, even when elite groups clearly dominate, and exercise their own shaping power in society at large. By the same token, changes in facets of society seemingly remote from formal politics may precondition political change, as well as the other way around. A fascinating correlation has developed, for example, between findings about shifts in child-rearing—based on new economic motives and new ideas about individuality reflected, for example, in less traditional naming patterns—and the kinds of political movements, pressing for greater opportunity and defiance of convention, that surfaced at the end of the eighteenth century. Once parents began to treat children as distinct individuals, giving them names apart from family tradition, those children, once grown, began to rebel against governments that constrained individual choice.

Social historians do not claim, of course, that they have identified all the connections that link family or leisure to more conventional historical topics, much less that they have unraveled all the links. They do claim not only that topics such as recreation or emotional norms are important in their own right because they provide historical perspective for key subject areas or policy concerns, but also that there are relationships across topics in which politics and formal ideas do not necessarily take precedence. Dealing with balances between elites and masses (the latter divided into various subgroups), and among various social institutions and social expressions, forces a more open-ended and a broader-gauged approach to the past. It also necessitates a more deliberately analytical style, as a mere recounting of data such as formal constitutional development no longer suffices to describe—much less to explain—how societies functioned in the past.

The rise of social history altered many staples of the past as well as adding whole new topics. The Industrial Revolution, for example, has been transformed from a story about a handful of heroic entrepreneurs and inventors to a more nuanced one focusing both on the processes by which large numbers of businesspeople and workers modified the ways they worked and on the reasons they participated in economic life. Industrialization is assessed in terms of its impact on a wide array of social constructs—on family and gender relations, for example—in addition to its more familiar results in the areas of technology and business organization. The essentials of this fundamental economic shift, and its causation, have been redefined and clarified, particularly through examination of its connections with wider social change.[5]

Not surprisingly, social history has also generated changes in the practice of older branches of the discipline, though without entirely displacing more conventional modes. Both intellectual and political historians have begun to talk about the interactions of their subjects with ordinary people, as recipients of key ideas whose reception could also shape cultural currents and as petitioners, voters, and political protesters as well as objects of state action. They also have begun to deal somewhat more directly with basic processes (an idea not foreign to intellectual history, which is attuned to general movements of ideas and not just individual thinkers); thus political historians now talk about major changes in the political spectrum rather than about one presidential administration after another, and attention to major alterations in the state-society interaction rivals the lists of new government agencies or individual pieces of legislation. A focus on basic processes and diverse strands of causation thus has begun to displace conventional narrative accounts and previous assumptions that politics (or intellectual life) was essentially a closed box in which political developments caused other political developments that only rarely came into contact with larger and less strictly political variables. Even in diplomatic history, where the "black box" of statecraft (diplomats causing diplomacy, with each major stage of diplomatic interaction following from the previous stage) remained hardest to penetrate, some bold pioneers ventured the possibility of linkages with the wider society in terms of popular value systems as well as changing economic or demographic structures.

As in the field of English, several strands of innovation have spurred the regeneration of research in history. Though less commanding than the social history approach, for example, psychohistory—the study of individuals or groups through use of psychological theory—has also produced some interesting findings. As in English also, the major new approaches in historical research have urged the exploration of factors beneath the conventional surface as part of a more penetrating inquiry into the ways in which cultures and societies really function. These new channels of historical inquiry, with social history atop the list, have generated an unprecedented explosion of historical knowledge and major revisions in the conceptual frameworks applied to the past. Finally, the new directions of scholarship have departed vigorously from the standard approaches and subject matter of the history classroom. Again as in English, innovation is not automatically equated with success; we have yet to address the real questions about the appropriateness of dynamic research for history teaching. What is clear is the opportunity for redirection, the challenge both to traditional teaching modes and to alternatives that merely contest the specific subject matter.

The development of social history, with its distinctive vision of the past and its expanded analysis, has been paralleled by growing historical attention to regions of the world outside the Western tradition. American historical awareness of developments in Latin America or Asia did not, of course, spring up entirely anew in the 1960s. Nevertheless, our growing international involvements, and particularly the new research funding briefly established in the wake of the Sputnik crisis, spurred substantial expansion in area studies programs, which normally include an extensive historical component. Historical knowledge of East Asia, Africa, Eastern Europe, and Latin America has grown rapidly, with American scholars making some basic discoveries in these fields. The new approaches to understanding non-Western regions are not confined to social history, but they normally focus on patterns among large groups of people and on behaviors such as peasant protest, kinship networks, or popular religious values. Major events, specific political forms and elite actors, and individual intellectuals are fitted into a larger picture. Also related to social history is the general interest in establishing firm ties with other social science disciplines, particularly anthropology.

The most important development of all, however, has been an insistence that major areas of the world be viewed as historical actors in their own right and not simply as recipients of Western impulses and guidance. Thus African history, to use the most notable example, did not begin with Western contact, and even in the age of active imperialism, Western contact did not define everything that was going on. This approach requires some of the same adjustments in conventional views of causation, some of the same attention to more complex outcomes, generated by the social history of Western Europe and the United States. Hesitantly at first in the 1960s, and then with renewed vigor in the 1980s, a breed of world historians has advanced ideas about international forces operating in the past as well as in the present and about the possibility of tracing and comprehending these forces historically. This world history approach, defined as something more than a collection of disparate regional histories, has by no means pulled every strand together, for coherent integration remains a daunting task. Nevertheless, new theories of international economic relationships and of cultural diffusion and evolution provide a challenging analytical framework that extends beyond the area studies specialties. The result increasingly has been to remake the conventional map of the past, to include world dynamics and a challenge to any West-centered myopia, paralleled by the growing interest in studying diverse groupings and behaviors within particular societies.

World history and social history are ultimately related. To be sure, some world history has focused on transferring Western categories of "greatness" to other societies, conveying a sense of civilizing accomplishments that may no longer be purely European but that continue to emphasize the achievements of the elites. Civilization itself is still frequently defined in terms of literary masterpieces and monumental art, though now Confucian philosophy and the Indian epics have joined the list of writings from Western classical tradition. But a fuller assessment of world history inevitably has forced major modifications in this approach, downplaying claims that Western measurements of civilization or ancient Greek paradigms suffice to capture global historical complexity. The idea of culture must be extended to include popular as well as elite worldviews, nonliterate as well as literary traditions. Historians who deal with African and Latin American social history, often interacting with anthropologists, have taken the lead in identifying the ways in which genuine world history forces us to undertake more than a geographic expansion of focus.[6]

The surge of social history and world history had political underpinnings, as the canonists who attack them obviously recognize. Many social historians hoped to elicit sympathy for lower-class groups or to aid in their empowerment. Many world historians had similar goals for various areas of the world outside Western Europe and North America. Traditionalists are not wrong, then, in identifying some political challenges embedded in scholarly innovation. All knowledge has political implications—for example, scientific learning certainly privileges certain knowledge groups over others and was correctly seen as intensely political three hundred years ago. The new humanities approaches are not simply or uniformly political, however, and they cannot be dismissed solely on such grounds. They also flow from new methods of inquiry and new explanatory models, and some of their leading practitioners have been either apolitical or moderate to conservative in slant. Radicals, indeed, often lament the political ambiguity of current social history—they see social historians who deal with adaptations and successful subcultures as infuriatingly, if implicitly, conservative in their neglect of injustice and struggle. Political debates cannot be avoided in the new scholarship, as we will see further when we discuss teaching implications, but the challenge to traditional humanistic formulas goes well beyond explicit political preferences to basic modes of explanation.[7]

Politics aside, the introduction of innovations like social history or world history into such an entrenched discipline inevitably caused a host of perturbations, which have been playing out over the past two decades. Faddish interests are not always tested for significance; not all the "new topics" that social historians have explored are necessarily worth the trouble, and in the meantime they have prompted accusations of triviality. Although social history has coined less jargon than the new cultural studies in English, it has developed coherence problems of its own. The proliferation of valid new topics has led to a sense of unmanageable fragmentation in our view of the past; this is an important complication, particularly where the teaching of history is concerned. Social history at times seems to be little more than the putting on parade of one historically neglected group after another, with little or no relationship among them. Exciting discoveries in area studies, often unleavened even by comparison with other cases, could have the same effect. Scholars may gain new knowledge about such places as southeast Asia or Turkey, but they fail to provide the linkages that would move these subjects beyond specialist's domain. In the schools and colleges, the results of this fragmentation are revealed in a host of courses on special topics like family history or surveys of individual civilizations—perfectly valid, but omitting the connections that would facilitate their coherent presentation to nonspecialists, and particularly difficult to translate to the level of high school or college-freshman teaching. It is also true that enthusiasm for genuine new discovery in historical research has diverted attention from the teaching mission. The most imaginative fervor has been directed at other targets.

Limitations of this sort are inevitable when the thrust of a subject area is being reconsidered and when substantial new knowledge is accumulating. When coupled with the outright opposition of some conventional practitioners and the even more widespread lethargy of many history teachers, however, these limitations have produced a widening gap between history as a source of discovery, not only of new data but of basic new approaches to the past, and history as a teaching discipline. It is this gap and its counterpart in literary studies, fed additionally by a recently enhanced agenda of values-inculcation, that raises the crucial questions about educational direction addressed in the following chapters.

Before turning to pedagogy directly, though, it is vital to note that research innovations, in maturing, have themselves yielded some important correctives to their more distracting initial impulses. Thus the tendencies toward fragmentation, based on the proliferation of new topics and the lack of a single unifying methodology, although not entirely excised, have yielded to important efforts at synthesis. These follow from the maturation of the field and from considerable self-examination, though, in fairness some of the pressures applied by external critics have played a role as well. Social historians by no means agree on a single frameworks—any more than old-fashioned political and intellectual historians did—but they increasingly have established their equivalents of major events as central benchmarks.

Thus historians like Charles Tilly have plumped for several "big changes" in the early modern West, which set in motion the essential social structures that have lasted, in Western society, into the present day.[8] The idea of looking for central developments around which a host of specific features of social structure, popular belief, elite-mass relations, demography, and even crime might be linked over long spans of time has gained ground steadily. Tilly urges the concomitant rise of capitalist social relations (with its key division between owners and nonowners of property) and the nation-state as the twin motors of social change from the sixteenth century onward in Western Europe. Others would modify this list slightly, in particular by adding a basic set of shifts in popular belief systems concerning the self, family, and the natural order, while agreeing that it is possible to find some central patterns in historical change over fairly substantial stretches of time. A leading Latin Americanist has proposed the effort to establish an effective central state, against diffuse social forces including Indian groups and Creole landlords, as a comparable unifying theme in Latin America from the colonial period into the twentieth century.

Another kind of integration, one that cuts through some of the various specific topics generated by social history, focuses on a consistent attempt to link social history and the basic forms and functions of the state.[9] Details of the political narrative still do not matter much in this approach, but substantial shifts in the ways key groups of people view the political process (not simply in modern democracies, but in older forms of expression such as petitioning or popular riots), in the ways they affect political decisions and personnel, and in the functions the state exercises over them, matter greatly—this hold true for leisure patterns or gender relations as well as political behavior per se. Just as the state is being brought back in, so are ideas and cultural values.[10] The burgeoning field of mentalities studies investigates deeply held popular values and their relationship to other social and cultural factors ranging from family behaviors (such as cutting or expanding the birth rate) to the styles and ideas preached by and for elites. Today's social historians have substantially recovered from an early aversion to purely cultural sources such as literary works, and many of them are eager to embrace major cultural changes, including shifts in elite-subgroup cultural relations, and to deal with the relationship between cultural change and other aspects of the historical record.

The visions of political and intellectual history resulting from the new syntheses are not conventional visions. Social historians maintain their belief that the history of the state is not always the central historical thread, and that state actions do not always provide the best measurement or explanation of what society is all about. Interest in the role of ideas does not mean automatic adherence to trickle-down theories of intellectual causation; sometimes beliefs change at the popular level without elite intellectuals having much to do with the process. Despite these caveats, there is no question that social historians are becoming more eager to establish larger visions of the past as well as exploring the ramifications of relatively new special topics. They are not simply attacking the narrowness of conventional portrayals, but supplying pictures of their own by putting specific pieces together into larger wholes. This newer version of social history has not ironed out all the wrinkles, for the new topics continually being generated will only gradually be linked to some of the larger themes—quite apart from the obvious fact that agreement on a single general framework will probably never be reached. The fact remains that social history is no longer the highly focused, research-driven movement that burst on the scene in the 1970s—and this means that social history increasingly serves as a basis for teaching about the past and for linking the past to the interrelated issues of contemporary society.

A similar integrative process has begun to emerge in history's new international outreach. Area studies remain vital centers of research, but more and more they are being joined through a growing array of comparative ventures that can help scholars and students alike deal with the past without passing through every major world region at a specialist level. The history of slavery has received particularly sophisticated comparative treatment, but work on slave emancipation, peasant protest, urban forms, and some other issues furthers this process. Another kind of integration is achieved through the use of particular concepts in various specific settings. Thus the discovery of popular belief in a moral economy—that is, a set of standards by which economic relationships were judged by ordinary people and, in periods of major change, often found deficient—developed initially as an explanation of the values that lay behind European protest surges on the eve of industrialization; but the moral economy concept has also proved fruitful in studying peasant reactions to commercial relationships and colonial legislation in various parts of southern Asia and in Latin America. This means that an understanding of moral economy conveys a substantial slice of world history, even for students of history who lack the time to develop full knowledge of all these regions of the world. Finally, world history itself—increasingly defined as more than a case-by-case summary of major regions—caps the integration process. As with social history, the result is not a single tidy package of the past but an enhanced ability to provide some theoretical guidelines toward greater coherence.

Developments in the study of literature and other media suggest that a similar process of integration and maturation, while preserving the essential vision of earlier innovations, is beginning to affect scholarship in the discipline of English. Some aspects of deconstructionism seemed more bent on trashing any framework based on identifying great works of literature than on creating an alternative structure. Increasingly, however, deconstructionist or post-structuralist theories work, first, to identify the historical context within which literary products take shape and, second, to use these products (conventionally familiar works as well as less famous ones and productions in media besides literature per se) to grasp the meaning of cultural relationships in a given society at a particular period of time. Literary scholars can generate theories about types of gender relations that are expressed, sometimes implicitly, in various cultural forms and can use these theories, in turn, to help students grasp the meaning of a given literary work in terms other than a faithful summing up of its surface content—its plot and characters. Theories about the relationship of literary or visual representations to human desire constitute another variable in understanding what a given work means or how the larger culture in which it was embedded actually functions. As in history, innovative research in literary studies has tended to build toward larger concepts after an initial flurry of irreverent bravado and a spate of often specialized, not readily accessible monographs.

In rough outline, then, history and cultural studies have moved from a somewhat iconoclastic phase in the late 1960s, in which conventional emphases in the humanities were attacked or bypassed and immense dynamism applied to alternative scholarship, to a more reflective phase. The energy persists but increasingly informs, in addition to new research, an interest in reassembling larger pictures. Conventional scholarship has not been restored, and the fiery tensions between new and old ways still burn bright. The innovators, however, are becoming ever more capable of offering their own visions, not simply to excited cospecialists but to a larger audience as well. The implications for teaching, beclouded in the early phase by the sheer fascination of innovative research, are becoming increasingly manageable.

Finally, the juxtaposition of recent developments in history and literary study suggests a new basis for considerable coherence in more general humanistic inquiry. Without oversimplifying various disciplinary terminologies and goals, it nevertheless becomes obvious that innovators in several disciplines are focusing on the issues of how basic cultural patterns shape the expressions, institutions, and behaviors of a particular society and how our own patterns affect our ability to understand.

One case in point involves gender, currently a driving interest in many branches of the humanities. Social historians are developing important new redefinitions of masculinity in American society during the early nineteenth century. Many of the attributes now associated with masculinity (and sometimes bemoaned)—including reluctance to cry or show emotions, sexual assertiveness, and a certain tentativeness in the domestic sphere—developed at that time, modifying or (as in the case of crying) actually reversing previous definitions. Social historians can also explain why these changes occurred. Scholars in the cultural studies area have documented many of the same developments and further point to their influence in a variety of expressions not only about gender, but about matters seemingly as far afield as race or foreign policy. The combined, interdisciplinary effect has been to establish a solid humanistic basis for exploring the nature, sources, and impacts of a new cultural definition of gender.[11]

The overlapping agendas in the humanities apply more broadly as well. Humanities scholarship, in its newer incarnations, argues strongly against any idea that the main purpose of inquiry is to master the great works of a given culture or to assume that such works in any simple sense define the values of that culture or its principal legacies. Social historians disdain "great men" as explanations for much, just as cultural scholars disdain a definition of great classics. This common reaction against older visions of the humanities is not, however, the main point. Scholars of history and of literary culture broadly construed can now talk to each other in terms of a new constructive agenda; their goal is to figure out how basic cultural assumptions shape political forms, scientific beliefs, even essential human experiences such as emotion and illness, and how these assumptions can in turn be studied by teasing out the fundamental meanings of particular cultural expressions. They see such expressions relatedly as products of an interaction between authors and audiences, for fundamental meanings do not flow from a simple, unidirectional act of inspired creation. The humanities, in this vision, gain basic coherence from their ongoing attempt to formulate the data and the theoretical approaches necessary for us to grasp how and to what extent cultures construct meaning. And humanists, as teachers and scholars, deal with the results of this construction not only on cultural forms themselves but also on wider reaches of the human experience.

Parallels in the key humanities disciplines need not be pressed too far. Students of literature accept cultural construction far more readily than do most historians. Does a social class, for example, evolve from new economic arrangements and political power balances and then create some common culture, or is it formed by the shared culture itself? Here is a current challenge to the practitioners of the social history of labor. Many historians would argue that shifting political and economic frameworks prompt new cultural constructions rather than the reverse, though they do acknowledge that the constructions themselves are significant; determining the direction of the flow is a crucial analytical focus. Disagreements among social historians and between them and even more relativistic literary analysts should not obscure the main point. The humanities do not produce tidy formulas. They do generate ranges of debate about how societies operate. New scholarship has now produced one of these ranges with fundamental implications for our understanding of the functioning of people and societies, and curricula can and should be formulated on this basis, with disagreements built into the mix.

The structures emerging in newer research areas like social history and the ability to discern solid hints of a unifying purpose in humanistic inquiry now redefined do not, of course, dispel all of the destabilizing effects of a generation of varied innovation. A newly founded collaboration between history and English, most obviously, remains more a potential gain than a reality, though a few pioneering teaching programs are implementing the connection with courses that blend social history, anthropology, and cultural studies. Pioneering scholars in English continue, in the judgment of many, to rely unduly on arcane jargon and, in some cases, to pursue too overtly a political agenda in deconstructing past culture to illuminate the injustices of prejudices based on gender, race, or sexual preference. Social history research does not always meet the highest standards of synthesis; in some instances, connections to wider concerns about the role of the state, belief systems, or other larger issues are merely tacked on. A few social historians, indeed, probably still work in the shadow of an earlier definition of their specialty, "history with the politics left out," that inherently complicates their relationship to the historical craft as a whole. Certainly, none of innovators in the humanities disciplines have persuaded all of their academic colleagues, or the interested public, of the validity of their claims; this is a central issue as we turn from the innovations themselves to the question of what should be taught. The inevitable confusion engendered by basic redefinition combines with a tendency toward obfuscation by some new-style researchers, bent above all on impressing a small academic audience, to complicate the issues of reception and impact.

Nevertheless, with all their warts, innovations in humanities scholarship have fundamentally redefined the fields involved, if not beyond recognition, than at least in substantial fashion. Social history, initially discounted as an interesting or distracting fad, has sunk durable roots into the practice of history during its twenty-five-year growth period. No major historical journal or history department or college-level text lacks substantial representation of the sociohistorical approach, and some are essentially shaped by this approach. Before turning to the contests over curriculum, therefore, we should sum up the essential qualities of new-style humanities.

The Focus on Analysis

Details of the achievements and limitations of social history or international history or deconstructionism or the new historicism are not, after all, the crucial stuff of curriculum formation, and my description of these movements has relied on selective illustration, not comprehensive exposition or defense. The main points, as they cut across specific disciplines, are not impossibly complicated, for they cluster around two central themes.

First, new-style humanists dispute the traditional canons of their disciplines. The new literary studies scholars argue against focusing solely on "great works" and even against the distortion of evaluation necessary to establish a list of great works in the first place. Their purpose is to develop wider theories of cultural expression and to determine how literary products of various sorts illustrate broader cultural dynamics, including the author/audience interaction. Definitions of English in terms of a *Beowulf* to Virginia Woolf pantheon, they claim, both distract and mislead us. Social historians urge attention to forces of change other than particular political figures or the specific ideas of individual philosophers, though they can sometimes enfold these factors within the larger categories they seek to establish. International historians insist that we recognize major values and institutions outside the Western tradition, even in its most extensive definition. Collectively, these emphases suggest a scholarly mission far different from the traditional one of memorializing a list of heroic figures or ideas from the intellectual and political past.

During the 1980s, as part of the canonists' reaction discussed more extensively in the next chapter, lists of essential facts were generated to provide guidelines for identifying properly educated people. One result, of course, was to highlight the presumed ignorance of most American students, who could not master the lists. The lists were largely populated by events and individuals in the Western tradition, especially the elite tradition; they assumed the special qualities of this tradition but also its trickle-down derivation from the minds of great thinkers and the heroic deeds of great statesmen and military leaders.

Most humanities scholars who had turned to the newer agendas were appalled at the narrowness of the lists. Some, as I mentioned in the introduction, were tempted to produce alternate lists that would reflect the extended range of their own subject matter. These lists could contain fewer elite and Western figures, more events and creative individuals from other world civilizations, and more trends—even some individuals—from the ranks of women and the lower classes. The result might be a world/social history list, in obvious contrast with a Western/elite list, and the gains, in terms of defining educated people and preparing guidelines for their training, would be considerable. For the most part, however, the new humanities scholars argued against creating lists of any sort, even better ones—which is why, despite the money to be made, alternative lists have not really been forthcoming. The central current of the new humanities research runs against facile attribution of significance to events and individuals merely because they happened or held some position of power, and the same current works against the idea that knowledge of items on a list reflects any understanding of the workings of culture and society. The goal, in other words, should not be primarily to replace one canon with a "better" one.

The positive side of the new humanities scholarship, which is growing more visible as the new research matures and its practitioners become less defensive, encourages us to use the study of cultures and of the issues surrounding cultural and social change as tools for analysis, as vantage points for raising critical questions about how human beings and their societies function. Analytical history, in this sense, is a more important category than social history or world history alone. Analytical history is not new; the best historians from Thucydides to Burckhardt have always tried to get beneath the surface, to ask questions about causation, deeper meaning, and results. What has happened, primarily through the agency of social history, is that more historians now seek this mode, with fewer being content simply to provide a factual narrative of events. Telling a story still counts in history, but now the stories are less straightforward, and they are more commonly surrounded by a formal analytical apparatus that raises questions about causes and impacts and that often seeks to link one pattern to others through comparisons or cautious generalization.[12] The historical record is no longer reproduced as literally as it once was, and we can no longer define educational goals so simply. Conceptualization has moved to the front of the stage.

In this formulation, to take a specific example, periodization replaces chronology. The latter, the staple of historical chroniclers since the days of the monks, lists what can be listed in order of each event's occurrence in time. This method offers easy targets for memorization. Periodization, in contrast, seeks to identify meaning over stretches of time. It seeks to discern when and why a change of pattern occurs and then to recognize when that pattern shifts in its turn. (Again, this is not a new approach—all good historians have used it to balance mere chronology.) Periodization requires analytical underpinnings to a far greater extent than memorization. It encompasses developments that occur in time but have no single date, and it describes far more of what the past was actually about than do the tidy lists.

A comparable analytical emphasis has emerged in literary study with the growing insistence on the importance of theory. A theoretical analysis of literary works requires more formal probing, less summary of contents, and fewer hymns of praise than in the old great-book school; critical questions become more varied as they attempt to penetrate beneath the surface and to link specific works to wider issues of cultural context and audience impact. Theories about gender or impulse override the more conventional categories, such as romanticism or realism, that once grouped literature into essentially descriptive genres. Where the understanding of history and culture is concerned, an educated person now needs to be far more familiar with analytical issues than with nominal lists.

Correspondingly, the central focus of the humanities has shifted from describing and pondering the value systems presumably embedded in the great thoughts and great deeds of literature, philosophy, and the past to considering how cultures themselves are shaped and how they in turn inform institutions, expressions, behaviors, and values. Analyzing the deeply held beliefs and assumptions that make up cultures—how they interact, sometimes within a single society; how they redirect and respond to patterns in politics, the economy, the physical environment; how they vary; and how they change—provides the central stuff of humanistic research. Some humanists see virtually all individual and social endeavors as culturally constructed. Others believe that cultural variety and change follow from some other causation, such as new economic relationships. Even in this view, however, cultural expression translates the essential meaning of more objective systems into human terms and causes additional adjustments in its own right.

Key areas of inquiry, such as research on human emotion, increasingly distinguish between innate responses, which are open to scientific research, and culturally conditioned reactions that can be fully explored only through a humanistic research design. Many demographers, similarly, move between descriptions of population behaviors, which require rigorous quantitative techniques, and the apparatus necessary to explain significant change in such behaviors as the birth rate, areas where human motivations—and therefore changing value systems—come into play. In technical terms, these researchers treat culture as a variable, not just a residual. As analysis reshapes the overall humanistic agenda, its cultural focus, broadly construed, has come to define the boundary line between the humanities and the sciences; both are analytical at base but feature different research methodologies depending on whether replicability is or is not possible. The sciences face deep-seated problems in dealing with cultural issues, just as the humanities cannot claim to explore essential physical phenomena. Both approaches, however, are concerned with generating explanatory theories on the basis of available data. Some individual disciplines like sociology and anthropology are themselves divided between scientific domains and those areas in which cultural analysis proves indispensable. In these fields, too, the new range and vitality of humanities research can provide innovative frameworks for interpretation and for interdisciplinary connections.

What has happened, we now see, is that key humanities disciplines have become sources of new knowledge and new kinds of methodologies, questions, and theories; they are no longer primarily repositories of received wisdom. It is of course true that humanities research has never precluded vital analytical insights, and it is certainly true that much new scholarship proves petty and ephemeral. Nevertheless, the balance of purpose has shifted. Correspondingly, one of the central challenges of the new scholarship involves transmission: How, and to what extent, can the new approaches be assimilated by nonspecialists and applied to the classroom setting? How can humanities teaching, long based on the idea of sanctifying established values through repetition of hallowed examples in history and literature alike, adjust to the new vision of the humanities as sources of new critical questions and vehicles for innovative discovery?

THREE

Sacred Cows

in Humanities

Teaching, and

How They Got

Grazing Rights

Disagreements over the new, analytical scholarship in the humanities are inevitable. They first surfaced in the 1960s and, with some oscillations, they have persisted among scholars themselves (with waning force, though the wounds remain fairly fresh in English). Older practitioners defend their turf and point out many gaps and infelicities in the more recent work. As suggested in the previous chapter, they have made some good points—amid many grumpy denunciations—and they have encouraged some healthy correctives without halting the momentum of the new research. Disputes among the new practitioners have scarcely abated, however, and as might be expected, the range has increased with time. Marxist social historians complain of upstart feminists and cultural relativists. Feminism ignites great scholarly passion, at times perhaps to the detriment of other topics and vantage points. The humanities, because they lack laboratory-replicable methods, are inherently disputatious, and innovation has hardly stifled this quality.

Disputes over scholarly direction, however, are not the same as the arguments over humanities politics that have received wider publicity amid the fulminations of the Blooms and the political correctness adepts. The disputes are not unrelated, but it is essential to distinguish between them. This chapter begins the process of sorting out the noisier, though in many ways more superficial, clamor. I have two main goals here. First, for those readers dazzled by current news about the sins of the academic left in its real or imagined political correctness campaigns, the chapter explores the earlier political current that deflected substantive implementation of the new scholarship at the curricular level and that continues to constrain educational debate; in other words, it defines canonism and its hold in the humanities domain. Second, the chapter offers some tentative analysis of the sources of canonism and its passions. The frenzy of some canonists goes well beyond the problems of facing down new scholarship; the context is larger. When Kenneth Jackson, a noted historian and a contributor in urban social history, invokes a return to the canon lest the United States splinter into Yugoslavian fragments—against all political common sense or probability—then clearly more than the threat of analytical history and deconstructionism is involved. Looking to the traditions of canonism but also its current social purposes helps explain the "other side" of the current political stridency, an agenda too often obscured by the civilization-salvation rhetoric of the canonists. The same examination moves us toward a clearer understanding of why responsible curricula must escape the canonist framework.

Others have already pointed out the self-serving sanctimony of some current canonists, who attack radical scholars as if they themselves were free of political partisanship and were concerned only with defense of objective, civilized truth.[1] Without accepting the entire multiculturalist counterattack, I agree that the unwillingness of many canonists to recognize their own political agendas is genuinely troubling. It impedes sensible debate. But the canonists do more than attack the scholars and students who seek a less elitist subject matter. They also assail, either explicitly or by indirection, the new scholarship in the humanities, seeking to close the museum doors against it. In this, they do an even greater disservice to effective teaching in the humanities fields.

We begin to trace these developments by picking up the themes of the new scholarship and the changes that they began to effect in planning course programs, only to be short-circuited by the canonist revival.

By the 1970s, as new historical discoveries and literary vantage points emerged, discussion of translating new humanities scholarship into teaching lagged behind the scholarship itself. Researchers had their own territories to stake out, and this task was sufficiently challenging and sufficiently exciting to divert their attention from immediate educational issues. Graduate programs, to be sure, quickly reflected some of the innovation, as new fields of study were added—Harvard defined a social and economic history area, open to examination, in the early 1960s—and new interpretations adduced. Mainstream college and high school humanities courses, however, changed little at first.

As the research agenda established itself more fully—in history, this followed major results in such areas as colonial family history, the history of slavery, and non-Western regional study—implications for education and popularization gradually solidified. In the 1970s the National Endowment for the Humanities began to sponsor teacher training and curriculum development programs for instructors at various levels, an effort that has continued, though more sporadically and amid fiercely competing emphases, even as the NEH turned against much of the new work. Several centers offering quantitative training in history and related disciplines cropped up. The Society for State and Local History sponsored an attractive training program for museum experts, designed to acquaint them with the relevance of social history to their presentations and outreach efforts, and a redefinition of historical museums along more sociohistorical lines has been fairly widespread.[2]

Textbook publishers were less susceptible to new scholarship because of their timid desire to make each new product only mildly dissimilar from its counterparts lest an established audience—or evaluators in critical states like Texas—be offended; nevertheless, even they found potential authors affected by the new findings to some extent. They were pressured also by new constituency demands, from such groups as women and African Americans, to include historical and literary analyses that went beyond the products and doings of the white male elite. This combination of factors produced, if not systematically new textbooks, at least special features sections that spiced conventional coverage with some social history or novel literary comment. By the 1980s, at the college level, some substantially reconsidered textbooks had emerged, surpassing the earlier patchwork response still characteristic of most school texts.[3] (As I have noted, even high school texts that trumpet a world history title still maintain a primary Western coverage, lest familiar Western signposts be lost; which means that teaching real world history at this level remains exceptionally difficult.) Finally other educational leadership agencies, responding to new scholarship and new student political demography alike, picked up the challenge. The College Board has made systematic efforts to promote social history in its testing program, often exceeding actual school coverage, while highlighting both social and world history and some newer approaches in literature in its recommended standards for students' college preparation.[4]

By the early 1980s, in sum, the new scholarship was beginning to reshape some humanities teaching. A definite lag persisted; the substantial redefinition that had occurred at the research level had yet to remake college programs and had barely penetrated most public school curricula. The various constraints that teachers faced—including available mainstream texts, the conservatism of a teaching corps most of whose members had been trained well before the advent of new scholarship, and the continued tendency of leading researchers to focus on their own discoveries rather than engage in curricular leadership—all limited the educational impact, but it was possible to imagine incremental progress. The logic of the situation suggested that a genuine rethinking of educational presentation to match the rethinking of the scholarly fields be undertaken. Logical development of this sort takes time, of course, and necessitates various compromises, but a decade ago there was no reason for pessimism. Indeed, several educators contended not only that teaching should catch up with scholarship in the humanities as a matter of accuracy—this was the thrust of College Board advice to the schools—but also that classroom translation of the same scholarship, properly done, could revivify student interest in the subject areas, and there was some scattered evidence in this direction from teachers who took the plunge of innovation. High school experiments with social history in the late 1970s generated enthusiasm among students who were intrigued by grappling with issues also familiar in their own lives, and some teachers, extending these same experiments, were able to move toward more sophisticated analytical training on issues of periodization or causation.[5]

Tentative gains were not entirely reversed by the 1990s, but it is obvious that far less advance has occurred than might have been anticipated a decade ago. Sheer lethargy continues to be an obstacle, but it has been joined by the tempestuous pedagogical counterattack. The humanities canon has been brought to bear on the advancing forces of change, and it has proved a fearsome weapon, misleading even its opponents into counterproductive strategies. So what is the canon all about?

Research innovation naturally begets reaction. It is not completely farfetched to compare the current situation in the humanities with the impact of evolutionary biology over a century ago. Darwinian theory ultimately forced a new way of teaching about biology, but only after a bitter struggle that even today has not completely ended. The theory seemed to undermine basic intellectual identities, particularly in its implications for established Protestant thinking about the Bible and creation. Although the current furor in the humanities has less explicitly religious ballast—even most conservatives reflect a more secular age—it has some of the same elements of impassioned defense of hallowed truths against a profane interloper. Darwinism, of course, also produced a host of dubious corollaries, particularly the racist, imperialist, and capitalist applications of evolutionary theory to the social sphere; and we will see that the new humanities scholarship generates its share of extremisms, though they are typically of the opposite political stripe.

Innovation, in other words, undeniably weakens some traditional controls over intellectual foolishness, and the results give heart to proponents of the status quo. But the counterattack is based primarily on resistance to the central innovation itself, not its more questionable ramifications. Conservatives feel that it is more important to defend established beliefs than to explore—and to encourage students to explore—what the new understandings may offer. This reaction may be inevitable, as the loose Darwinian analogy is meant to suggest, but it is nonetheless troubling, for it delays and might even prevent us from addressing the real challenge of making new forms of analysis available to students who, willy-nilly, face the question of what culture is all about.

At the same time, the most critical attacks on the core of the new scholarship have not been scholarly (with some exceptions, again, in the field of English), but pedagogical. Traditionalists have raised some valid points about social history—such as the non-sense of leaving politics out—but their comments have helped the field mature. Pitched battles about the new approach itself have dwindled. The teaching target, in contrast, has proved more vulnerable, allowing arguments that could not pass muster at the research level (about the causal role of heroes, for example) to be revived amid the complex contexts in which curricula are discussed.

Adapting new scholarship to teaching requirements is demanding in itself, for it requires choices about omitting familiar materials and decisions about identifying appropriate levels of understanding. The adaptation is nearly impossible in an atmosphere of obscurantist counterattack. This counterattack, then, must be addressed before the more constructive tasks can be renewed.

The passion of the canonists' belief is unquestioned, as demonstrated in a number of recent books and editorial broadsides. A professor of Italian writes, in a book awarded the annual prize of the American Association of Colleges, that students need study only the history and literature of classical Greece and Rome to gain their humanistic insights, but this history and literature they must study thoroughly, without the distraction of subsequent writings, much less current controversies.[6] Only unadulterated tradition, this view seems to say, can shelter us from the sad facts of modernity.

A blast at academia by a journalist, although making a number of valid points, cites as its principal aim "to expose these recent developments in the academic study of humanities for what they are: ideologically motivated assaults on the intellectual and moral substance of our culture."[7] This writer's solution (not closely examined, on grounds that it should be self-evident) is a return to the single, unified, coherent tradition that provided clear and glorious standards of truth.

Bringing the charge to a still-simpler level was the conservative columnist Charles Krauthammer. In a 1990 commentary (before Saddam Hussein provided a briefly distracting demonological target), Krauthammer cited deconstructionists, along with peace advocates and environmentalists, as the chief threats to the American political order now that (in his perhaps overhasty view) the cold war had reduced the outright communist threat. Joining the peaceniks and antipollutionists, and probably exceeding them in menace, were the new radical academics bent on tearing down belief in the common values of Western civilization and American democracy. Good Americans, the implication was, should come to the aid of the military, capitalism, and the Platonic-Thomistic-Cartesian-Federalist intellectual tradition that had generated beacons of light in a world of darkness.[8]

Clearly, by the late 1980s a vital set of assumptions had come into play, in defense of a particular kind of humanities curriculum and in fevered opposition to innovation. The coherence of these various assumptions was not as immutable as some of their proponents seemed to take for granted, which does not prove that the assumptions themselves, in their curricular implications, were wrong. The defense of Americanness, for example, has not always been rooted in the idea of a continuous Western tradition. Education designed to boost the principles of the American political system, as it developed in the early stages of the new republic in the late eighteenth and early nineteenth centuries, did not emphasize a larger Western civilization, for the simple reason that Western values to that point had been, in the main, neither republican nor democratic. Selected classical writers might be cited in defense of a mixed constitution or of political virtue, but there existed no belief that the American Revolution had sprung from a time-honored Western core. Although classical culture and literature were honored, more recent West European history was shunned in an effort to establish the novel purity of current American virtues and institutions. As a result, not surprisingly, education tended to stress (in addition to religion) the distinctiveness of the American experiment, its advantages over Old World systems that, however impressive and culturally sophisticated, lacked the innovative qualities and youthful vigor of the new United States. Avoidance of European contagion warred with continued admiration for the continent's intellectual and artistic achievements, but even the admirers of a larger Western civilization granted the need for great selectivity in educational matters.

The idea, current in much canonist thought, of genuine harmony between American democratic and Western cultural values is of rather recent vintage. As the United States gingerly entered world diplomacy in the twentieth century, often in opposition to European chaos, its leaders frequently viewed themselves as defenders of a unified Western tradition that their country exemplified in purer fashion than the parochial British or French. This perspective gave new American ventures in world diplomacy a larger purpose. It also evolved as a result of the country's new wealth and power in the wider world as the United States began to share the privileged international position earlier carved out by France and Britain. A virtual abandonment of emphasis on the United States as a revolutionary or at least anticolonial society, in favor of more conservative efforts to join in the defense of Western economic interests in the world at large, facilitated this merger of American and Western traditions and, essentially for the first time, allowed full-scale Western civilization courses a prominent place in American educational curricula.

It is also true that, as even friendly critics of the canon have pointed out, the current fixation on a single "canon" of must-read works and must-know historical data is itself inaccurate. Even traditional humanities programs always allowed considerable variety in the authors covered, changed emphases periodically, and conveyed a certain tentativeness in their judgments of what materials were significant and what works met the highest standards of intellectual excellence.[9]

The fact that many current canonists either distort the educational record or really do not know how they have simplified past curricular complexities is more than an amusing blemish. It behooves those who insist on teaching students the real essence of our past to know, and to convey, what that past is—or at least so it would logically appear. Many canonists, however, are not really defending some essential tradition against iconoclastic onslaught; rather, they are inventing a tradition (partly from genuine elements of past curricula, but partly from whole cloth) to combat real or imagined political problems in contemporary society.[10] Without trying to offer a detailed history, it is time to see how this most recent vision of an intellectual canon emerged.

ffectively, the first definition of the humanities in Western education was a product of the Renaissance in Italy. Classical authors and educators themselves had cited various authorities in developing their own work, and they certainly honored precedents— as when Romans hearkened back to Greek achievements. But they did not project a sense of a particular corpus of learning that must be mastered, beyond largely technical essentials like rhetoric or grammar.

The germ of a canonical idea emerged during the Middle Ages, precisely because the deterioration of education and intellectual life prompted a new sense of awe at past achievement and a new desire to find ways to master and convey the grandeur of earlier intellectuals, particularly of the Church Fathers—theologians such as Augustine and Ambrose—but also of philosophers like Aristotle. Because the primary emphasis was placed on faith as a source of knowledge and on divinity, rather than humanity, as a foremost intellectual goal, this first version of a canonical orientation was not centrally humanistic.

This was where Renaissance thinking, with its attendant redefinitions of education away from strictly church-run schools, came into play by the fifteenth century. Without attacking religion, Renaissance thinkers increased their use of man as the measure of things. They made literature and some branches of philosophy, including political theory, their central intellectual pillars as they distanced themselves from the most rigorous theological systems. And they judged that a mastery of classical style, language, and thought provided a crucial basis for the schooling of educated gentlemen and for further intellectual endeavor.

At an extreme, the Renaissance educational vision assumed that all essential truth, all relevant models of beauty, and all necessary historical examples could be gleaned from exposure to the literature, art, and history of classical Greece and Rome. The assumption rested at once on the real veneration in which classical models were held and the need to find an alternate respectability against the more rationalistic and religious emphases of the Middle Ages. The stress on ancient history thus allowed Renaissance educators to bypass the messy medieval interlude without confronting it directly, though in the process the task of providing a comprehensive historical picture was neglected. History in the Renaissance curriculum entailed mastery of key subjects—particularly political and military events plus major biographies—from the ancient world, along with the ability to draw analogies with similar potential situations in contemporary political, military, and personal life. Systematic analysis was not necessary, and indeed the crucial assumption of the analogical approach—that the frameworks of ancient and Renaissance society were sufficiently alike that knowledge of one could carry over without difficulty to the other—was neither openly presented nor tested. The further assumption was that knowledge of particular sets of data about particular historical episodes and exposure to certain kinds of literary and philosophical writings, such as those of Cicero, would inculcate necessary values and understandings in the process of achieving of factual mastery.

Renaissance educational emphases carried a threefold message. First, of course, was the quintessential focus on the arts and letters as the sources of truth and the foundations of education. Both theology and science were downplayed in the fervent faith in what the disciplines we now call humanities, from their Renaissance humanistic roots, had to offer. Small wonder that humanists in later periods, including today, look back on Renaissance formulas with loving approval—their interests have never since won such unadulterated esteem.

The second message was the belief that reading literature and descriptive history would convey understandings that would improve and guide students as they moved into adult careers. This was unspecialized, generalist training, yet its advantages seemed too obvious to warrant explicit comment. Just how understanding emerged from the memorization of literary passages and the recitation of historical data was thus not explored. Some contemporary canonists echo this Renaissance dictum in arguing, for example, that learning certain historical facts will convey a larger appreciation of political values and options, without really explaining how this occurs—how memorization and understanding combine. The fascination with biographies of great men—for example, Renaissance students dutifully read classics like Plutarch's *Lives*—offered a specific case in which exposure to the facts (sometimes selectively presented for maximum uplift) was designed to provide inspirational guidance. Here is another link with current canonists, who are bent on restoring heroes to the curricula for the benefit of model-starved American youngsters.

The third ingredient of the Renaissance humanities formula was its explicitly elitist quality. The fact that only a small number of wealthy families could afford extensive education was not new to this period—it was characteristic of the Middle Ages and, indeed, of most agriculturally based civilizations. The Renaissance, however, added a new scorn for the uneducated masses, whose culture was now defined as crude and vulgar, possibly dangerous. The withdrawal of educated elites from their prior willingness to share in popular culture was one of the crucial turning points reached in the Renaissance. Not surprisingly, this change in attitude tended to encourage a sense that mastery of certain classics, including, of course, the Latin and Greek in which they were written, were vital means of distinguishing the gentility from common folk—whether or not the former actually had any measurable advantages in wisdom.

The second and third features of the Renaissance humanities formula—the plea for classical wisdom and the unabashed elitism—

could easily clash. It was possible to argue, for example, that the gentry's distinction from the hoi polloi on the basis of their ability to make learned references and to quote extensively revealed the unique understanding that this learning conveyed—through the values imparted by historical analogy, a mastery of literary classics, and an appreciation of the biographies of the ancient greats. It was also possible, however, that in practice the enthusiasm for the status features of classical training might outweigh any consistent concern with understanding. Indeed, if the status criteria functioned well in assuring appropriate jobs for the sons of the wealthy, more substantive probing would be unnecessary. No one would be in a position to ask whether a classically trained scion of the aristocracy had really learned much along with his Latin tags. The tension between status-conscious exposure to rote learning in the classics and widespread assumptions that the classics almost automatically generated enlightenment was neither faced nor resolved as the Renaissance humanities tradition continued to shape European elite education for several centuries. Many aristocratic or aspiring wealthy business families, however, who concentrated on purchasing beautifully bound books by classical authors for libraries that were not always actively used, tended to come down on the side of status assurance. Books owned could count more than books read, just as, for students, memorization could count more than critical understanding.

Quite apart from ongoing religious concern about its excessively secular qualities, the Renaissance tradition was challenged by about 1700 on several related fronts. The belief that education could focus almost exclusively on reading in the works of classical authors and ancient history—a canon, in sum, though not so labeled—was complicated by a growing interest in science and by the scientists' well-supported claims to be able to produce new knowledge, not merely to replicate older learning. Renaissance education, though it had largely shunned the scientific sphere, did accept the widespread and longstanding belief that scientific training should focus largely on mastery of ancient authors, such as Galen in the field of medicine. This harmony had been shattered by the seventeenth century, as scientists like Descartes deliberately shook off older authority and demonstrated their own ability to generate new truths.

Education was not immediately affected, however. Leading scientists did not explicitly claim an educational role, and many of them, as amateurs, maintained a strong if somewhat inconsistent interest in the humanistic canon. New technical training advanced alongside the humanities—for example, the civil and mining engineering schools in eighteenth-century France—but although these institutions foreshadowed a larger ultimate trend, they were not immediately critical. The rise of science did begin to break up the near-monopoly that the Renaissance had conferred on the humanities in education, though the process was a gradual one until well into the nineteenth century, both in Europe and in the new United States. Throughout this period, the humanities segments that persisted were not necessarily rethought. Science at the college level might follow a secondary-school training in the classical humanities or might somehow combine with it. Indeed, many educators, particularly but not exclusively nonscientists, gloried in a traditionalist humanities program precisely because it provided an alternative to the inherently innovative, substantive courses in the new science. Status considerations played a strong role: A gentlemanly cachet won from mastery of the humanistic classics could override the new-knowledge claims of scientists without subjecting its bearer to the chore of dealing with the unfamiliar.

The rise of science, in the long run, did not just reduce the place of the humanities in education and in intellectual life more generally. It tended to confirm many educators, both those opposed to science and some of those enamored of it, in their belief that the humanities' role was to be an unchanging anchor. As science periodically shed its old skins, the classics would remain constant from one generation to the next—an attitude that many scientists, force-fed on a humanistic great-books diet, still maintain. In this view, the humanities, in addition to their inherent differences in subject matter and methodology, were distinguished from science by their stability; their glory lay in *not* changing.

A second challenge to the classical focus of the humanities, also following from the rise of new science, undeniably complicated the humanistic disciplines' new service of providing educational ballast in a time of change. As early as the 1690s, a number of philosophers and literary figures began to carry the iconoclastic implications of science into the halls of humanism. They argued that philosophers and writers, like scientists, could improve on the work of the ancients. The resultant "quarrel between ancients and moderns" reverberated in Western Europe for several decades. The "ancients" maintained that classical culture had been a humanistic Eden; it was blasphemy to suppose that the like could ever again appear on earth. The Greeks and the Romans had achieved cultures unsurpassable not only in general, but in every essential particular. The "moderns"—advocates of progress among men of letters—granted the impressive achievements of classical civilization but insisted that modern Europeans could surpass them, even in areas of style and beauty. New literature or philosophy, in other words, partly because it could build on past works, might be better than old. Novelty, according to the extremist moderns, might even be a plus.

Officially the moderns won the debate. Writers felt increasingly freed from purely classical stylistic or thematic models. A more radical version of the debate in France in the 1820s saw romantics attacking even classical stylistic norms—and, again, winning out. Philosophers in the eighteenth and nineteenth centuries alike, although they still usually cited ancient example, could discuss the possibility of constructing new and greatly improved political schemes. Artists proudly began to depart from classical models, particularly after 1830. Humanistic endeavor proceeded, in some areas, with no explicit bows at all to the classical canon.

Education, though slowly, came to reflect some of these ideas. By the nineteenth century, some modern or relatively modern authors were studied along with the classical greats. Shakespeare was a case in point; after many decades of relative neglect, he gained neoclassical status by the later eighteenth century. Modern languages were taught alongside the ancient tongues, then instead of them—first Greek, then Latin began their nineteenth-century decline. Most of this change, however, was amazingly gradual. Despite the vigorous new work being done in literature, philosophy, and even aspects of history, education never fully reflected the moderns' victory—and, as the vigor of canonism testifies, it has not done so even to the present day. The gap between what was actually being done in humanistic areas and what was taught, though greater today than in the past, first opened in this period. The inertia of older generations of educators who defended materials they themselves had learned, the true beauty and insights many students and educators continued to find in a substantial diet of classical works, and the status or prestige associated with the classical education combined to ensure that a list of largely classical authors and substantially ancient history maintained considerable dominance. As new groups penetrated traditional institutions like the British public schools—which grudgingly opened to scions of the business middle class by the 1860s—pressure to maintain the classical focus actually increased in some instances. Having won access to a new educational sphere, the insurgents had no desire to see its status value diminished through a reduction of the classics. A bit of science is acceptable, perhaps; but in the humanities, give us the tried and true—along with a respectable alternative to unadulterated religion.

In the United States, one result of this ongoing humanistic tradition, upon the advent of mass high schools, was the creation or preservation of special "classical" programs or of separate schools open only to a tested elite; another was the vigorous role of expensive elite liberal arts colleges as alternatives to massive state schools in which, in the main, innovative programs have won more common acceptance (and still do). In general, democratic education has wavered between a mission to extend knowledge of a humanities core—leavened by appropriate nationalist pride—to the masses, and an attempt to use a more extensive core to continue to mark off an elite educational status. In other words, status concerns as much as truth and beauty explain why the "moderns," though victorious in the creative humanities, never fully won out in education.

The inconclusive outcome of the battle of ancients and moderns in humanities curricula—a battle that extended from its advent around 1700 to the incorporation of new materials, including science, in the schools through the mid-nineteenth century—presents some important dilemmas. The fact that a "modern" victory *did* not erase the strong classical emphasis in school humanities might be taken as demonstration that it *should* not, that the values of the classics override vulgar modernism in the larger culture. So many canonists would currently argue, with deep sincerity. Yet the inconclusiveness of the battle had unhappy consequences, in that it separated humanities emphases from some of the strongest currents in intellectual life, bent on innovation, and tended to relegate them toward museum status—places pleasant to visit but too musty for regular use after childhood. The rise of science made some cultural schizophrenia inevitable, for humanistic learning cannot proceed along strictly scientific lines, as some misbegotten efforts at proclaiming "scientific history" have recurrently demonstrated. Yet the degree of dualism between humanities largely valued for their ancient pedigree and sciences esteemed for perpetual renewal is unfortunate, even dangerous, for on balance the new wins the day every time. It would have been happier had the results of modernism carried through more fully in humanities curricula two centuries ago.

The results of the moderns' incomplete triumph were not so confining for humanist scholars. Indeed, the persistence of a conservative humanistic tradition in the schools may have encouraged some scholars and essayists to seek more critical vantage points in their own work. Conflicts with "school" art and "school" literature, and more recently "school" history, posed important political challenges to the mainstream. Some of this tension between humanities education that can be widely enough agreed upon to serve as standard school fare and the wider critical obligations of individual humanists will doubtless persist in any imaginable setting. Nevertheless, the gap that had opened by the eighteenth and nineteenth centuries proved needlessly large, unduly limiting the humanities fare available to students and in some cases constraining academic research as well.

Not surprisingly, then, the battle of ancients and moderns may need to be refought in the educational sphere, even though a clear winner emerged in humanistic endeavor, on the creative side, by the mid-eighteenth century. Humanistic education was not thoroughly reconsidered, as the "battle" should have assured. New ingredients did accrue, significantly modifying a purely Renaissance definition of the humanistic core, but they tended to be assimilated into this core, not used to challenge it. Thus, to continue the obvious example, Shakespeare became a classic, to be studied alongside Greek thinkers and with comparable awe. Methods of studying literature changed little, save for new acknowledgment of the English language. Indeed, by the early twentieth century the dominant mode of literary criticism advocated "explicating" a text in its own terms, with due reverence for its formal beauty.[11]

The third challenge to the Renaissance-derived humanities canon in education, along with science and modernism, came from quite a different source, arising even more recently in time, and it generated the most substantial curricular change—but still no sweeping reevaluation in the long run. During the nineteenth century, education became a mass institution, first at the primary and then, with the United States in the lead, at the secondary levels. This development raised inevitable questions about the traditional humanistic canon: What role did a classical emphasis, almost deliberately fashioned for an elite, have in the radically new educational environment? The answers were threefold, forming a pattern that in essence has persisted into the twentieth century, even after the addition of mass college education (again with the leadership of the United States) completed the conquest of previously elite terrain.

First, the humanistic focus obviously had to be reduced in favor of a larger number of subjects suitable for masses of students who needed a clear or at least plausibly asserted relationship between education and future work. Courses in technical areas and basic skills, along with increased exposure to elements of science, began to curtail the amount of time spent on the essentials of the humanities (and, of course, religion). Home economics and secretarial training were two new offerings in colleges as well as high schools around 1900. The rise of even more utilitarian majors, from physical therapy to business and commerce, among undergraduates in the late-twentieth-century United States maintains this trend with a vengeance. Between 1968 and 1988 the number of bachelor's degrees awarded grew by 56 percent, but those in the humanities fell by 39 percent. By the late 1980s, one in sixteen, instead of the previous one in six, college graduates had majored in the humanities. Clearly, a massive reduction of the educational role of humanities classics was underway, but that reduction maintained a clear trend beginning with the advent of mass schooling in the nineteenth century.[12]

A reduced role did not mean, however, that the remaining humanities courses and programs, even when they had become vestigial by traditional standards, had to be reconsidered. The second result of mass education was to increase the insistence on a reasonably traditional humanities program in elite settings, so that the familiar task of distinguishing really educated people from the lesser (though now usually literate) rabble could be retained. To be sure, even the crème de la crème dropped Greek and Latin requirements; some change did occur. But the fundamental desire to equate quality and personal distinction with exposure to a set of identifiably classic humanities traditions persisted strongly nonetheless. The same held for the education one would want for one's child, whether the goal was maintenance of one's status or, by the best American-dream criteria, advancement. It was vital in either case to have a reasonably stable humanities program to swear by.

Many liberal arts colleges continue to emphasize this educational-social function through great books programs in literature courses, or heroes-of-history emphases in Western civilization courses, or some combination of both.[13] Even latter-day programs like the Advanced Placement in such disciplines as history have shown a pronounced tendency to be more traditional, if higher-powered, than mainstream offerings because the clientele likes the status implications of fairly traditional coverage. With this specialized adjustment to a radically new educational content, in which humanities are used in novel ways to bolster elite status—though possibly for real enjoyment and understanding as well—in the mass environment, certain classics could become even more classical. Shakespeare, already well on the way to enshrinement, thus around 1900 became an object of near-worship by middle-class aspirants, who taught the lower classes to maintain proper reverence and decorum toward the great man and, in the process, killed off what had been a lively if rowdy popular urban interest in the Bard.[14]

The third adjustment—ultimately the most important one of all —affected masses and classes alike, particularly in primary and secondary schools. The humanities classics were redefined to include fewer purely ancient materials, but the older tradition was joined to a newfound use for literature and history: preaching nationalist loyalty. In this area the same respectful mastery could be enjoined, but for a different range of materials. Elitism was downplayed, for this was democratic education with a vengeance. Ancient history persisted, but now as a backdrop for the sacred national experience; no other historical strands were seriously considered. Biography joined national figures to remnants of the Plutarch pantheon. National authors replicated an essentially classical tradition, to be read with docility and in the confident knowledge that this was Good Literature, quite probably Best Literature. The humanities, now serving elites a bit more uncertainly than in the past, began largely to serve the state.

Once again, although the materials covered were massively redefined in this process, the fundamental educational approach to the humanities was not. Humanities learning still consisted of memorizing historical episodes chosen (by curriculum planners) for their inspirational value or reading through selected great books chosen to illustrate prime literary quality and good values, defined now in terms of classical pedigree and citizenship training. Most nationalist-humanities programs, at least in the Western world, directly linked the new materials with the old, a connection facilitated by the fact that the essential approach was the same. French students thus were taught a boiled-down version of ancient history and selected classical writings, which had existed (the implicit message read) to provide the seedbed for the glories of French culture itself. American students in the twentieth century, as we have seen, were urged to associate their glorious national history with a larger Western tradition, the whole anchored in the classical experience, which providentially had pointed the way to democracy, individualism, rationality, and other virtues that would reach perfection across the Atlantic. The icons of American political history flowed from a selective treatment of Athenian democracy and British parliamentarianism, the whole to be reverentially memorized.

(An aside: Again and again students in my freshman world history course tell me about their high school teachers' theory that civilization has moved steadily westward. Starting in Mesopotamia, the center of civilization shifts sequentially to Greece, Rome, France, and England, and then to the United States, where it presumably transmigrates from East Coast to California until—and here I go beyond what has been reported to me—it splits off in an earthquake and sails to Japan. The theory is just plain silly in ignoring Asian and other civilizations and in so blatantly enshrining our contemporary American selves, but its apparent propagation in some classrooms is downright frightening.)

The basic reactions to the challenge of mass education, particularly when joined with the rise of science, produced some interesting overlaps and confusions in the teaching of humanities. This teaching declined in importance overall, but it was vigorously defended for both its democratic and its elitist functions. The canon was redefined to include more modern history and recent national literature, but the idea of a canon persisted strongly. The elitist fringe continued to urge, at least at the college level, a more traditional, classically oriented curriculum that would enable the really educated to identify one another amid a larger mass, with which it could simultaneously agree that American culture—or at least Western culture—was close to best. The central idea, born in the Renaissance, that there were lessons to be derived from exposure to great facts and great works survived, despite the introduction of a host of new complexities and a dilution of the humanities' overall role in education.

This charting of the canon's evolution constitutes a thumbnail sketch, to be sure, and to canonists surely a tendentious one. The long and impressively flexible history of reliance on a sense of classics in defining the humanities leads, even briefly outlined, to several main conclusions.

The first acknowledges the durability of something like a classical tradition. Some educated people have been and continue to be genuinely inspired by encounters with great works of literature and exposures to a mainstream historical narrative. No tradition of this sort could survive otherwise. The passionate conviction displayed by advocates of the canon owes much, at least in many cases, to the rewards those same advocates have won from their own romance with the classics. Too, a classical approach to the humanities can lead to acutely critical vantage points, as the canon by no means necessarily induces slavish acceptance of the existing political or economic order. The Socratic tradition, adapted by medieval scholastics and then generalized by seventeenth-century modernists and by classic nineteenth-century liberals, urges questioning of any so-called established truth, and this skepticism is an ingredient in any sound educational program; it should be firmly cherished. Finally, although many of the people intellectually stimulated by an experience with classical humanities are members of a definable elite—wealthy white males who were able to attend a prestigious private university—the joys of traditional humanities have in no sense been confined to this group, even though the canon itself, as its critics laboriously note, is almost exclusively a white male product. Women often defend a classical humanities program more vigorously than men. Autodidacts in the working class or among freed slaves gained not only a new sense of literary beauty but also vital political grist from reading the great philosophers of the Western tradition.

The classical approach to the humanities should no longer define basic teaching programs, but we should not deny the value of the approach itself, nor our potential loss if it is significantly reduced. Critics who belittle the inspiration of the great Western traditions not only fail to persuade those whose educational experiences suggest otherwise; they also needlessly distort and narrow their own message. There is no question that a concentration on the humanistic canons has worked well for many people, and for a fairly diverse constituency, from its Renaissance inception to the present day.

By the same token, canonists have been using their educational tradition to good advantage in criticizing a number of features of contemporary American schooling. Those who savor great works or who want students exposed to key historical moments, however conventionally defined, readily mount attacks on the undiluted diet of massive textbooks that has come to dominate in college as well as high school classrooms. It would be folly to pretend to disagree with their critique or to disavow a common purpose in urging a wider, livelier array of reading materials, even though we might seek alternatives somewhat different from those the canonists propose.

The need to revivify humanities teaching, to encourage imaginative attention to this aspect of the humanities mission and to promote greater attention to humanities courses in the overall curriculum, is one point on which constructive canonists and their critics can agree.

In sum, any attack on the canonist position should not entail either myopic dismissal of its great strengths or the tactical folly of a down-the-line dispute. On some key issues there can be a united effort, and on others, as we will later suggest, some possible compromises may emerge. The successful and adaptable history of a basically canonical approach to the humanities is a challenge to the forces for change, but it is also a legitimate warning not to press the attack too far.

The second corollary to the long history of the canonical approach to the humanities is less friendly. The traditionalism of this approach, even when relieved by adaptations to democratic education and to science, can be severely constraining. The deep roots of the canonical tradition in our educational past help explain the tenacity of its adherents' opposition to anything more than cosmetic innovation, but they do not justify it. Some defenders of the canon profess surprise at accusations that their cause is political; truth, in their judgment, has no partisan bias. Yet the fact is that the canonical tradition has always carried elitist overtones, even in a democratic educational climate, and this fact raises some legitimate concerns given our manifest inability to draw "the masses" into extensive or respectful engagement with the presumed classics of our culture. The elitist features of the canon, as conveyed within the school system and in the wider culture, limit its effective impact on many students; preaching Shakespeare has not generated mass audiences for his plays in the modern context, and memorization of the American Constitution has not produced active citizen involvement. These things provoke the canonists' ire, but this is by the same token a poor basis for remedy. Criticism of degraded taste rarely inspires the degraded, particularly when their taste is partly an intended reaction to elitist pretensions in any event.

Furthermore, traditionalism can risk outdatedness. As most critics and some advocates note, a curriculum based on the humanities canon made more sense when more Americans were of European origin than is currently the case. Far more Americans now than even in the past come from non-European cultural traditions, and they understandably seek inclusion of their own canons in the educational mainstream. The Western-focused canon also made more sense when the United States was reasonably isolated in world affairs, and when Europe was its main point of reference outside its own boundaries. The geographical blinders on the tradition have long since lost their utility, yet precisely because of the tradition, the canonists are slow to react.

For example, an intelligent, reasonably flexible canonist argues that the United States is and will remain in the European tradition, a product of the European Enlightenment; students must know this cultural tradition and how it came to be. "This involves reading not only texts that are of great value, like those of Plato, but many less valuable that have been influential, such as the works of Marx" (a characteristic classicist putdown, these final phrases). But this basic concentration does not preclude some vague outreach: "You do not understand your own tradition if you do not see it in relation to others. Works from other cultural traditions need to be studied as well."[15] The last statement, however, offered with neither passion nor specifics, is a clear afterthought and an inadequate one. An alternative curriculum is proposed by another rhetorically flexible canonist, who realizes that the relevant world is no longer confined to the West alone but simply cannot bring herself to a full adjustment. In her recommended fifty-hour core program, Lynne Cheney advocates six credit hours on Western civilization (Pericles through the Reformation and the Reformation into the twentieth century), plus another three on American civilization. This would be matched by six credit hours on the rest of the world. The combination is, one hastens to note, better than nothing, and it is certainly more concrete than a vague injunction to study works from other cultures "as well"; some good specific suggestions are attached. But the collective recommendations are illustrated almost exclusively by established curricula in Western culture alone, and there is no question where the heart of the writer lies.[16]

Clearly, the very durability of the canonical tradition can pose a serious constraint. Many canonists simply oppose outright the idea of including anything non-Western in a required curriculum core. One even argued, with exceptional obscurity, that because the Western tradition is unique among the great civilizations of history in looking with any tolerance at other cultures (a claim that is, by the way, completely inaccurate), we should not bother studying other cultures today; pride in our own tolerance will presumably suffice. Even when some bows are made to new or newly realized needs, such as the desirability of teaching students something about the wider world, they tend to be grudging and curt. The compelling force of a belief in an essential (and Western) canon prevents more thorough rethinking and allows only the most limited kind of compromise with new coverage demands.

The joys and genuine intellectual liberation that some students have found in a canon-based humanities program must be balanced against the constraints and rigidities of a hoary tradition. Without playing cheap historical games, we can nonetheless see that it is improbable that a basic educational approach devised by an elitist society in which most people were illiterate peasants—and at the time when the West was just beginning to have significant contact with the world beyond its borders and was still largely rural and agricultural in social and economic focus—would remain appropriate in a highly international, industrial, and democratic context. Of course, the tradition has retained some value and, without question, it has demonstrated considerable flexibility, particularly in its incorporation of nationalist classics and the ideal of devoted service to the nation-state, but its viability has become increasingly limited.

Indeed, the very tension between two intellectual cultures—to repeat C. P. Snow's dichotomy that so marks our education and larger cultural life—owes something to the disparity that has grown up between scientific inquiry, which possesses a distinctive methodology but is also open to steady innovation in theory and subject matter as a matter of principle, and the humanities, which are defined as valuable precisely because they change so little. The division has often been cited as a complexity in modern education, one of the factors promoting specialization and a lack of sweeping intellectual dialogue. The same division has also worked, on balance, to the humanities' disadvantage. Although some points can be made for the humanities as defenders of timeless cultural values, they yield on balance to the more dynamic claims of science, given our progress-minded outlook. Again, traditionalism imposes unacceptable limitations.

Finally, there is the third corollary of the canon's historical record: Education based on devotion to classics has already served a number of purposes beyond its professed goals. This may be true of any large educational scheme, but it certainly defines the canonical tradition and, most decidedly, its contemporary manifestations. The role of classical emphasis in defending and measuring elite status and the more recent, admittedly more tortuous modification of the canon to include inculcation of national loyalties have long ago diluted any claims to purity in humanities teaching. And if *purity* sounds too far-fetched, we can at least say that they have distorted easily accessible accuracy.

The extracurricular goals of the canonist tradition routinely force omissions. The glories of Athens are presented with only passing reference to the dependence of this same culture on slavery, for a more complete presentation might distract students from the central lessons to be learned about the magnificent pedigree of Western rationalism or democracy. (It is worth remembering that significant attention to slavery in American history texts was lacking until about thirty years ago.) Or, if slavery is too tendentious a point, we can also note that the Athenian message is rarely diluted by examination of the extent to which the city's political experience was atypical and, in the judgment of most educated (and proaristocratic) Greeks, positively undesirable. The larger goals of canonical education have long promoted a highly selective historical portrait, with the warts and complicating factors left off.

The same extracurricular goals also encourage outright error. Students who emerge from a canonical program that combines emphasis on ancient history with the constitutional highlights of American political history routinely believe that democracy has evolved in a fairly straight line from its Athenian roots, changing only to add further perfections. The complexity of the actual historical record and the notion that a major political episode can be resolutely Western and yet not democratic or even antidemocratic is shocking to these students, often almost impossible to assimilate within a their deeply rooted school framework. This means that they routinely confuse medieval parliamentary traditions, which limited royal government by institutionalizing the rights of privileged minorities, with democracy; if it's Western, it must be democratic. Movements like fascism are dismissed as aberrations, not part of a "real" West. The same standards are applied to individualism: clearly good, clearly part of the Western tradition beginning in ancient Greece, and therefore to be discovered in every intervening historical era. Athenian society is thus incorrectly seen as individualistic, as well as being incorrectly judged typical of classical Greece; the newness of our individualism, and therefore its real causes and impacts, are not readily grasped because of this hallowed-Western-values syndrome. An educational program so bent on hammering home a few key values that historical accuracy is sacrificed—even granting a range of inevitable disagreement about what constitutes accuracy—raises serious questions.

Most important of all, however, is the extent to which the larger social and political purposes of the canonical tradition have commonly promoted passive retention and memorization. This is not the avowed purpose of a canonical curriculum, and it does not describe the experience of those students who have found great personal meaning in their exposure to the classics. Nevertheless, because part of the function of the canon has been to demonstrate elite status or patriotic loyalty (or sometimes both), memorization has played an important role. The person who could quote some lines from Virgil or the Constitution, or who knew the proper order of the presidents, had at least covered the desired material. Whether the desired understanding had also been conveyed might well prove secondary.

The final great adjustment of the canonical tradition to the apparent demands of democratic education—in the United States, at least—simply enhanced the likelihood of superficial retention. Mass education required mass testing, yet it has never seemed possible to pay for the kinds of generalized tests that would demonstrate real understanding of major works of literature or key political institutions of the past. Happily, a surrogate was available in a multiple-choice format. The canon required coverage of certain literary products and certain historical events; therefore, rather than probing for comprehension through some oral or essay examination format, it seemed logical simply to ask factual questions. How did this plot run, who was this character, what genre did that book fit into, what were the dates of the Pelopponesian War? Students who knew these things could be certified as educated, at least in the sense of having been exposed to the right descriptive data and having demonstrated, through knowing the proper tags, their elite standing and/or mastery of a patriotic common fund. Knowledge of prescribed data, not the more open-ended qualities of critical understanding, provided the keys to the next educational kingdom.

This is not to argue that memorization of factual tags is dreadful and certainly not to downplay the importance of factual knowledge for analysis, which we will get back to later. Regurgitation of dates, names, and plots of novels is not wisdom, however, nor does it hint at a larger understanding; yet presentation of culture in terms of Items That Must Be Known—in turn a practical translation of the canonical approach—has too often been our highest educational aim in the humanities. This was not, to be sure, an inevitable result of canonical emphasis: European testing programs, no less canonical in the early grades, are characteristically less fully rooted in memorized knowledge. Mass-testing passion in the United States, however, has seemed to require a fact-grubbing program, to which the canonical tradition lent itself fairly readily because it had already outlined an agreed-upon range of coverage from which the facts could be drawn.

Another American trend has also pushed testing in the same direction: the search for measurements that will keep teachers honest while also testing the achievements of their students. As we have seen, this impulse has gained footholds in some state testing programs in recent decades and may acquire still others if simplistic national standards campaigns advance too readily. Teachers, according to this argument, could not be relied upon to evaluate essays or oral discussion, for this would assume they had the stature to make such difficult judgments. Rather, examinations must be developed that were independent of teacher control, and once again the machine-gradable, factual-mastery approach worked best. School officials and the general public could judge how well their schools were doing by listing how many wars the students could identify on multiple choice tests. Such tests have formed the basis for school reports on deficiencies in the social studies in recent years, reflecting the assumption that memorization measures knowledge. Standardized achievement tests, which inherently do little more than assess memorized facts, thus have not only rated students for such purposes as college admission; they also have been introduced to various primary and secondary grades as a means of evaluating teacher and school performance for a skeptical audience.[17]

Testing programs understandably usurped much of the task of determining the range of subject coverage in humanities classes as well as in other areas, but because they largely emphasized great literature, Western culture, and American politics, no great outcry ensued. One of the great anomalies of the College Board during the past ten years is the gulf that exists between the board's sincere advocacy of updating the content and analytical purpose of humanities training in the schools and its continued reliance on fact-testing programs (not even adjusted for the altered coverage recommended in its own curricular statements) for college admission. The goals are inspiring, but it is not surprising that actual courses are defined—more and more, given the increasing pressure on students to get into good colleges—by the fact-based testing realities.

Memorization tests rule, and their sway increases. Although sensitive canonists also deplore these prosaic, mind-fogging, teacher- and student-deadening results, they have trouble suggesting real alternatives because they share the assumption that the humanities can be boiled down to an agreed-upon set of items to cover. They want more besides, but they can't deny the basic premise. The student who knows when Pericles lived can't be entirely ignorant.

To sum up: The canonical tradition carries baggage in the form of larger social and political goals, and this has caused considerable distortion of courses in the humanities, particularly through the substitution of factual surveys for real understanding. Students are more likely to know lists of novels than literary values, constitutional amendments than political purpose. The situation gives us grounds for rethinking the curriculum.

Finally, this same baggage helps explain the striking public currency of canonical preachments during the past two decades in the United States. The undeniable popularity of sometimes turgid educational tomes and mind-numbing fact lists must be grappled with in any discussion of educational alternatives that hopes to do more than just shout loudly. That same popularity returns us to the mixed bag of advantages and drawbacks that the canonical tradition has borne for many decades. Why have pedantic canonist claims caught the public eye? Why have otherwise sensible scholars jumped on the canon-or-chaos bandwagon?

There is, first of all, the power of personal experience and sheer tradition. Most leading advocates of the humanities canon, and many of their audience, themselves had literature courses dealing with at least English-language classics and history courses that seemed to highlight the emergence of American democracy, and they benefited from this training. They want the same benefits for the current student generation. Faced with various appeals for innovation based on the new humanities scholarship and other, more overtly political impulses, they naturally close ranks around the tradition they know and favor.

The sheer weight of tradition may extend beyond a generous desire to share delights and insights. It is always tempting to urge on the next generation what one has experienced oneself. Even pain can be rationalized: "If I endured it, and emerged the marvelous person I am, then you can endure it too." This was the impulse that prompted Henry IV of France to urge regular spankings for his son—he had no other reason, as the boy was quite docile; and some of the same thinking goes into canonical pleas. Physicists, thus, may support a canonical humanities program—even though they would bitterly resist traditionalist constraints on their own discipline—because it was crammed down their own undergraduate throats and they were persuaded that the experience was, if not pleasurable, at least salutary.

Traditionalism also builds on a combination of genuine commitment and routine-mindedness on the part of many teachers. In recent decades, efforts to persuade high school teachers and many in the college ranks to seriously reconsider their curricula have rarely been successful. Since the 1950s, a whole series of experiments have attempted to bring new life into humanities teaching, ranging from the use of novel materials to new curricular emphases. Workshops and other devices have proliferated. An important group of exciting, innovative teachers has indeed emerged—it is important not to ignore the real vigor in some quarters. Yet most teachers have budged little, if at all. The mediocre training administered to much of the teaching corps, the limited recruitment of new humanities teachers since the 1960s, and the huge constraints on teacher time all add up to a conservatism that is hard to shake.

This conservatism is partly canonical. Many teachers are sincerely devoted to at least some of the familiar materials they have been covering for years. Urge a group of American history teachers, for example, to revamp their eleventh-grade survey course, and nine times out of ten they will, unless compelled by outside authority, emerge with a program almost identical to the one with which they began. They have to cover the Constitution, the Age of Jackson (complete with arcane bank crises), and so on, partly because they have difficulty imagining an alternative (and, in some cases, they shun the effort that learning new material might entail), but partly because they really love the material they grew up with. This is the American story, and without being systematic canonists, these teachers nevertheless want to socialize their students to this story as they themselves were socialized a generation before. Similarly, many high school teachers, prodded to convert their Western civilization course in to world history, adopt the new title while changing almost nothing of their previous subject coverage; the world simply becomes a new label for the West, which is what many Americans tend to think anyway.

The same conservatism describes many school board authorities, who are, again, often poorly trained in the humanities or trained some time ago, and who are eager to maintain a familiar structure that they, their teachers, and potential parental critics can all recognize and agree upon, if only as a lowest common denominator. As with the teachers, this sluggishness is not precisely the same as a committed canonism, but it has much the same effect in maintaining an essentially great works/great events focus in school humanities.

Finally, this is also a framework that most successful commercial publishers are loath to tamper with. Textbooks in the humanities, particularly at the school level but to some extent at college level as well, are orchestrated with a keen eye to what already exists. Publishers' committees effectively write most school texts—regardless of what authors' names appear on the cover—and college products, though genuinely written by scholars, are also monitored. The goal, with some rare but happy exceptions, is a product only marginally different from existing texts. Because the investment in mammoth textbooks is considerable, risk taking is shunned, particularly at the high school level. Textbook adoption committees are presumed to discourage innovation—the statewide adoption system in Texas is particularly influential in this regard—and thus familiar coverage is largely maintained. Cosmetic changes do appear—for example, gendered language has been scrupulously pruned, so that *man* becomes *human* (without the text's paying serious attention to women, however), and reading levels are periodically adjusted down or up—but the subject matter evolves modestly. The effect parallels the canonical emphasis on stable coverage, though the bland quality and sheer bulk of many texts can, as noted above, offend canonical purists as well.[18]

A tendency toward stability in humanities coverage, based on teacher, school board, and textbook routines, lends itself admirably to the fact-gorged testing programs. The eagerness to endorse tests that measure student and teacher competence largely on the basis of factual retention, has spread widely in humanities programs. Testing that initially measured grade-school skills acquisition or knowledge of subject matter appropriate to memorization, such as basic geography, has now permeated secondary school humanities. Along the way, it has reinforced the need to define humanities teaching in terms of coverage of a familiar range of materials—with great authors and great events heading the parade. The testing impulse has been spurred on by reports of lapses in student knowledge, but also by the growing involvement of state governments in school funding. State-level monitoring agencies seek standard measurements to assure that taxpayer dollars are buying at least minimal attainments, and multiple-choice questions addressed to standard curricular materials provide the readiest response. The tests do not require students to be steeped in the humanities canon—the really devoted canonists deplore testing, along with conventional textbooks; but there is no question that testing programs reflect a version of the classic books-and-events approach, adjusted to some minimum range of memorization that seems in turn to attest to basic competency. The fact lists that have accompanied the canonists' counterattacks in recent years both demonstrate and encourage this impression that education in history and English consists of fixed, memorized knowledge.

The devotion of some canonists, as advocates and audience, is thus supplemented by various bureaucratic routines that assure the retention of traditional coverage goals, in turn reinforced by the dictates of fact-testing programs. Confronted with various possible alternatives proposed by advocates of the new humanities scholarship or by partisans of different kinds of literature or history, the sources of educational conservatism readily join in praise of the status quo—or at least the status quo modestly modified. Educational conservatism is not exactly canonism; it somewhat uneasily unites real devotees of a classical canon with pragmatic school officials willing to settle for a more superficial run-through of conventional materials. Despite internal tension, however, the various adherents of conservatism certainly account for the relatively slow pace of significant curricular revision that contrasts so vividly with the huge shifts in humanities scholarship; and they help explain the popularity of the recent canonical counterattack.

Yet the passion of this counterattack has other sources as well, as does the increasing impulse to more rigidly define the canon as a set list of works to be covered and facts to be known, rather than as a somewhat looser program designed to steep students in literary and historical classics. The equation, scholarly innovation equals conservative educational response, explains part of the surge of canonism—including the specific term itself—but by no means all of it. Additional factors have helped produce the bestseller canonical statements and their popularity among an educated readership. Conviction plays a role, as does routine-mindedness, but, as in earlier periods of history, additional canonical goals enter in as well.

Emphasis on a canon—on the idea of a set of books and historical coverage that will promote agreed-upon values, including cultural Westernness and American patriotism—has responded to the national uncertainty that followed defeat and bitter disagreement in Vietnam. Ironically but understandably, American educational flexibility in the curriculum area that is primarily responsible for inculcating values lessened in the wake of the decline in self-confidence. Adults who had shared in the humiliation of Vietnam and who wondered about America's international decline hoped to use the curriculum to produce a younger generation that would be properly guided despite the new uncertainty. The same adults who increasingly questioned most traditional sources of authority, from doctors to politicians, as America's place in the wider world grew shakier yearned for an education that would generate a definite consensus, a measurable public faith. Their desire was one source of the enthusiasm that greeted canonical apostles.

The new international context that followed the Vietnam war simply added fuel to this fire. By the late 1970s, Americans accustomed to an unchallenged economic supremacy found themselves faced with new, non-Western rivals. Legitimate competitive concern about Japan's rise was enhanced by a racist element that exaggerated the focus on countries of the Pacific rim; continued German advances or high rates of British investment in the United States passed with less notice. This setting helps explain the otherwise strange hyperbole that has accompanied the canonical reaction to innovation in the humanities, under such headings as (to cite an *Atlantic Monthly* subhead) "the assault on the foundations of Western culture."[19]

Another source of the popular reaction to canonism grew out of particular concerns about the younger generation, resulting from the student unrest of the 1960s and early 1970s. These unruly students offended adults, and the memory their activities affected the later judgments even of people who had been rebellious in their own youth, but who were now repentant and noisily respectable. Amid complaints about student disaffection and ill-disciplined adolescents, education was called upon to instill appropriate values. Because the sixties had seen widespread attacks on core curricula, the reaction against this mood of revolt called for a restoration of basic requirements; and although the new requirements might vary from their predecessors in some individual cases, many advocates of a core curriculum also urged its definition in terms of the humanities canon. Requirements, rigor, and curricular reaction went hand in hand, all charged with reducing youth chaos and aimlessness. A canonical program could even be seen as having a punitive tinge, particularly when, in the schools, it was accompanied by more frequent multiple-choice testing. Hammer home the proper values through required coverage of humanities staples, the thought seemed to be, with student inquiry limited by the desperate need to prepare for the next round of systemwide examinations, and the generation gap might be forced closed.

Here, indeed, was an additional reason for the association of canonism with lists of facts designed to show how deficient today's youth have become. The shock at apparent knowledge gaps was genuine, and the new zeal of state educational authorities to find ways to evaluate school programs and require accountability was not necessarily misplaced. But the enthusiasm for attacking youth on the basis of cherished fact lists and coercing them, through related testing programs, into compliance with mandated definitions of what they must memorize to demonstrate education marked an interesting new phase of generational conflict, an old-fogey retaliation for a previous decade of youth initiative and ongoing concern about the habits of the young. Like earlier efforts to discipline modern youth, the fact-list measurement aimed both at "other" youth—those lower-class and nonwhite youths who were considered particularly close to barbarism—and the discipliners' own progeny, also uncertainly monitored. At least, armed with lists of 1,000 facts that any educated person should know about the world, or (to top that) 1,001 necessary facts about the United States, we could label ignorance even when we could not coerce compliance.[20]

In addition to the factors listed above, the passionate urging of the canon responded directly to changes in American demography and the racial composition of the student body in decades of overall birth-rate decline. Since 1960 the United States has been experiencing its highest immigration levels of all time, and the origins of new immigrants have become predominantly Asian and Latin American.

Massive immigration around 1900 spurred vigorous efforts to use the school systems to acculturate the newcomers, but also to discriminate against them using ethnically biased testing and tracking programs. "Americanization" was the watchword, both in school systems and in employer schemes such as the Ford Motor Company's grand plan. Such blatancy is now unfashionable, except for the partisans of David Duke and Pat Buchanan, but ever greater immigration—less and less of it from European sources—inevitably influences mainstream thinking and helps explain the passion behind the pleas for a Western-focused canon that will defend the gates of civilization against the barbarians. The same reaction applies to the differential birth rates, among native-born Americans, between blacks and whites, which has led to an increasingly strong black component in urban schools. Again, the impulse to stress Europeanness, to emphasize humanities programs that will promote presumably secure American political values, results from massive changes in the student constituency, which trigger fearful middle-class assumptions.

Emphasis on the canon thus continues to answer a multitude of purposes, from genuine effectiveness as a teaching approach, through rigid layers of sheer traditionalism, to a barely concealed political agenda aimed at a series of new or renewed issues in American society. The uses to which the canon can be put in a climate of new national uncertainties may help explain the urgency of canonical attacks, even as the larger tradition helps to explain how canonists infuriatingly can claim nonpartisanship, imputing political agendas only to their opponents. Canonism seems to allow its proponents to have their political cake and to eat its objectivist frosting, too. Reasoned opposition to curricular innovation plays a role in all this, but it hardly dominates. There are far more Americans who embrace the canon out of routine-mindedness or political anxiety than there are those who really feel enriched by Ciceronian rhetoric or enlightened by article-by-article coverage of the Constitution. This wider explanation does not invalidate the canonical approach—all large educational frameworks have a multifaceted constituency—but it does suggest the desirability of a new and more open-ended dialogue. The canon may prevail; thus far, however, it has not been preserved because of explicit popular consent to its content and intellectual implications, but rather because of educational inertia and public anxieties. The substantive debate may yet be joined.

For the history and the current implications of canonical thinking, particularly when they are linked with subject coverage and testing goals, raise some obvious questions. It is too easy to turn the canon into a "Jeopardy"-like array of tag words and great names. This was true even when the canon was largely confined to an educated elite, and the tendency may be even more pervasive in a mass-education environment.

The canon omits too much; it pulls values out of context and ignores aspects of historical reality. To study American democracy without grappling with the problem of slavery, as was done in school and college courses alike until black political pressure and the discoveries of social history forced some modification, was simply unconscionable. Quite apart from their omission of black history, such surveys provided no training in the actual and ongoing complexities of the American democratic tradition. Because of its consistent desire to define literature and history in terms of values training, the canon limits and distorts the humanities—and, indeed, invites backlash from students who know, from their own experiences or from later education, that American and Western life is more complicated.

In confining the humanities to the role of guardian of sacred truths, the canonical approach places the actual subjects of the humanities at a disadvantage in an educational culture that otherwise stresses innovative training and new knowledge. The popularity of appeals to the canon has not ratcheted the humanities into a higher place in the American educational lexicon, save perhaps in helping to justify some increase in high school history requirements. The same conservative politicians who voice praise for the educational canon have yet to put their money where their mouths are, save to deny most of the meager funding available to humanists with a different vision.

Two other results of the canonical domination of history and English classrooms follow from the canon's inherent limitations. First, mere emphasis on the hallowed story of the American republic does not create informed citizens or eager voters. This is a matter of record, with which the canonists refuse to grapple except to imply that classrooms have turned aside from their sacred trust. Yet American classrooms have sedulously fostered stories about the Founding

Fathers and the Constitution through a largely political and largely laudatory series of narratives for generations. They were doing so in the early 1940s, when a significant percentage of draftees did not know who the president was.[21] They were doing so in the 1950s, when the percentage of voters among eligible adults began to plummet. They were doing so in the 1970s, when polls revealed that a majority of high school students advocated censorship and other violations of the Bill of Rights, and that a majority of Americans identified unlabeled sections of the Declaration of Independence as Marxist revolutionary rhetoric and thus subversive. Teaching the canon does not assure the transmission of democratic ideals or relevant understanding. We will return to education's function in a democratic society, for curricula and school organization unquestionably have roles to play, but these limitations on the canonists' claims—the fact that canonism has not translated into effective citizenship—add to the empirical burden of their own argument.

It is also inescapable that canonical humanities classrooms—sometimes admittedly deadened further by the factual memorization approach—are needlessly boring. They help persuade many students to dislike history or literature, partly because of the tedious fact lists, but partly because of their own perception that the explanations being offered are inaccurate and irrelevant to the society they inhabit. This is true of many bright students, who tire of the propagandistic qualities of American history. It is true of many working-class, or black, or women students, bright or not, who know that the hopeful lessons of equality and mobility are whitewashes, incomplete truths at best and destined at worst to make disadvantaged groups feel that inequalities are the faults of individuals, not features of a social system that has many good qualities but that can and should be assessed critically in its historical origins and its current functionings.

To be sure, good teaching can bring the canon alive for some students. In the main, however, the presentation of history and literature as a series of masterpieces, more to be wondered at than analyzed, turns students off—and too often no alternative vision ever rescues their interest. Teachers who have offered such a vision by venturing outside mainstream American history staples, for example, see many of their students wake up and began to accept a new kind of engagement with the past and with the insight of historical study. The proper goals of the humanities are, as we will show more fully later, compatible with heightened student interest.

Most damning of all, at least in the contemporary context that characteristically views culture of all sorts as something to be consumed and enjoyed rather than actively engaged in, the canon tends to promote passivity. The best canonists argue otherwise, but the practical educational translation of an emphasis on standard texts and themes promotes memorization over participation or active understanding and urges admiring assent over critical debate. The grandeur of the Western tradition, the greatness of Shakespeare, and the glories of the American panorama are laid out for viewing, with approval assumed and with learning measured by an ability to recite the labels. Although a host of factors can be called up to explain this result, including assumptions about the organization of American mass education quite apart from the canon, canonical thinking in the humanities undoubtedly plays its role. For at base, the canonists seek an appreciation of eternal truths—for their own sake and for their potential utility in taming suspect hordes—rather than active analysis. This limitation does not just exclude most students from anything more than rote involvement with the plots of novels and lists of historical dates. In an environment that has also stimulated a critical, highly analytical humanities scholarship, it is also unnecessary and inexcusable.

The canonical tradition was born during the Renaissance in a burst of critical fire directed against narrow scholasticism and the increasingly mindless rehashings of the Church Fathers. It integrated the goals of scholars with those of educators. The tradition has responded to change in part because of the vigor of Renaissance culture, in part because it was able to tie into concerns about science, then into elitism and nationalism. As translated through contemporary curricula, despite the valiant intentions of some proponents and real success in some classrooms, it increasingly contradicts its own life principles. The canon favors the status quo; it promotes catechisms; it divides its students from the excitement of research; it serves concerns about race, youth, and international position that, if valid (and in my judgment they are not), should be addressed more frankly and by other means. The canon, as it has evolved to survive, has shot its bolt.

FOUR

Answering
the Canon Fire:
The Debate
Miscast

Response to the canonists has been strident and predictable. The pieties of Republican education officials, and particularly of the NEH, have drawn fire, and the prophets of doom and makers of canonical fact lists have been ridiculed. Criticism has come both from academics in the humanities, bent on defending their own agendas, and from political interest groups that seek adequate representation in literature and history courses. The critics have scored many telling points, correctly noting deficiencies in the canonical approach, both in principle and as applied to schooling in the contemporary United States. At the same time, their criticism has been inadequate, unable to win out and incapable of defining a vigorous but coherent alternative humanities curriculum. This chapter, while briefly echoing established anticanonical claims and reaffirming their value, must also assess their deficiencies.

The central thrust of anticanonism has emphasized the importance of cultural diversity, as opposed to the single-mindedness of a Western high-culture focus. Elite Western values, in this vision, omit too much of the world, too much of Western society, and too many alternatives to serve as the foundation for appropriate humanities curricula. A Stanford professor of comparative literature writes that canonists like Allan Bloom and William Bennett "are advocating a narrowly specific cultural capital that will be the normative referent for everyone, but will remain the property of a small and powerful caste that is linguistically and ethnically unified. . . . Few doubt that behind the Bennett-Bloom program is a desire to close not the American mind, but the American university, to all but a narrow and highly uniform elite with no commitment to either multiculturalism or educational democracy."[1]

According to the anticanonists, the teaching of American culture must be opened to the writings of women and minorities in a strongly pluralist framework that works against any notion that culture is the creature of the privileged and powerful alone. The teaching of culture more generally must refocus from the West to the world. Women and people of color must be able to discover in literature and history "the reflection or representation of their images" and "hear the resonance of their cultural voices. The turn of 'the' canon, the high canon of Western masterpieces, represents the return of an order in which my people were the subjugated, the voiceless, the invisible, the unrepresented. . . . Who would return us to that medieval never-never land?"[2]

The canon, clearly, is politically incorrect and demographically unrepresentative, and so it will not work. It symbolizes not only limits but outright oppression. Some educators have urged that the canon not only be rejected but attacked at the curricular level by substituting, for example, a required African civilization course for the traditional Western civilization offering. In this scheme, canonical narrowness is to be prevented by blocking formal exposure to the historical tradition that gave it birth—a tidy solution, if nothing else. Alternatively, some Afrocentrists argue, African origins of the Western tradition must be uncovered even as, somewhat inconsistently, the West is still being attacked.

Other critics combine political radicalism with a version of deconstructionism that insists on absolute relativism. A list of great books is wrong because it imposes a hierarchical order in which the products of more ordinary people are downgraded. Books not on the reading list will be unfairly regarded as less adequate, and the values they represent unfairly dismissed. The exclusion of women and minorities as canonical authors (at least until quite recent literary periods) demonstrates canonical narrowness and renders it politically unacceptable. The humanities should challenge the established order, not confirm it. "What is in question here is not merely a defense of a particular canon, but the issue of struggle and empowerment." White, male domination should be exposed and clear alternatives provided. At the same time, this position may add to the charge by insisting that the humanities must demonstrate the relativity of all truth claims—nothing is certain, and humanities courses are where students must find this out. An American Council of Learned Societies pamphlet, *Speaking for the Humanities*, issued by several professors of literature, blasts the very idea of objective truth: "As the most powerful modern philosophies and theories have been demonstrating, claims of disinterest, objectivity and universality are not to be trusted and themselves tend to reflect local historical conditions."[3]

Debates of this sort have been most pervasive among scholars of literature, partly because literature lends itself to a stiffer interpretation of the canon in terms of set "great books" than does history —where even a resolute focus on the progress of Western civilization has always accommodated a certain untidiness—and partly because deconstructionist theory has applied mainly to literary criticism. Obviously, though, many historians have joined the chorus of humanists who lament the narrowness and political unrepresentativeness of canonical thinking. They want multiple voices to speak from the past, not those with a single set of values, and they want the world as well as the West to be heard.

Some recent attacks on conventional historians' truth claims echo deconstructionist and post-structuralist positions. All historical work, some post-structuralists argue, is essentially invention, which means that conventions such as making rigorous efforts to define the representativeness of sources or testing generalizations against extensive evidence are mere window dressing. History can be written to openly demonstrate current partisan positions, and evidence can be chosen almost at random to make the best and most convenient case according to the writer's political beliefs. Few of these critics have directly ventured a curricular translation of their views, though they vigorously join anticanonical debates within history departments to advocate admitting the voices and views of feminists, gays, and others. In such a climate, the potential exists for an attack not simply on any particular historical coverage but on the idea of authoritative history in any form.[4] Some historians, including innovative social historians, are deeply concerned about this relativist thrust.[5]

Attacks on the canon are related to less systematic efforts to generate humanities curricula that diverge from classic core traditions.

The revived Harvard University core program, constructed in advance of the most fervent debate over canonism but helping to inspire it, seeks to offer students specialized courses noteworthy both for their diversity and for their avoidance of systematic standard coverage. The list of literature courses (from which at least one must be selected) thus includes African American Women Writers, Beast Literature, and Epic Fiction International; it does not cover nineteenth-century English novelists, Virgil, Milton, or Dostoyevsky. Nor do core history courses deal with Greece and Rome, the Renaissance, the Enlightenment, or the American Civil War. The purpose of this curriculum is to expose students to a wide array of choices in key humanities disciplines, not to insist that they learn an extensive or conventional battery of facts. To the canonists, the result has proved anathema—an example of requirements that are worse than useless. Though much maligned, Harvard educators have stuck to their program, providing an explicit reminder that canonical thinking, despite its convenience in defining revived core programs at many institutions, has by no means won the day.[6]

The attacks on the canonical revival and the suggested alternatives to its prescripts are persuasive in many ways. They remind us of the distortion involved in pretending that a single cultural tradition, whatever its richness, defines everything we need to learn about American values, and they compel our attention to the necessity of learning more about the world beyond the West. Insistence on a wider range of cultural contacts is thus timely and appropriate. The desirability of teaching students about the time-bounded qualities of certain habits of thought—including some that are widely accepted today as virtually indisputable—can be traced back to elements of the critical strand in traditional Western culture from Socrates and then Abelard on down; and that desirability has been reinforced by findings in humanities scholarship in recent decades. Even basic scientific, medical, or economic assumptions—perhaps particularly such assumptions, because of their common sanctity—must be problematized by studying their original cultural contexts.

Recognition of the political implications of canonical thought is also valid, even if some of the common corollaries—for example, that humanities education should be deliberately political in intent, albeit in the opposite, radical direction—do not necessarily follow. It is even possible, depending of course on one's personal politics, to see something refreshing in the frank consciousness-raising interests of the "academic radicals." Their advocacy of using curricula to change American political thinking is quite open. Even if some results seem bizarrely exaggerated to all but the converted, the contrast with the canonists' invocation of purity and their reluctance to acknowledge their own political agenda, is striking. Canonists, after all, conceal much of their political purpose by self-righteously wearing the mantle of saviors of Western civilization. They ignore the extent to which they have selectively browsed among Western cultural traditions—which, after all, embrace many episodes of intellectual intolerance and many periods of attempts at radical innovation. The editorial uses of canonism to identify new enemies designated to replace cold war communism are surely as blatant as the political goals of the antiestablishment radicals, and potentially more misleading if unthinkingly translated into classroom choices.[7]

If forced to choose between the principal implications of the anticanonists and the strictures of the canonists as the basis for a lively and useful humanities curriculum, then, I would on several grounds frankly urge the former—shorn, however, of the intolerant claims that have accompanied recent critiques and that must still be addressed below. More strongly still, though, I would hope that the choice need not be made. The limitations of the curricular innovations, both of the anticanonical critics and of such alternatives as the Harvard program, simply cannot be ignored, even without the predictable canonist counterattacks. The problems fall into several categories.

In the first place, not surprisingly, the political goals of the anticanonists, though overtly expressed, go well beyond educational issues, and they burden some of these issues with their larger agenda. Response to changing student and national demography and resultant demands for attention to African, Asian, and Hispanic experiences, use of important aspects of the new humanities scholarship, and outrage at the simplification of the "Western tradition" by many self-serving canonists all play a role in the anticanonist agenda. But so does a lingering interest, 1960s-fashion, in using academic unrest to affect national politics well beyond the educational sphere. By the 1980s, academic radicals found themselves immensely frustrated by the substantial neglect of academia—outside the purely technical fields abundantly subsided through Department of Defense research contracts—on the part of Republican administrations and even a large segment of the meek Democratic opposition. Military buildups, the dismantling of many domestic programs, and a more aggressive foreign policy, all answered feebly if at all by leading Democrats, revealed how far not just radical but even liberal academic social scientists and humanists had been pushed out of the political mainstream.

The decline of feminist political clout during the 1980s similarly reduced many academic supporters to battles within university confines. Small wonder that agitation within academic ranks, where the powerful dissenting voice could not be denied, boiled up and over. A sense of bitterness and injustice, induced by conditions in the wider society, gained all the more intensity for being imprisoned in academe. Yet this same context, however understandable, raises some questions about the educational soundness of the anticanonical alternatives. One might, for example, respond more readily to the political pain the dissenters expressed than to the actual educational arguments they advanced. And it is difficult *not* to distinguish between the overt political purposes of the Afrocentric and multicultural movements and the much more complex educational agenda provoked by the new humanities scholarship, which overlapped with academic radicalism to a degree but could not be contained by it. In other words, the wider agenda of many anticanonical humanists did not necessarily provide a firmer educational foundation than did its canonical counterpart. And the resultant polarization was more likely to damage humanities teaching—or to leave its daily routine unaffected amid the sound and fury of theoretical debates—than it was to lead to intelligent rethinking.

These points must be phrased with care. I share many of the political goals of the anticanonists, though not all their fervor. I also agree that any curriculum is to some extent political. I do not, however, therefore agree that sweeping political radicalism constitutes a valid or a practical curricular approach. This means that the politics in my educational goals (about which I will say more in the conclusion) are less detailed in terms of contemporary issues, as well as less strident, than those of the current wave of academic radicals. I try to separate (for example) my personal hostility to several aspects of current American foreign policy from what I teach about the evolution of this nation's world role in the twentieth century. I would hope for my students to question established beliefs (conservative and radical alike) but not necessarily to reach my conclusions. This is a political goal, too—but not that of most anticanonists.

Other implications of the anticanonical critique focus more directly on curricular issues. If their goal is significant curricular change, the radicals surely press too far in their desire to adopt revisions deliberately hostile to conventional values. They clearly enjoy their iconoclasm, but they risk sacrificing their impact on all but the smallest educational enclaves. Short of outright revolution, it is impossible to imagine a society willing to give up its desire to use the schools to inculcate mainstream values. The reformers' wish to find alternatives may be quite sincere, and their pleasure at rhetorically tweaking the canonists' noses may be intense. In certain settings, furthermore, pleas for humanities programs that emphasize African civilization over Western civilization or urge a primary focus on the voices of discontented women and homosexuals may win constructive political credit. In the larger society, however, such approaches have no realistic chance of success without massive and potentially haphazard dilution. Their advocacy merely inflames the canonists and gives greater credence to their own program, concealing its narrowness and bias.

The radical critique, in effect, strains against political reality and risks sacrificing essential reform and even coherent discussion in the process. And it unduly downplays society's legitimate needs for the transmission of conventional values; this is a point to which we will return, recognizing that no society reasonably can be expected to endorse curricula that simply encourage students to rebel. This is not to argue that the canonists' option is therefore the correct one, but simply that the radicals do not provide a viable alternative.

Political pressures for multiculturalism do have an impact on school curricula.[8] Increased attention to the historical contributions of African Americans—with the school canonization of Harriet Tubman as one icon—has occurred as a result of real changes in student demographics and the political pressures that followed. But such changes do not silence the canonists and therefore may prove fragile. They are often random—a brief unit on the Sudanic kings may be tossed into a course that focuses medieval Europe—and so of doubtful impact. It remains true that the most ambitious radical revisions, and particularly those being sought at the college level, ask for the educational moon. Their success is unlikely, and the stimulus they provide to canonist counterattack can be positively frightening. We must find ways in which real political pressures can be more fruitfully harnessed.

Key elements of the radical critique are also hampered by the emphasis on relativism. Teaching about the specific cultural assumptions inherent in basic intellectual approaches is a vital ingredient of the humanities' educational task. This is not the same thing, however, as espousing no truth claims whatsoever, so that education becomes a grab bag for whichever group has greatest clout. This relativism obviously antagonizes the canonists, contributing to an ideological polarization that makes mutual interaction impossible. It risks, in fact though not in principle, an unfortunate amplification of the science-humanities division in which science is reified as truth seeking, the humanities as sloppy and contingent theorizing. (To be sure, relativists direct part of their attack toward Enlightenment assumptions about science as well, but it is doubtful that they will find an extensive audience anytime soon.) Most important is the fact that no clear curricular structure emerges from the pure relativist stance; indeed, absence of structure may be the main point.

Yet curricula almost certainly must have some structure, some basis for selecting one course over another and for a certain ordering of topics within a course. Structure of this sort need not preclude critical assessment of the bases of truth claims. But most humanities research continues to strive for a certain level of truth. Because postulations about the nature and role of culture cannot be precisely confirmed by laboratory experiment or repeated observation—each cultural moment is, to some extent, unique—there is no question that humanities educators must grapple more openly with issues of accuracy and knowability than their scientific colleagues. Yet findings of high probability have emerged from the new research on historical contexts and audiences in relation to literature and from the efforts of social historians. The level of theory has improved, and the range of evidence appropriate to generalizations in the humanities is becoming steadily more extensive. Humanities curricula have gained alternatives to the rigidity of the canon on the one hand and the flaccidity of pure relativism on the other. The truth seeking that follows research advances in the humanities should be self-conscious and appropriately tentative and questioning, but it is not a matter of mere individual whim.

The fact is that the relativist impulse has generated a great deal of heat in several humanities disciplines, particularly with its urgings about the gendered nature of knowledge.[9] But it has produced very little light. Not only have no real curricular alternatives emerged from the movement; little interesting research has developed from the most extreme relativist claims, either. In history, work in the extreme relativist mode has been whimsical at best, labeling materials as representative because they are politically convenient (or simply involve little work), rather than worrying about available evidence.

Modified relativism, incorporating attention to the assumptions of humanistic and other scholarship, is another matter. As was discussed in chapter 1, analysis of cultural construction—the role of assumptions in determining seemingly "objective" patterns—is a vital focus of humanistic study. But unadulterated relativism, using whatever approach supports a preferred political slant, will not prevail as a significant current in humanistic research or as a serious curricular foundation.

Even some critics of the canon who do not yield to pure relativism too often jeopardize coherence, despite its legitimacy as a prerequisite of curricular structure. The temptation to ignore coherence requirements is understandable, for the canonists' central failing is their insistence on lockstep coverage and oversimple formulas about what Western civilization and American political values consist of. If this is coherence, then some chaos might be welcome. Yet alternatives to the canon do not have to resemble the random collection of courses outlined in the new Harvard core curriculum, which suggests little more in the way of principle than that any instructor willing to participate should be allowed to do his or her thing. Nor do they have to transform world history surveys into an almost random juxtaposition of regions. We can decide on some basic guidelines, as long as these are also exposed as partially heuristic devices, open to discussion and not hidden from view under an aura of sacred timelessness.

The point can be explored using American history programs as an example. Canonists tend to urge an American history agenda with a uniform emphasis on mainstream political values, in which the narrative moves from one agreed-upon period to the next. The American consensus—an ability to agree on basic issues because of the population's enlightened national spirit—illuminates virtually every moment except the Civil War and contrasts with the political polarization and ineptitude of most other societies, past and present. Stability is presented as a central political value and also a key product of the United States's unique version of democracy. This approach is unquestionably coherent, but only because it leaves most American history out of the tale.

To counterbalance this traditionalist approach, anticanonists (including many who believe passionately in historical truth, and for whom relativism is not an issue) propose a multifaceted American history in which the idea of a mainstream essentially disappears. American history, in this version, presents a collection of scarcely related group experiences—each race, each ethnic group, and both genders have their day in the curricular sun. The advantages of this diversity are immense, for different groups do have distinct pasts, each enhanced by a wealth of new information, and different students can connect with different phases of the story, depending on their own gender, ethnicity, and so on. This aspect of the multicultural alternative to canonism is valid and important. But the victim of an undiluted diversity approach is, obviously, any sense of unifying threads. American history becomes an almost unmanageable hodgepodge of discrete stories. Yet some central developments, including larger patterns of racism and other discriminations, ensure that the choice need not be between canonical narrowness and maximum diversity. The former is inaccurate, the latter unassimilable and even, despite its virtues, unnecessary—a disservice to what we know about larger forces of historical causation and some reasonably definable stages in American evolution that affect the mainstream and diverse groupings alike.

The alternative to canonical American history, in sum, is not a grab bag of group accounts, proliferating with each advance in knowledge or with each accession to political consciousness. Individual groups must be given their own pasts, but also their often complex relationships to larger power structures and larger value systems. Some of the most intriguing facets of African American history describe a separate culture and experience, but some others involve acceptance of widely shared values on such issues as education or social mobility (wherein African Americans often differed from European immigrant groups), juxtaposed with the tragic constraints of racism.[10] African American history is not just the story of separate values and reactions, and therefore it must be taught in balance with larger forces.

Multiculturalism need not, indeed should not, be an excuse for randomness. Links to larger patterns do not always evoke the simplistic pieties of the old melting-pot imagery. Decisions about how many groups to represent in relation to larger developments depend, of course, on both size and importance—in various periods, some groups have proved more significant than others—and on the level of curriculum being considered, as management of detail should improve in more advanced surveys. Manageability and coherence remain relevant factors and achievable goals even when we use something other than the traditional consensus as our central thread.

These factors apply not only in reconsidering American history, but also in other areas of the humanities. World history, for example, does not need to study a procession of individual civilizations—a pattern often mandated, ironically, by state educators who have managed to dispense with a full Western civilization emphasis, as if the alternative to a single emphasis is a random list. Instead, students should be encouraged to find patterns and generalizations that link and relate the experiences of different civilizations. Literature courses, likewise, need not present random lists of books chosen simply to please diverse constituencies; indeed, cultural theory dictates principles of coherence even as it attacks great books lists. Disputing a narrow structure does not mean that we should have no structure at all in making humanities courses responsive to new findings and new needs.

Finally, some of the new approaches to humanities scholarship manifest a self-indulgent obscurantism that does not permit curricular translation of any sort. The scholars involved do not venture teaching statements, save perhaps to carp at the canon. Their own work, however, is filled with a politicized jargon that is unintelligible to the noninitiated, so dependent on prior conversion that widespread pedagogical application is impossible. The drumbeat against the inherent horrors of gendering, sexual preferencing, and, of course, pervasive racism is couched in language as abstract and recondite as possible. The result is often simply silly and provides ample grist for canonical lament. The fact that this sort of theorizing occurs most commonly in literary studies and has some genuine links to relativist thinking helps explain the particular discredit applied to innovations in this field. Theory itself is sometimes misused in the new cultural studies field. Some scholars so emphasize theoretical formulations (obscurantist or not) and issues of methodology that they ignore literature of any sort, canonical or otherwise. But no discipline can prosper by formulations of theory alone; theory must be applied to evidence, in this case varied works of literature and other forms of expression. The alternative, realized not only in some scholarship but in some curricula, is that cultural theorists talk only to and about each other, ignoring or even attacking literature rather than carefully applying their theories toward fuller, less purely hagiographic understanding.

It is important to note that these extremes *are* extremes; they do not tarnish the better recent work in English. The excesses never-theless complicate the task of defending new approaches in human-ities teaching, and it would be folly not to recognize this fact or to try to explain away the more lunatic fringe. Intelligibility and some balanced judgments continue to be legitimate prerequisites for writ-ing in the humanities, and they form the only sound basis for a teaching agenda.

xtremist sound and fury aside, the limitations of the dominant anticanonical critique remain substantial. Political feasibility and even desirability, in light of the need to examine socially approved values as part of a critical humanities approach; the flaws in undue relativism; and the need for analytical coherence—all these are cru-cial challenges to humanities educators who plan alternatives to the canon, and they are not fully met by the radical critique. The final challenge is even greater: The fact is that, though related to the new humanities research, the anticanonical position does not fully flow from it. Ironically, and perversely from the canonists' standpoint, the radicals often share their impulse to reduce curricular goals to formulas for subject coverage.

Humanists who plan course programs on the basis of sheer rela-tivism, skipping happily from one work to another according to personal preference, may avoid the coverage trap, to be sure. Those, however, who seek to use humanities programs to sensitize students to the experiences of women and of minority racial and sexual pref-erence groups frequently display a passionate attachment to their particular subject matter. They may not have a single set of repre-sentative works to use in competition with the canon, but they cer-tainly insist on adherence to a common range of materials and on historical coverage of such predetermined units as stages of fem-inism or cycles of racial struggle. They project, in other words, a somewhat canonical anticanon, which they insist that a well-trained student must have mastered.

The suggestion that African history be substituted for Western civilization is revealing in this regard.[11] Its advocates undoubtedly believe that the Afrocentric alternative will amplify student under-standing of vital social and cultural issues, but on its face it will sim-ply replace one set of privileged facts with another. Indeed, at the high school level, introduction of African history has just given students another parade of kings to learn—along with the clear and desirable message, however, that Western society is not the only one capable of producing organized states and regal persons. Apart from the fact that Africa is no more representative of the whole world than the West is or was, exposure to African history without deeper attention to the goals of learning history simply provides a new list of memorizable datapoints. The modest gains of learning a distinctive vantage point and providing legitimate sources of pride for African Americans (though not necessarily for other minorities) cannot be denied, but the overall learning results will not change simply because of a shift in the subject matter covered.

A radical canon, seemingly a contradiction in terms, may indeed emerge in the battle against conventional coverage, and some of the Afrocentric or cultural studies theory formulas suggest precisely this. The fight for diversity can produce a belligerent rigidity: If you don't cover women, minorities, and sexual alternatives my way, with my intensity and using my range of data, then you aren't presenting diversity at all. Variant diversities need not apply. Here is the source of so much of the intolerance recently displayed on some American campuses in the name of greater tolerance; here is the source also of the tendency to convert antagonism to the conventional humanities materials—the great works and great people—into prescriptions about what should be covered instead. All that changes is what specifics are to be committed to rote memory.

This is certainly how the concern for diversity is currently being translated into middle school and high school curricula. Just as canonism too often blends with routine-mindedness, so now do the most politically popular features of the anticanonist crusade, and with results almost as numbing.

Thus California eighth-graders learn to identify not only George Washington but also Mercy Otis Warren, Sacajawea, and Absalom Jones. This usefully reminds them that women, Indians, and African Americans existed and functioned during the American Revolution. But it tells them little about power positions or other basic social interactions. Or, on the world history front, Minnesota students repeat that King Mansa Musa of Mali was a powerful ruler with lots of gold, alongside their encounters with Pericles and Caesar. This is useful to a point in reminding them that Greece and Rome were not isolated from the rest of the world—but do a name and a treasury constitute what should be grasped about premodern Africa? Conservatives object that these new names will conjure up racial hatreds and distract students' attention from mainstream values. The more obvious objection is that they will be fitted into a redefined main-stream and added to the memorization lists. There are certainly worthier additions to the new California and Minnesota curricula, and there are some signs of desirable flexibilities in related textbook programs. On balance, however, the main analytical point is still missed. The roster changes, the political service broadens, but the chores remain the same. New beauty marks appear, but our approach to the past is still a cosmetic one.

Clearly, the radical critique of humanities education yields no like-lihood of constructive dialogue with advocates of the canon. In one sense the radicals are not radical enough, for they do not push sufficiently for understanding. More obviously, the excesses of the radicals merely drive the canonists into further hyperbole. To their credit, canonists rarely talk about banning discussion outright, which some radicals tend to do in their eagerness to assure that proper thinking and inoffensive labeling alone prevail; but the can-onists do reach toward comparable extremism in their references to attacks on the foundations of Western culture and other impli-cations of dire subversion. The two camps risk converting the con-sideration of humanities education into a winner-take-all battle-ground. Between the iconoclastic extremism and the frequent silliness-cum-dogmatism of the radical humanists and the defen-siveness and often stuffiness of the canonists, there is no prospect of constructive compromise or exploration of additional options. Mu-tual extremism cancels out—and the result, if left untended, will surely be a failure to reconsider humanities programs in a more imaginative fashion.

Several observers have legitimately bemoaned the potential paral-ysis of the current debate—indeed, the frequent absence of direct debate courtesies of any sort. They note the imperviousness of both major camps to each other's criticisms, though their well-meaning pleas for tolerance seem inadequate to the task.[12] Some current can-onists have recently ventured a superficial conciliation. Of course, they say, there will be multiculturalism; the question is whether it will be done right. This stance may mask an unchanged underlying intent, or it may reflect a complacency that offers crumbs to the bar-barians while intending no real rethinking. The fact is that anti-canonists who are involved in curriculum discussions will yield no ground (in contrast to their research colleagues, who have more to say but have yet to translate their messages into systematic pedagogy). The further fact is that canonists either demonstrate equal stubbornness or, even if they are mildly conciliatory, relegate noncanonical themes to vague afterthoughts. A vigorous middle ground has dropped from view, and curricula that in practice try to draw from both camps are in danger of becoming mere collages, collections of bits and pieces with no underlying vitality.

Furthermore, the paralysis of polarization is not the only result of inadequate debate. Neither the canonists nor the radicals are taking fundamental features of the new humanities research into account. Radicals have the edge in subject matter, for it is surely true that humanities courses based on current scholarship must deal with a variety of cultural voices; and they have dealt seriously with the need to approach literary works and historical events through new theoretical perspectives. Yet the tendency to anchor alternatives to the canon in distinctive subject coverage, to replace one set of memorized facts with another, very different set, gives short shrift to the real options in humanities education. Accumulating new lists of heroines and literary works simply should not be the main goal. A larger danger of the current polemics is that mongrel mixtures—a smattering of canon, followed by a dollop of multiculturalism—will emerge as the only viable alternative to a humanistic hundred years' war.

The battle over the canon has become too bitter to permit of constructive result, and the debate is miscast in its tendency to focus less on analytical style than on subject coverage. The excesses of contemporary critics do not demonstrate the validity of the canon any more than the respectable pedigrees of the canonists automatically refute some of the telling critical claims. Neither side manages to achieve the central task of converting humanities education into an active agency for cultural analysis. Replacing the mission of sacred trust with one of diffuse revolutionary dogma will not suffice. It is time to bring the larger implications of humanities research into fuller play.

FIVE

Clearing

the Decks

for Creative

Planning

The task of peeling back the layers of outdated tradition, pedagogical addiction to routine, and now the politicized debates between canonists and their critics is unquestionably demanding. In a sense the charge involves more than simply bringing humanities teaching in line with the basic thrusts of exciting new research; it must also be kept abreast of the knowledge needed by an advanced industrial society. Just as science teaching in Europe had once to be weaned from its reliance on classic texts in light of experimental advances,* so now the humanities require a genuine conversion not just to incremental accretions of new subject matter, but to active recognition of their own role in generating new knowledge. The way station that allowed the humanities' initial survival in industrial society—the identification with nationalism and special educational service to the elite—still functions, admittedly, but on increasingly shaky grounds and at the cost of neglecting tremendous new opportunities.

Simply combating the temptation of many teachers to stick to the

---

*The field in the nineteenth-century United States was born, however, on assumptions of new discovery, because classical sciences, featuring the authority of the ancients, never penetrated our fledgling universities.

tried and true—an understandable temptation, given frequently inadequate subject-matter preparation and the tremendous time demands of teaching many hours each day, often before an unruly student horde—is difficult; without a valid alternative vision, it may be impossible. When this challenge is compounded by the frontal assaults of canonists who have the support of authorities from key government agencies and the backbiting distractions of some anticanonists who have their own rigid definitions of suitable coverage (with friends like these, who needs enemies?), it is small wonder that the gap between imaginative scholarship and most teaching remains yawningly wide. For scholars themselves, it is easier, more exciting, and more rewarding to continue to extend humanities research than to tackle its implications for teaching, aside from very specialized courses. We have had distressingly few commitments to curricular discussions by major researchers. Partly their reluctance stems from the undeniable penchant of major universities to value research over teaching in doling out salaries and granting tenure. But partly it results from the sheer density and unpleasantness of the current curricular structure and the debates that surround it. The key mission of humanities teaching really is to apply some of the same enthusiasm and creativity to curriculum development that have for decades marked research. Those who attack research as a distraction from teaching, although they are not wrong in all cases, generally retard the very connection they should encourage.

It is revealing that most discussions of improved teaching (not only in the humanities, to be sure) focus on better individual performance and the rewarding thereof, not on the substance of what is taught. Good teachers do need encouragement. Some good teachers, however, teach bad stuff: vigor and popularity with students must not be our main goals. Curricular design is a vital part of the teaching equation, and too many teaching advocates are dropping this more complex and substantive ingredient—perhaps because it has become too controversial, or perhaps simply because it is collectively more difficult.

Overcoming tradition, routine, political counterattack, and the oversimple definitions of quality teaching adds up to an awesome task. The task must be shouldered, nevertheless, if the humanities are to hold their own, certainly in the classroom and ultimately in scholarship itself. The urgency of the task calls for new effort.

There are, fortunately, also a variety of more encouraging signs. Teaching in its broader dimensions is beginning to receive some welcome new attention. In a recent book, Ernest Boyer, the head of the Carnegie Foundation, predicts that the 1990s may become the decade of the undergraduate in American higher education.[1] The reasons for the change are not all good news—they include the prospect of some indiscriminate reduction in research support, ultimately the lifeblood of stimulating teaching, as well as of new knowledge, in modern society; this is, in fact, already occurring. The transition also involves some frankly silly claims, such as the president of Stanford University's argument that teaching will replace research as the major criterion for faculty promotions —a most unlikely development at places like Stanford and one that would upset the proper balance of responsibilities at major universities as fully as does the present overemphasis on publication quantity.

But there are also some solid reasons for new interest in teaching. Until 1995 at least, undergraduates must be actively recruited by most colleges and universities, because the size of high school graduating cohorts is continuing to shrink for demographic reasons. With research monies becoming more uncertain, tuition funding is demanding more attention—and this means, or should mean, a constructive interest in curriculum quality as well as teaching prowess. These developments should in turn encourage new teaching interest among humanists, but also—because in fact most humanities disciplines already take their teaching functions quite seriously—they should attract new attention to the humanities as guides in the teaching endeavor.

Until recently, for at least the past two decades, the humanities have been squeezed by a growing emphasis on technical subjects at the state college level, combined with disproportionate attention to science facilities in the leading universities. The costs of science facilities and faculty, in turn, have limited the resources available for humanities teachers, even as college costs and revenues seem to soar. As a result, class sizes in the humanities have grown while faculty sizes stagnated or shrank. If an emphasis on teaching is revived, some rebalancing of priorities will be a key measurement of its force, and humanities faculties can only benefit from the process as their ratio with students becomes more reasonable. (Though some good teaching advocates also propose increasing class size for economic reasons—a troubling prospect overall.) Improvements in the framework for humanities teaching currently are speculative at best; the restructuring has not yet occurred beyond a rhetorical level. We are not yet assured of a similar reconsideration at the high school level, where the clearest crisis mentality applies to science courses and testing procedures, not to humanities training in a larger sense. But if colleges begin to send new signals, they may reap results in the form of more general benefits to teachers in the schools.

My goal is not to oppose humanities and science instruction in some simple antagonism; attention to quality in both areas is vital. Indeed, recent rethinking of general education science courses in college, which would refocus them on basic analytical modes rather than watered-down coverage of entry-level physics or biology, parallels humanities reforms in exciting ways. Nor is it to oppose research and teaching in either science or the humanities. Critics who have posited such an opposition profoundly misconstrue the role of the humanities in generating new knowledge and insights. If teaching does gain ground, however, its enhanced position may facilitate a more fruitful linkage between research and the classroom and, in specific cases, give a welcome boost to the teaching function, as opposed to the often mindless concentration on the numbers of books and articles published. Furthermore, the result could be a more useful curricular discussion between the humanities and science sectors on the grounds of shared needs and shared endeavors. These are results to be hoped for, should the educational climate change somewhat.

Thus Boyer anticipates a new blend of discovery, integration, and teaching. He believes that the new concern for teaching will reduce purely specialized research endeavors, not only by elevating the status of the classroom but also by requiring new attention to connections and syntheses within and across disciplines, illuminating specific research findings in ways accessible to students and nonspecialists. These issues have already attracted the attention of innovative researchers in the humanities, because of the common blend of teaching and research interests and also because of the dynamic of new knowledge generation, which ultimately requires attention to larger, synthetic frameworks. If the university context does change such that more scientists become interested in these demands as well, the result could be a wider canvas for those humanists already attempting more general statements and those relatively easily attracted to curricular and classroom concerns.

The process may be further enhanced if some of the more farsighted plans for stimulating American education bear fruit. The interest in new national testing programs has already been mentioned.

Such programs pose a danger, but they also offer promise. Enlightened advocates of testing argue against rote memorization exercises, and for a more diverse array of student expressions through some system of student portfolios that will include essays, oral responses, and other creative work. Their goal is precisely the opposite of the routine memorization so often emphasized in the past. Social and economic needs have changed, so this argument runs, and necessary intellectual skills have been redefined in the process. Analytical capacity and the ability to learn quickly now hold pride of place, and assessment mechanisms must change fundamentally to take these priorities into account.

This prospect is tentative at best. It does not exclusively address the humanities or define the humanistic versions of the desired capacities. Nevertheless, the more imaginative formulations for new ways of assessing students' knowledge are engagingly compatible with the emerging directions in humanities education, which point away from memorization and toward a new ability to marshal evidence for analytical goals. They argue for new beginnings at the middle school and high school levels, which the assessment process would encourage and on which it would ultimately be based. They suggest, further, some ultimate compatibility in science and non-science education, with both directed away from the simplest skill requirements. It may not be totally utopian to see some common movement at both school and college levels, based in the one case on new assessment initiatives and in the other on broader encouragements toward imaginative teaching, which will work toward new curricular integrations of research methods and results.

In the humanities specifically, this trend has received further encouragement from some of the more enlightened canonists. At the National Endowment for the Humanities, the tone has changed, if slightly, from the stridency of the early 1980s. Too much attention continues to be lavished on canonist training; basic goals need considerable adjustment. But the narrow, rather petulant defensiveness of the William Bennett years has yielded to somewhat wider concerns and even to a certain willingness to compromise. As we have noted, this mood falls short of truly embracing new goals; it does not promise an adequate reformulation. But it has generated a heightened interest in creative teaching that, in turn, has identified important targets in need of remediation.

Even while we continue to explore a curricular vision very different from a slightly revised canonism, it is important to recognize the validity of many of the canonists' points about classrooms themselves. Lynne Cheney joined other authorities in blasting the mindlessness of many textbooks, which are so loaded with facts that instructors are discouraged from making anything but fruitless attempts at coverage, students from getting beyond data to meaning. Cheney's proposed solutions, concentrating heavily on the need for more reading in elite cultural texts, remained too narrow, but her initial focus deserves real applause. Cheney similarly zeroed in on training programs for precollege teachers in the humanities, which are weighted down with education requirements but are tragically short on stimulating content in the disciplines that are ultimately to be taught. This is another vital focus, around which humanists who seek better education can make common cause. Other obstructions to building a solid humanities program include sheer time-wasting on courses or segments devoted to consumer education or "futures learning"—stopgaps directed particularly at "learning resistant" students who are assumed (often incorrectly) to be incapable of achieving a more serious understanding of social patterns.

In sum, Cheney, along with a number of canonist colleagues, correctly identified problems in humanities courses that result not from excessive innovation but from excessive routine. Her predecessor politicized his goals by suggesting that poor educational quality resulted from the ill-considered incorporation of social history or the new criticism into humanities classes; courses in check writing seemed to equate, in his mind, with courses exploring the African American experience. Cheney largely moved back from this stance, though her 1992 outburst against political correctness as the chief problem facing universities was a bizarre reversion related to the presidential campaign. But canonists have made valid points. Mind-numbing textbooks, poor teacher preparation, and frivolous distractions in the essential humanities courses are targets that require redress. Renewed attention to education, although it has hardly produced agreement on new goals, nevertheless has turned a welcome spotlight on some fundamental preliminary concerns.[2]

Finally, there are signs that some of the more innovative scholars in the humanities are awakening to the twin tasks of developing an educational vision appropriate to the new scholarship and opposing some of the simplicities of the current debates over the canon or political correctness. After a few years of relative silence, they are beginning to develop a response to the spate of fact lists claiming to establish real educational credentials. Eric Foner, a leading historian of Reconstruction, correctly places much of the current debate over student ignorance in a longer continuum: "Ever since the Puritans some Americans have feared that this country has been in the midst of social and cultural decline. The latest version of this long tradition is a series of best selling lamentations." This analysis does not prove that the canonist critics are wrong in their approach to current problems, of course, and certainly should not be taken as a sign that they are mistaken in all particulars. It does offer a high probability, however, based on an analytical use of historical perspective, that their concerns are exaggerated and their reasoning confused. The canonists' charge of diminishing patriotism—which must be compensated for by a still-more-nationalistic humanities teaching agenda—has also been debunked simply on the basis of current evidence. But the scholarly counterattack is by no means entirely negative. Other historians such as David Thelen, the editor of the *Journal of American History*, distinguish between processes of memory and the establishment of meaning. Pure memorization, encouraged by the routine tasks emphasized in the schools and by some teachers' desire to pound patriotic lore into their students' heads, can in fact, these scholars say, impede the development of an ability to assess factual information and select from it the evidence to answer significant questions.[3]

There are powerful indications not only that existing educational approaches are faulty, but that the faults are not novel and that some of the most widely publicized critiques point in exactly the wrong direction. More memory, more lists of data, or, as one *New York Times* writer urged (after sneeringly dismissing "big-time scholars"), a revival of mnemonics are not only not the answer; they do not even respond to the significant questions.[4]

Straws in the educational and humanities winds are beginning to blow less wildly. Attention to good teaching—and, it is to be hoped, to fresh curricular planning—may be on the rise, and this in turn could bring humanists together in a new kind of educational mission. The attempt, visible in the current assessment debates, to gain some sense of what abilities our society needs to develop in students (whatever the past utility of rote achievements) is a step in the same direction. Real initiatives like the high school CHART and Pacesetter projects mentioned in the introduction, or California's move to begin serious social studies training in the later primary grades, have exciting potential.[5] At the university level, non-Western historians finally are beginning to develop coherent alternatives to ethnocentric traditionalism, rather than contenting themselves with potshots at Western civilization programs alone or confining themselves to equally narrow area specialties. Perceptive observers of the humanities, though by no means agreeing on all goals, are joining together to address some common educational issues and are beginning to perceive the limitations of the most widely publicized frameworks advocated during the 1980s. Utopia has not yet arrived; disagreements remain vast, and the current effort to use political correctness as a club with which to attack humanities innovations could retard the potential progress. A basis exists, however, for building new agendas.

Warnings: How Not to Proceed

New agendas, however, are not easily formed, in part because of the hold still exercised by older debates, and in part, of course, because of significant disputes among some advocates of change. It is easier to identify what *not* to do than to formulate new plans. And it is tempting to settle for some patchwork compromise as a means of uniting educators of good will in what must be, ultimately, a common endeavor. Before turning to the central issue of what the goals of humanities education should be, it is essential first to address the preliminaries.

The pitfalls are, by now, reasonably clear, though a few considerations—such as the problem of coherence—will still need to be raised after a positive agenda is more firmly established. Pitfall number one, suggested by some of the thoughtful responses to the fact listers, involves getting the context right. The idea of formulating humanities curricula on the basis of a belief that the quality of education has massively deteriorated and that the humanities must serve as the bastion of a beleaguered civilization is misplaced. Student achievement may have worsened in some respects, and without question we still need to address massive problems concerning what students know and can do. But a defensive, possibly punitive mentality is worse than useless; it is empirically incorrect. There is no systematic evidence of a worsening of achievement levels when present-day student groups are compared with similar groups in the past. More important, an approach based on the assumption that our youth are deteriorating is unlikely to motivate the students who need motivating, and it will not teach them what they need to know about society and culture. Without jettisoning all the traditional features of history and English courses, it is more fruitful to consider what students need to learn from the humanities in order to face the social conditions that exist today and are likely to exist in the future. We have never been able to make the masses of students into Athenian aristocrats, and we are unlikely to profit greatly from a renewed effort to make sure they have memorized the names of the leading Roman emperors.

In addition, the humanities should not constitute a curricular museum, designed to provide the one stable core in an educational program otherwise geared (at least in principle) to evolving demands on education and to an expanding knowledge base. Museums, as places that deliberately preserve past treasures (though many actual museums are themselves trying to escape this confining definition) have a role in the transmission of culture, but not as primary definers of what the humanities are all about. Our nation is not threatened by massive disloyalty or the collapse of substantial agreement about shared beliefs, and it is unlikely that ideologically inspired education could repair the damage if it were. Rather, we are hampered by an inadequate grasp of how societies function and a considerable passivity in social and cultural arenas. These arenas constitute part of the present and future needs that humanities education can and should help address.

The biggest problem with humanities education in the schools, and in some colleges, is its lack of inspiration and experimentation. Routine, not radicalism, is the enemy, as even the more sensible canonists recognize. Faddism has afflicted education in a few instances, but it is more often debated than widely implemented. In a society wherein large numbers of high school history instructors, for example, are primarily athletic coaches, it is hardly surprising that efforts to introduce changes in subject coverage or teaching techniques have had limited impact. Though the secondary schools present the most obvious examples of routine-mindedness, colleges that offer required courses in which the only assigned reading consists of mammoth, fact-filled textbooks are little better. Here, too, goals of coverage and memorization predominate, and the instructors are sometimes too burdened, sometimes simply too unmotivated or too lazy to rethink their approach beyond possibly experimenting with a different text-clone in the interest of superficial variety.[6] Exceptional teachers at all levels, whether actively innovative or not, must qualify any blanket criticism; but the fact remains that survey courses continue to be the major source of humanities fare for most students, and many survey courses have changed little over the past forty years.

Curricular proposals based on assumptions that student deficiencies are the result of huge changes or oscillations in coursework, or those that try to beat back innovation by implying that it has already triumphed in the classroom, with tragic consequences, are simply off the mark. The biggest recent changes in actual humanities training (as opposed to proposals and experiments) have not instituted massive new subject coverage; instead, they have come about either from the testing mania in the schools, which focuses primarily on conventional coverage and basic skills, or from the re-installation in some colleges of a core curriculum, which is founded more often than not on the Western history and great books approaches predominant in the 1950s, with only minor modifications. These changes have not replaced routine-mindedness in humanities education overall, and in some cases they have reinforced it. Future proposals for genuine change must take the immense inertia of the curricular setting into serious account—which of course is why shortcuts like national assessment programs are so commonly sought.

Routine-mindedness bedevils humanities teaching in many guises. It shows in the widespread reluctance to introduce new topics, new materials, or new approaches—or the tendency, when forced to yield, to give up as little of the familiar as possible and to prefer relabeled old coverage to the genuinely new article. It shows above all in the fondness for equating coverage with adequacy. A student's ability to memorize a battery of familiar points eases the teacher's task, facilitates comparative testing, assuages many parents who want Junior to learn what they once were supposed to learn and have since forgotten, and imbues the whole enterprise with the comforting sense of the familiar. Coverage of a required range of subjects is the bane of constructive humanities teaching. Plays and novels are not mastered by regurgitating characters and plot lines; history is not learned by cramming in the maximum number of dates and names. Following this same line of reasoning, we can see that humanities goals are not served by increasing the number of plays covered or—for history is a more common victim of this thinking than literature—by expanding the number of reigns, wars, or important ideas to which diligent students, for a time at least, can apply brief tag lines. Facts are vital to the humanities, but they function best as ingredients of analysis, not through sheer quantity. Many key humanities goals are best met by simplifying factual coverage, not by extending it—though the simplification should include careful guidance in where to find additional facts when needed.

Facts, after all, are readily available in compendia, libraries, and, increasingly, in computerized banks. Not so easy to come by is the motivation to seek the facts, the knowledge of what kinds of facts are needed, and the ability to use the facts to address interpretive issues. The temptation to insist on factual retention constitutes the most insidious hold of routine. Even innovators who espouse new topics like women's literature or world history fall into this trap, urging expanded coverage instead of generating more imaginative alternatives. Correspondingly, textbooks fatten at the expense of effective, challenging teaching. Even routine-minded teachers recognize that the amount of material to be covered has become impossible, but they resolve their dilemma simply by leaving things out —for example, by ignoring the twentieth century, or at least the decades since 1945, in history surveys. This is haphazard selectivity (and in fact, as we will see, selectivity of the worst possible sort), not the kind of innovative planning needed to undermine routine.

Coverage goals defined in terms of factual retention are not the appropriate organizing principles for humanities curricula. Their convenience, easy testability, and mistaken association with a mastery of historical and literary canons explain their prominence but do not, however, excuse it. As subject matter changes, particularly with the move to add multicultural topics, the factual-coverage syndrome may render humanities courses still more numbing and even more incoherent.

Students need facts, but for a purpose, not for the sake of the facts alone. Students who delight in memorizing dates or material from baseball cards or names of tragic heroines need not be discouraged. If this helps them locate themselves in the humanities, or simply entertains them, fine. But these students, as well as others more immune to the charms of data lists, must be taught, beginning in appropriate ways early on, that in the humanities strings of facts in and of themselves do not suffice.[7] They count only if they can be employed to answer larger questions, and this use requires selectivity as much as massive demonstrations of memory skills. Datadrops, those most convenient of crutches for students who work but don't quite know why, are second only to complete ignorance as problems in good humanities teaching.

This point needs to be stated carefully, because appropriate humanities goals that focus on analyzing cultural and social patterns require factual knowledge. There has been a small trend of late—though it has receded somewhat in the past several years—toward teaching students "critical thinking" skills without significant content. The ability to express an opinion coherently, regardless of its empirical base, is privileged in this approach.[8] But fact-free analysis is not a valid goal, however well the student may editorialize, and both humanities courses and student assessment mechanisms should legitimately probe the ability to find, interpret, and use data to form an analysis. The trick is not to be trapped by the need for data—to assume, or encourage students to assume, that the usually short-lived ability to recite facts is a substitute for useful knowledge.

Clearing the decks for planning valid humanities education programs does not, then, mean that we need to get rid of facts. It does mean that we must actively alter the current balance, so that facts cease being ends in themselves. It means resisting the shock techniques of routine-minded canonists who try to scare both educators and education consumers away from change with their alarmist messages about what students do not know. This reorientation is difficult. At a meeting of social studies teachers, a historian, friendly in principle to analytical goals, introduces a conversation stopper: At his Ivy League college, a student who had demonstrated outstanding skills in dealing with analytical issues in American history unwittingly revealed, in a casual conversation, that she thought Pearl Harbor was somewhere in Latin America. Shocked gasps ensue, or at least they are supposed to ensue. Of course we all wish that college-educated students knew the location of Pearl Harbor. (Though keep their age in mind; how many of us know, as our parents or grandparents routinely knew, where Verdun is?) We must, however, resist the easy reaction, which is to assume that this relatively modest deficiency proves that Ivy League (or even bush league) history courses should return to or reconfirm factual drills. There will always be important data that students do not know. Emphasis on new topics and appropriate analytical habits may conceivably increase sheer factual ignorance slightly, though this is not a proven result.

Despite all the momentum of routine classroom habits, we must distinguish between mere factual exposure, mere factual retention demands, and the habits that enable students to interpret and use facts. This is one of the most challenging reorientations required for constructive curricula in the humanities.

Routine-mindedness and its common companion, fact-think, constitute the recurrent bugbears of effective humanities curricula, but they have additional comrades. Heedless lip service to teaching can, ironically, pose another stumbling block, as we have seen. A focus on teaching is welcome, but efforts to establish polarities between research and teaching in the humanities are counterproductive. In many instances, the real problem is how to acquaint humanities teachers with research findings and principles. Not all humanists are eager teachers, and a few researchers undeniably bow out of teaching as completely as possible. Most humanists who do research, however, both expect and want to teach. Advocacy of greater rewards for good teaching and for imaginative and effective curriculum development makes excellent sense, but it should be presented as an adjustment to the present system, not as a frontal assault. It should be balanced by efforts to involve teachers who are not able to participate directly in research and to enable them to keep up with their fields in demonstrable ways, however popular their classroom performance. In innovative, advancing fields—which the major humanities disciplines now are—learning cannot end with the completion of initial teacher training, even if this is upgraded.

On another contextual front: Extreme caution is necessary in evaluating the current curricular climate in American universities. Radical tendencies are not nearly so widespread as they are often portrayed to be, and they often involve interactions among students more than actual classroom planning. Further, they correctly point to the need for new flexibilities in many programs, and they usefully challenge both unconsidered routine and the pressure for still greater emphasis on a literary and historical canon. There is no need to base a curriculum on the perceived necessity of beating back real or imagined radical challenges. At the same time, students at some elite universities unquestionably do feel constrained by political correctness pressures. More to the point for this book, curricular plans in a few instances have been distorted by a desire to see the humanities defined as the basis for attacks on the established order or as sources of identity for beleaguered groups. Any curricular approach has political implications, but the humanities should not be co-opted by either the elite or the elite's varied challengers.

Many of these points are widely recognized, though of course by no means uniformly agreed upon. They constitute essential preconditions for the positive task of identifying appropriate educational goals in the humanities. Yet obviously they do not fully define such goals, much less lay out their curricular implications. Because of the distracting furor of recent debates, and because of the effort by many canonists to use a more conservative political climate to beat back unwanted or misunderstood changes in humanities scholarship, the critique of erroneous assumptions has overridden the establishment of viable alternatives. We must understand what not to do and then build on this understanding.

The Limitations of Compromise

The above said, the next move might logically be toward seeking a reconciliation between the more sensible canonical statements and the more moderate radical pleas. Humanists of various stripes can indeed agree on certain points, such as the need to improve teacher training and provide appropriate teaching incentives. Some of the canonists have begun to distance themselves from the most adamant positions, and particularly from undue association with the advocates of memorization. Why not take these gestures one step farther and talk about how diverse philosophies can be blended to make a framework of common devotion to high-quality learning?

Two related kinds of compromise might be considered. The first, ventured initially in the late 1970s, calls for combining new styles and old in the humanities—combining social history topics, for example, with conventional political coverage in high school American history survey courses. The second, potentially more complex, focuses on the possible integration of canonist goals with some reasonable set of diversity demands.

In the long run, curricular compromises may be possible. They may well, in future, build a growing constituency for what should be done. It is indeed vital to find some way of achieving humanities goals that avoids the extremes of both canonism and diversity claims, and compromise would be a logical means of steering an apparent middle course. Yet despite its surface charms, compromise is not the way to begin; it should at best be a later result of more fundamental initial innovation. Although I cannot complete this argument until I have outlined the proposed innovation itself in the following chapter, some preliminary warnings will indicate why we should not move immediately to a tactful middle ground.

When social historians first began to talk seriously of integrating their findings into mainstream curricula rather than presenting them in new, topical college courses, they roused interest among teachers and textbook publishers—but, with some striking exceptions, interest of only the most limited sort. The majority impulse was to introduce snippets of new material, but not to rethink conventional coverage. Thus textbooks introduced special feature sections intended to give students some information on women in the past or on aspects of daily life. The text itself continued to highlight political developments.

In survey courses, similarly, teachers might insert a brief social history segment as an attention grabber or diversion, spending a couple of days on leisure in premodern society and then, at some later point, a day or two on women's domesticity during the Industrial Revolution. The effort was not inconsiderable, in the sense that some conventional topics had to be cut back slightly and several new lesson plans prepared, but there was little real restructuring of the course as a whole.

As a way station, the snippets approach made some sense. Revolutions do not occur overnight, and a few new lessons one year might lead—in a few bold cases, *did* lead—to an entire unit the next. For the most part, however, adding an occasional snippet to textbooks or to course syllabi proved counterproductive in that it excused history teachers from giving any real thought to combining old and new. Students, for their part, though they often reported feeling a particular engagement with some of the new materials, readily discerned that the real meat still sat on the old counters; political history provided the only coherent thread in the survey and usually constituted the only materials subject to testing. This kind of limited compromise did not generate substantive change.

The introduction of snippets or special topics segments failed two key tests in the history course. First, it failed to offer the continuous treatment of major social history themes that would have made analysis over time possible. The topic of leisure, for example, might draw student interest. But the basic transformations in popular recreation, from significant community festivals—the staple of most preindustrial societies—to the limitation of leisure outlets during early industrialization, to the commercial leisure emphases of more developed industrial societies, simply were not conveyed. Interpretation of change over time, or even comparison of modern leisure values and content with prior historical examples, was impossible.

Second, snippets almost by definition failed to link new topics with old; political developments continued to be seen as self-contained units, not only overshadowing other facets of social behavior but also unable to mesh with a wider social context. Yet leisure history, to pursue the example in this second respect, frequently has vital political implications. The festival tradition served to promote community bonds, while also giving certain groups a place to let off steam: youths, for example, could periodically ridicule the power of elders; farmers could mock the pretensions of landlords in the latters' indulgent presence. The decline of the festival tradition signaled a new nervousness about popular revelry on the part of those in authority and also encouraged many discontented groups to turn more directly to political action to vent their grievances. The rise of subsequent new leisure outlets, such as ballyhooed spectator sports, along with the measurable decline in classic industrial protest forms suggests yet another relationship between leisure enthusiasts and protest manifestations, one that should be explored as part of a larger effort to relate contemporary society to the broader historical perspective. Leisure history is important in itself for what it reveals about community life and standards of pleasure, but it also crosses over into other historical spheres, including the conventional category of political behavior. Introducing an occasional descriptive segment on leisure cannot convey this link—meaning that, on yet a second front, an analytical opportunity is lost. Because of the sheer weight of traditional coverage, a sincerely intended compromise attempt failed. History coverage and its goals were not really altered. The effort did clarify, however, what genuine change would require.

That the most undemanding combination of the innovative and the traditional should fail to advance a more imaginative humanities agenda is hardly surprising. The experiment is worth noting, however, because it demonstrated—to the surprise of many initial advocates—the empirical limitations of patchwork compromise, and because even apparently more substantial efforts risk falling back into a similar pastiche. The power and convenience of routine easily overwhelm even the more conscientious efforts at partial innovation.

The same dangers inhere in more recent compromise proposals.

One example has been offered already. In the Bradley Commission's report, historians concerned with widening the reach of history in the schools offered essays on a conventional Western civilization course and on world history. The implication was that both would be desirable, and in principle, over a sequence of history offerings, this is indeed the case. Simultaneous presentation, however, begs two crucial decisions. The first, obviously, is what goes where? Most high school teachers and the majority of college teachers who work in this survey area are familiar primarily with the Western civilization course. This familiarity is buttressed, in some instances, by the vigor of recent canonical arguments. Without explicit guidelines about the placement of a world history course, teachers at each stage of student preparation are likely to call for what is easiest and, often, dearest to them—good old Western civ. As noted earlier, they will often in fact convert curricula labeled as world history into a barely expanded Western civ approach—a self-deception encouraged by the many textbooks that call themselves world history while devoting the majority of chapters to the Western experience alone.

A compromise between Western and world history approaches too readily obscures priorities—the need to choose and to rethink. Even were decisions ventured on some definite world history–Western civilization sequencing, a second and more subtle set of choices must address coherence of approach. A genuine commitment to world history entails a distinctive treatment of the Western experience. It requires more explicit comparison of the West with other areas, as opposed to conventional but untested assumptions of Western uniqueness and often superiority. It also requires more analysis of the West's involvement in the wider world, not just as master during the centuries between 1450 and 1920, but as exploiter and even, in these centuries but more obviously before and since, as apprentice. Simply juxtaposing a good world history segment and an unexamined hurrah-for-the-West survey leads to confusion or at least a sense of unconnectedness on the part of many students; to continued ethnocentrism, as the lessons briefly sketched in world history are ignored or contradicted in the Western segment; and, once more, to a tendency on the part of many teachers to incorporate even less innovation than is officially called for, as apparent compromise blends into unexamined familiarity. Juxtaposition, in sum, although in principle involving more change than the addition of a snippet of novelty here or there, differs from rethinking. As such, it hopelessly burdens the compromise approach.

This is no mere theoretical dilemma. Recent curricular experiments have tried to combine more global coverage with some attention to the West through mechanical rearrangements. New York State's global studies program, for example, answers the desire for an emphasis on world history by relegating Western civilization to the final quarter of its tenth-grade course. The result pleases no one, which might suggest a good compromise. The more extreme diversity proponents object to any explicit unit on the West, while canonists deplore the brevity of the segment as well as its end-of-term placement. In fact, the problems go deeper, resulting from the failure to offer an overall framework into which the West would appropriately fit.

The same dilemma of compromise sketched out but incompletely realized bedevils some interesting attempts to think through the American history survey. In 1989 a New York State task force on minorities reported that history programs emphasizing Eurocentric and elite histories contributed to low self-esteem among minority children in urban schools. Appalled, Diane Ravitch and Arthur Schlesinger responded by forming a "committee of scholars in defense of history" to monitor the state's curriculum revision process. Their brief attacked "the politicization of history" and blasted any notion that history courses should be seen "as a form of social and psychological therapy whose function is to raise the self-esteem of children from minority groups."[9] Strong words. Yet Diane Ravitch also contributed substantially to the Bradley Commission report, which eloquently justifies a use of history to "satisfy young people's longing for a sense of identity and of their time and place in the human story."[10]

Ravitch, in fact, seems to value some consideration of non-elites in American history while fearing a balkanization if mainstream national history is not dominant. The combination of interests is understandable enough; what is missing from this potential compromise framework is a clear statement about how the various concerns can be melded into an adequate whole, at once reasonably coherent and sensitive to the actual diversity of the American experience. Somehow what should be an invitation to explicitly blend old and new fails to work, producing contradictory statements instead of a satisfactory overall structure. The Bradley Commission report similarly fails to generate a single framework, urging conventional survey coverage in one place while noting the importance of appealing to varied identities in others. This is yin and yang, not the kind of harmony that depends, even in its "traditional" elements, on imaginative synthesis.

One final example along the same lines: One of the leaders of the Bradley Commission has recently ventured a slightly more structured statement of compromise, explicitly combining the need to study mainstream political evolution and the current attractiveness of the diversity approach. Paul Gagnon urges that social history be used to provide the necessary multicultural education, with political history providing the necessary education for democracy.[11] The twinning constitutes "the final pair of ideas we must keep in our heads at once." The proposal is attractive, suggesting some movement in the right direction, particularly as it is supplemented by urgent pleas for an accurate rendering of the political record rather than values glamorization. Yet the foundation remains flawed by the now-familiar pair of dilemmas. First, while Gagnon talks two ideas, he himself is overwhelmingly interested in the political record alone: "Knowing political history is the absolute precondition for political sophistication, which in turn is the absolute precondition for free choice and the exercise of political power." Multicultural needs are granted only briefly and rather grudgingly, so that what seems to be a pairing is actually a definite hierarchy of goals. If this is Gagnon's best shot at compromise, it would fall even further short if translated into day-to-day curricula, in which the teachers' familiarity with political staples, largely descriptive and defined in terms of coverage goals, would readily take command. Objection one, then: The compromise is too feebly stated and would not adequately redefine the history survey against the massive inertia of routine.

Second, the bifurcation is inaccurate and needlessly confusing. Social history is concerned with far more than diverse groups. It also studies the interaction of leading institutions like the state with these groups. The honest political history that Gagnon sincerely intends is impossible unless it is merged with social history in order to determine how state activities really affected workers or women or racial minorities and vice versa. The merger required differs fundamentally from the dualism Gagnon seems to imply. The division between social and political history is misleading but also unnecessary; fuller integration requires an additional major step, which seems to be impossible from a slightly half-hearted compromise platform.

If compromise between the canon and innovative scholarship falters even when both desire to cut through the most numbing classroom routines, direct compromise with routine itself is still more hopeless. College Board experiments largely bear this out. The Advanced Placement programs nobly attempt to mix essay and machine-graded tests, with both new and old subject matter. Essay segments, for instance, have particularly stressed newer materials on the grounds that their more open-ended framework would be fairer to students trained largely in conventional materials than multiple-choice questions; the hope was that the experiment would gradually move teachers toward the new topics as well. This was true in some cases, which means that the experiment was better than nothing. It was not, however, a real success. Because conventional materials were still honored in one part of the test, many teachers focused on these alone, loudly resenting the board's attempts to twist their arms with other subjects. Seeing the multiple-choice formats, many teachers concentrated on fact coverage, hoping that students could wing it in the more analytical segments. Blending programs have only a marginal effect on humanities teaching, for routine too often distorts the blend, and the blend itself is developed too mechanically.

Many of the goals of compromise are valid. Curricula that are genuinely international should not exclude the West; diversity must be addressed without pretending that political power does not exist; new approaches in literary criticism can be applied to some familiar "great works"; and—definitely—analysis must combine with some mastery of facts. Valid compromise goals, however, have thus far failed to generate acceptable implementations. Too many plans contain no protection against widespread impulses to return to the familiar. Too many plans are themselves half-hearted, in that they prefer conventional goals while rather grudgingly recognizing their inadequacy in light of current student needs and research advances. Too many plans, finally, are needlessly incoherent, juxtaposing ingredients that need a single but innovative and imaginative recipe. The ability to talk of compromise is a gain, signaling the more favorable climate beginning to emerge among the less routine-minded canonists. Even when it is not invoked to camouflage essentially conventional aims, however, the compromise approach does not sufficiently inspire. It also fails to eliminate forcefully enough some of the leading pitfalls to a dynamic humanities curriculum, from the factual coverage impulse to the larger commitment to routine. A fresh start is essential.[12]

SIX

Education:

The Central

Mission of the

Humanities

The purpose of courses in the humanities and related social sciences is to teach skills and convey insights about how people and societies function.* This purpose should transcend any vestigial impulse to regard the knowledge of a set body of facts as proof of student self-discipline or cultivation. Facts are vital for inculcating the skills necessary to analyze cultures and societies, but they are tools, not goals in and of themselves. Facts are not long retained if they lack meaning, and they are not worth retaining if they do not further understanding. Critical analysis, not mere descriptive knowledge either of conventional materials or of newer topics, should be the central goal of humanities curricula from the middle school level onward.

To be sure, some factual definitions are essential, simply because they come up so often that ignorance of them would needlessly re-

*These skills and insights are not, to be sure, "objectively" definable. They are themselves cultural products—as indeed are scientific methods, however confirmable they might be. There is, in other words, still an inescapable political ingredient. I continue to argue, however, that this ingredient is less detailed and confrontational, and certainly more open-ended, than both the wider political agenda of many academic radicals and the conservative implications (however garbed in nationalist and civilization-saving rhetoric) of the canonists.

tard one's progress.[1] Students in history need to know what a state is, for example, and what culture means. Some of these definitions can be introduced in grade school, through concrete examples, and developed more formally later. Aside from this intellectual infrastructure, however, descriptive or factual presentations in the humanities should always be subject to justification: What understanding does the presentation advance? How is it given meaning?

The basic analytical function of humanities education relates to two additional guidelines. The humanities must be taught as sources of new knowledge, not simply as repositories of established information or hallowed values. They need not be equated with science; indeed, explicit distinctions between methods of inquiry and subjects of study will help students get more out of both their science and their nonscience programs. As with science, humanities courses cannot be uniformly devoted to new inquiries, for students must acquaint themselves with existing methods and theoretical concerns before proceeding. As with science also, however, students must be given some sense of open-ended discovery, and teachers must see their subject as a dynamic one, not as a tidily and durably prepackaged product. As one excellent recent discussion of history teaching put it, the humanities must be approached as an ongoing series of inquiries, not as "a closed catechism, a set of questions already answered."[2]

The knowledge and analytical skills that we most need to derive from the humanities, finally, are those that allow us to interpret the way societies and cultures—and their peoples—function today. This is not to prescribe a diet of presentism. Humanities courses teach us about society and culture by using diverse examples and by exploring past patterns in some detail. To understand today, we need to know what yesterday was like and to have a real sense of how the two connect. Some humanists' resolute resistance to the present is a part of the creativity of the disciplines involved and certainly need not be denied. Nevertheless, the educational mission of the humanities requires some application of analysis to the present, and not merely in the form of vague pointers or wistful analogies. Course segments that explore connections between classical experience and contemporary life must do so in part explicitly; segments that establish social, political, or literary trends that presumably extend into our own day must analyze those extensions directly. Precisely because the humanities should not focus exclusively on preservation—exposing students to past cultures or institutions just because they were there, or even because they ought to be vaguely inspiring by their antiquity—the links to current concerns must be made part of the curriculum itself.

These fundamental goals—provision of analytical skills, attunement to further discovery, and linkage to contemporary social and cultural issues—are not entirely novel. The best canonical programs, for example, teach critical analysis through examples from classical texts and political experience. The idea of building a curriculum on these goals in combination, however, does depart from most current formulations. It suggests that the humanities, like the sciences, must be regularly updated. The disciplines are not static, and teachers who work in the humanities must not only be trained initially in the newest materials; they should also expect to have to refresh their own knowledge throughout their careers. The need to establish links with contemporary developments means that the history program that never gets beyond 1945 or the literary program that takes refuge exclusively in time-tested classics will no longer suffice, for students need experience in applying the skills partly developed through a study of earlier patterns to the society and culture around them.

Above all, humanities curricula should be generating assessments quite different from those most commonly applied. The central question is not how many historical periods or literary genres the student has been exposed to, but what kinds of analytical problems he or she has encountered and learned to manage. The ability to use data, including relevant understanding of how to find it, clearly takes precedence over any capacity to regurgitate. Defining interpretive problems and working toward their resolution, not maximum memorization, should set the basic guidelines. To evaluate course segments in terms of how they add new analytical experiences is to unseat the more common sequencing structure of periods or genres. In order to deal sensibly with causation, of course, students in history must gain some sense of what fundamental patterns follow what prior patterns—innovation is by no means complete; but the basic point is to work from one analytical level to the next, and in some cases this method may prove compatible with outright deviation from the traditional sequence.

When analysis is stressed over coverage, a key injunction becomes: Dare to omit. No history course can possibly cover everything, yet instructors often come to feel that what they *do* cover is sacrosanct. Courses in literature are in this respect better off, for selective sampling, even among the recognized "great" works, is unavoidable. Historians, including those who are devoted to new approaches in their own research, have a harder time shaking off the blanket syndrome, which assumes that maximum coverage is essential against educational nudity. Students may be hazy about precise dates or unable to flesh out some famous names, yet still have an excellent command of the essential tools of historical analysis. Some of the time now devoted to covering standard survey material must be used instead to hone conceptualization skills, and the required shift in our assessment priorities may be even greater than the accompanying adjustments in syllabus coverage. Always, the goal should be transmission of the ability to use facts, not an insistence on maximum retention.

Two years ago I overheard a student in my world history course, which is designed for freshmen, telling another, "This analysis is really pretty interesting, but I keep waiting for them to get to the history." I took the remark as a compliment, but also as an indication that I needed to convey more clearly what the study of history is about.

One useful testing mode, even at the high school level, would involve a willingness to hold open-book tests, so that students would not be hindered in their handling of analytical problems by a slightly tenuous recollection of specific facts. For such tests to work effectively, prior acquaintance with the facts is essential, otherwise students will not even know what to adduce and what to look up, but this mode of testing reduces the sheer recall element while accentuating the primary analytical goals. One teacher, bent on emphasizing methods of interpretation over the mere recounting of facts, actually offers general guidelines on which facts to include; she finds that the resulting stimulus to organized argument "can excite and motivate today's high school students" and carry over into subsequent exercises.[3] The same approach could be applied to literary criticism, replacing memory-probes about plots and characters. But a sea change from the conventional coverage syndrome is an essential precondition for this new approach.

The remainder of this chapter will spell out the curricular thinking necessary to implement basic changes in humanities education. Until we develop extensive experience with the new curricula, some issues must remain indefinite, though we will move toward more explicit translations in the following chapter. We will need to experiment to determine what kinds of analysis will work for students at various educational levels. For too long, high school teachers have found themselves pitching toward the lowest common denominator. In one instance, an able teacher boasted of a long exercise devoted to having his sophomores first digest, then evaluate the impact of the fact that rivers in Russia run from south to north —in a mere two to three class sessions. The goal—a specific analysis of geographical factors in shaping society—was valid, but the time allowed for exploring the topic reflected a distressing lack of ambition.

The analytical approach, based on what humanities methods and knowledge demonstrably contribute to understanding, assumes a willingness to work toward greater challenges at the middle school, high school, and collegiate levels alike. Many students are capable of readier responses than we currently expect of them, and a program that asks for more thought and less rote recital can engage them in this direction. If we ask only for memorization, we will get nothing more—save, among many students, an additional harvest of resentment or apathy. If we approach humanities materials in terms of problems to be addressed, and if we extend a given question across several cases and into the contemporary arena, we will find that many students can go considerably beyond the factual retention—the "concrete operational thought," to use the fashionable jargon for presumed student limitations—that is currently promoted. But exactly what can be achieved at which levels, or how many cases will be necessary to drive home a basic analytical concept, cannot be determined in the abstract.

We can stipulate several key features of a problem-driven humanities approach, not with the intention of constructing a single ideal curriculum, but rather with the aim of setting some parameters for a wide variety of specific efforts. We begin with the issue of choosing topics, particularly the problem of balancing new subject matter with old. Closely related to this subject is the necessity of introducing theory, an area in which another set of innovations is vital in order to develop analytical capacities in the humanities sector. Next we will address the most direct manifestation of the plea for conceptual focus: a list of some of the basic analytical skills the humanities should engender at all schooling levels. Finally, an examination of the problem of coherence will cap this initial sketch.

The Need for New Topics

The excitement of humanities research in recent decades and the goal of presenting some open-ended issues to students, instead of their usual steady diet of cut-and-dried humanities staples, both dictate the introduction of new topics into the curriculum. History courses must begin to include materials on areas of the world still often ignored in surveys and on topics seemingly far from the political skein that still predominates. English courses must include more varied readings than the standard "great works" and must take a look at media other than formal literature. The subject matter of the humanities is far broader than was once the case, and it is still expanding.

It is possible to imagine a situation in which innovative research programs at the university level coexist with limited, traditional curricula in the same subjects in the schools; this situation has to some extent prevailed in France for several decades. French leadership in social history and deconstructionist literary analysis has had only a limited impact on school approaches, which remain heavily focused on nationalist goals and standard coverage of political themes and "great authors." The disparity partly reflects the much smaller ratio of French students admitted to college than exists in the United States, where the gap between high school and college is already dangerously wide in terms of work demands and could become impossible to bridge if there should be greater divergences in subject matter. Even in France, the disparity has had its costs, revealed in a widening gulf between routine humanities learning and more innovative technical programs and in a growing loss of effective historical sense beyond high-level memorization. The example, despite the prestige of things French, is not one to recommend.[4]

Yet this has been the drift in the United States in recent years, except for some social history coverage of minority groups and a certain current of interest in world history at the precollege level. Proposals to add new subject materials continue to clash not only with routine habits, but with the coverage impulses of the schools. This division is one source of the lifelessness of much humanities teaching, which has been substantially cut off from evolving trends in scholarship and, as a result, from imaginative leadership. A recombination is essential, and it can only come about through the expansion of subject matter in basic humanities programs. But enlivening the curriculum is only part of the solution. Students themselves must be made to see the potential for social understanding in some of the new topical areas and to see that the humanities share with the sciences the task of expanding our knowledge base.

One of the newer areas of interest among historians, philosophers, and sociologists serves as a case in point. Humanists (broadly construed) are beginning to contribute actively to an understanding of how emotions function in social contexts. Sociologists have been exploring the interaction between social relationships and emotion; one researcher has detailed efforts to manipulate emotion to affect job performance—as in the training of flight attendants—and the different expectations of gratitude that develop in contemporary families amid changes in work and household functions. Cultural anthropologists deal with the often radically different emotional formulations of various cultures. Historians work on patterns of emotional change. They have found, for example, a number of shifts in emotional standards in Western society during the eighteenth century: a heightened valuation of romantic and parental love; a growing distaste for anger within the family (captured by the invention of a new word, *tantrum*, to identify unacceptable outbursts); and the increasing use of guilt rather than shame to discipline children and to define criminal punishments. For the period 1920–50, other changes have been revealed, including a growing distaste for public displays of grief and widespread efforts to control the emotional training of young children.[5]

Work of this sort adds a major new dimension to the evaluation of culture and cultural change. It brings together humanists and social scientists in wide-ranging debate with behavioral scientists, who focus on unchanging and therefore laboratory-replicable manifestations of human emotion: Where do "basic" emotions stop and cultural conditions take over? Such questions assert the fundamental relevance of defining and testing cultural constructions. The humanistic work suggests vital directions for further research, including the application of existing findings to other time periods and cultures, more general examination of the causes of diversity and change in emotional cultures, and further exploration of the impact of diversity and change on other facets of human and social behavior. This is, then, a frontier area of humanistic research that has already produced substantial findings.

This, in turn, is precisely the kind of scholarship to which students should be exposed after some basic training in humanistic research and analysis. The type of research problem, not the study of emotional culture per se, is of paramount importance. There is no need to parade every substantial area of new research before non-specialist students. Instead of the work on emotional culture, we could as easily have cited the exciting findings about the nature, origins, and evolution of modern consumerism or the pathbreaking findings on historical changes in human sexuality, two other areas where various humanists, along with social scientists who are sensitive to cultural factors, are making major strides.[6] The important thing is to keep any list of humanistic topics flexible, to allow for new research areas, and deliberately to expose students—even those in high school—to some sense of the humanities on the cutting edge, where new topics are being opened and where new issues about the nature and function of culture are being raised.

Some relatively unconventional topic areas (unconventional, that is, in terms of standard survey courses, though not in terms of existing humanistic research) absolutely demand inclusion in the basic humanities agenda. Gender is an obvious case in point. This subject belongs in the curriculum not because of feminist political pressures or even the desirability of giving female students a greater sense of identity and the opportunity to explore relevant issues through education, but because gender has become a fundamental unit of analysis in cultural studies of all sorts. Knowledge of cultural constructions of femininity and masculinity—including the diversity among different groups and societies and major changes in standards over time—is vital to understanding how people and societies function. Such interactions describe not only women's conditions, but also basic male values; and they shape definitions in religious and political institutions. *Patriarchy* thus becomes an essential addition to the terms required for understanding most civilizations, including our own. The fact that contemporary society has vigorously disputed various gender constructions only serves to link historical and literary scholarship with exactly the kinds of current conditions that students should be able to analyze in applying humanistic learning to the world around them.

Obviously, the addition of gender studies as a humanistic staple raises some problems not associated with, say, the study of the American Constitution. Research findings are newer and, on the whole, more subject to dispute. The relationship of gender to other topics, including standard political themes, has not been fully worked out. These problems obviously must be dealt with in the appropriate curriculum segments, but they do not constitute reasons to back off. They usefully challenge students to relate current political debates—over men's and women's family responsibilities, for example—to the wider humanistic perspective. A good curriculum can, with reasonable clarity, establish boundary lines between widely accepted findings, areas of incomplete research and analysis, and areas (however vital) of bitterly partisan scholarship. Thus it is both possible and essential, in dealing with basic social and cultural frameworks, to reveal some of the general and agreed-upon features of a patriarchal society while noting that the reasons for the initial establishment of patriarchalism are not entirely clear and that use of the term *patriarchal* to describe recent or contemporary gender relationships is more politically charged. All three points are worth knowing: the fundamental, the incompletely explanatory, and the politically volatile.[7]

The need to introduce new topics into the standard humanistic curriculum is neither random nor infinite. Two principles should govern our choices. The first is a belief in the importance of conveying the energy of the humanities, their exploratory and innovative qualities; studying a topic like emotions or social mobility could achieve the desired results. The second principle involves recognizing a finite number of additions to the subject matter, like the gender perspective that now must be conveyed as part of instilling a basic understanding of how societies function. Some teachers may want to add a third desideratum: the addition of relatively new topics, such as the serious study of leisure or of childhood, that don't quite meet the second criterion and are not essential to the first but have the potential to command unusual student interest, to lead students more readily to higher levels of analysis, or simply, by evoking the enthusiasm and special interest of the teacher, to add vigor to the classroom presentation. Even these three criteria do not require humanities curricula to embrace every significant new facet of literary, historical, or philosophical research. Selectivity is essential, and there are guideposts to help us accomplish this goal intelligently.

Even when we are selective, though, the addition of new topics, combined with the need for ongoing flexibility, will require us to compress or jettison some existing staples. The study of twentieth-century media will reduce the number of classic literary works that can be covered. Giving attention to gender matters will mean less time for canvassing the European Renaissance or nineteenth-century American railroad development. Greater rigor in the classroom may allow some additions without correspondingly full deletions. In history and related social studies, an outright increase in course work, now widely proposed, or the reduction of Mickey Mouse interruptions and detours into such areas as consumer education, also widely proposed, may free up some useful time as well. There is no getting around the need for a genuine reconsideration of conventional coverage, however. New topics must not simply be spliced in or confined to the odd Friday when students aren't paying much attention anyway.

The reevaluation of existing subject coverage is hardly new to the humanities. The amount of attention devoted to the classics declined long ago. In more recent times, our altered understanding of historical content reduced the amount of space given to British constitutional and political history, and even the canonists have not suggested that this somewhat arid theme be revived in full. Admittedly, the adjustments needed now are particularly sweeping because of the dangerous lag between research and curricula, but they are not entirely unprecedented.

The first step in adjusting our present curricula should follow the same basic guidelines proposed above for governing the addition of new topic areas: What conventional topics must be covered for students to gain an accurate sense of how societies operate and to develop a progressive ability to analyze social and cultural issues? These criteria are quite different from more conventional formulations about which facts students should be exposed to in order to parrot the standard lists. Understanding how the Constitution shaped the United States and the extent to which it created a distinctive political society is quite different from the ability to recite each item of the Bill of Rights in the appropriate order. The Constitution can be "taught" more quickly than is often now the case, especially if students have previously learned about civil societies, traditionally constituted, that required no such self-consciously formulated fundamental contract.

The second step in adjustment blends the selectivity already found in conventional areas with that required for selecting new topics. Humanities courses, beginning in the high schools, must work to show connections among new topics and old. Political constitutions, for example, do overlap with gender relations. In eighteenth-century Western society, changes in thinking about social hierarchy prompted reconsideration of standard patriarchal dominance and of traditional monarchical authority, and the two lines of thought clearly intertwined. Correspondingly, actual changes in political structure by the end of the eighteenth century prompted further disputes over gender relationships precisely because the reform principles were less fully and systematically carried over into family relationships. Not all aspects of gender can be neatly linked to categories of political analysis, but genuine and extensive relationships such as this can show us the way to combine old and new in humanities programs—once the new is thoroughly introduced and its implications genuinely understood. Students and teachers alike must confront the task of synthesis, which is why a purely mechanical process of subtracting some conventional subjects and adding new ones will never work. Creative imagination is essential to the changes required.

A willingness to introduce new topics and to rethink current and conventional subjects constitutes only the opening move in reorienting the humanities curriculum toward its appropriate goals. If we pay too much attention to this preliminary process, we risk limiting the change to purely mechanical adjustments and vitiating the movement away from memorization criteria. Humanities programs will not serve their function if the only change made in them—however great a change in and of itself—is a redefinition of coverage. Openness to new topics is not an invitation to scholarly innovators to substitute their list of essentials for the current list; nor should it serve as a catalyst for some combination of conventional and novel topics that will fill every day of the course, every page of the mammoth text, with facts that should be known. The inclusion of gender as a causative element invokes a vital analytical ingredient; it does not immediately prescribe mandatory knowledge of such (admittedly interesting) details as the growing exclusion of women from the European craft guilds during the later Middle Ages. That particular data set may or may not be useful for students to know as part of their examination of how gender factors operate in society.

For the importance of factual material is its use in supporting the ability to answer questions about how societies change and how systems of belief and representation develop and function. Every scholar worth his or her salt has developed arsenals of factual knowledge without which he or she would feel bereft, and from which students can clearly benefit. My own list would include not only materials about emotional standards and gender in craft guilds, but also demographic patterns, military technologies, and a host of data from my own more conventional humanities education that I am glad I know—the list is long. Translating scholarship into effective education, however, means holding back parts of these lists in favor of asking the overriding questions whose exploration will benefit students even more. New topics are essential to an energetic humanities curriculum, not because they meet a revised definition of coverage, but because they are vital elements for conveying how cultures and societies develop and operate. The purely conventional lists of topics, which revolve around the structure of the state and elite taste, are simply too narrow even if we reorient them toward the basic analytical goals. But some conventional topics unquestionably belong with the materials that must be involved in the analytical process, for among the questions that students should be able to handle are such items as the relationship between political constitutions and other social characteristics.

The goal is to select factual categories that fit the questions to be addressed and the analytical skills to be honed. This goal dictates the omission of vast reaches of potentially interesting data. It requires consideration of some new topic areas and some old; it encourages relevant synthesis of new and old; it demands openness to new combinations as scholarly emphases and findings change—though not on a whimsical or faddish basis; and it urges that no syllabus be overfilled, lest the simpler measurements of coverage preempt the goal itself. The basic American history course at Case Western Reserve University focuses on only three episodes. Each is explored in depth in order to arrive at an understanding of three major themes in American history, but especially to convey a sense of the issues involved in analyzing the combinations of factors that shape a complex society around questions of race, gender, or political culture. Students emerge from this course not knowing about some other parts of American history; but they emerge also with a sense of the kinds of processes necessary to analyze how our society functions. Stanford's non-Western history course explores only three areas—Mexico, China, and Nigeria—in order to achieve its basic goals: in-depth consideration of non-Western societies, including the impact of past patterns on the present; understanding that these societies differ and change over time—that the "non-West" is not a stagnant lump; and the honing of comparative skills. Full world coverage, an impossibility in any event, is deliberately bypassed, in contrast with some knee-jerk world history sketches (including a recent "national standards" draft) that propose mind-lessly "covering" one society after the next. The point of these examples is to show the difficulty of identifying a single formula governing which episodes or cases to cover or how many to tackle; rather, we should insist on the reorientation of purpose behind any intelligent selection.

Survey courses can retain a legitimate place in the curriculum, but they must be rethought using the twin criteria of admitting essential new topics and targeting goals other than maximum coverage, whether conventional or newfangled. Graduate students, including potential teachers, still need this survey knowledge—though they too must absorb new findings along with older staples—so that they can make intelligent selections in their research and in the classroom. Before the graduate level, mere command of survey materials must not be the main goal, and in some instances the whole survey form could legitimately be replaced with more targeted analysis. Whatever the choice of framework, however, room must be left for new issues, new slants, and creative use of the factual materials that are presented.

Theory

Many conventional humanists long prided themselves on their avoidance of theory. History and literature, in their view, called for description and narrative, not theoretical flights of fancy. The purpose was to describe the facts, to lay out the story. The humanities thereby contrasted with some of the newer social sciences, in which theoretical interests often predominated, leading to numbing jargon, neglect of the distinctive details of real human experience, and lifeless generalization.

It is easy enough to show that whole sets of theories have in fact always been intertwined with traditional humanistic scholarship and teaching. The privileging of democracy involved theoretical assumptions. Analogies between classical and desirable contemporary values involved others. American history was commonly researched and taught on the basis of a theory of American exceptionalism, which argued (though usually implicitly—overt comparisons were too demanding) that our national experience, though derived from and closely related to patterns in Western Europe, was nevertheless distinctive, a civilization in its own right. A related emphasis on consensus over polarization in the American experience relied on vigorous if unanalyzed assumptions about what to include and what to omit in teaching American history and about the desirability of avoiding conflict. Teleological assumptions were often prominent in frameworks of this sort and in many Western civilization courses as well. History was seen (again, often implicitly) as a progressive march toward steadily greater enlightenment, at least in recent centuries, in which societies became more humanitarian, better educated, less superstitious, and more democratic. Previous historical stages are seen as building blocks that allowed progress in these and other areas in more recent times. When an advocate like Paul Gagnon urges attention to the origins, evolution, and advances of democracy, noting that there have been periodic retreats but claiming as well that "only in the last half-century have we achieved democracy in legal terms," he touches base with vital theoretical assumptions about continuities and even purposes in patterns over time, at least in the West and the United States.[8]

On a related front, conventional coverage criteria in history courses, though rigorously nontheoretical in tone, nonetheless embody theoretical assumptions about the importance of state-building and state activity in defining societies. Politics is presented as the central cause and mirror of more general social and cultural patterns. This is a defendable proposition, but it certainly involves a number of major assumptions. Like the child who discovers in an English course that she has been writing prose all along, humanities teachers can and should be brought to recognize their own involvement with theory even in the status quo.

In the status to come, theoretical demands will expand. The new humanities education needs to pay more formal attention to theoretical concerns, introducing theory and its evaluation extensively into nonspecialist courses. This innovation is less well defined than the challenge of introducing new topics. It may be more difficult to envisage, for in addition to demanding some class time, attention to theory involves another recasting of approach. Difficult or not, though, a more theoretical orientation is absolutely essential.

The reasons are several. The existing use of theoretical assumptions needs to be made explicit and examined so that students and teachers can make an intelligent selection of the assumptions to be retained. History may be teleological, moving in some evolutionary progression to higher levels of civilization. But there are many theorists who argue against this proposition, and the assumption should be analyzed, not merely conveyed. Also, students themselves are equipped with a number of essentially theoretical assumptions derived from general culture, including previous schoolwork, by the time they enter high school or college humanities courses. Many, for example, implicitly accept what can be labeled as modernization theory, the belief that some societies are better than others because they are more fully modernized (having developed democratic political structures, industrial technology, and mass consumer cultures) and that a logical historical framework is one that looks at the progress of these societies from less modern (less democratic, less industrial, culturally more religious and particularist) to modern. Modernization theory may be correct, at least in some respects, but it has been widely attacked. Insofar as it is assumed, it should be examined and its drawbacks noted.

Some new scholarship in the humanities invokes and develops theory more formally than was the case with more traditional work; this provides the second reason to introduce theoretical frameworks and theory-testing as part of a staple educational diet, adjusted appropriately to student level. Social and world historians maintain considerable skepticism about sweeping theories, though they have dealt with modernization and also with a newer world economy theory that organizes a major part of modern world history in terms of differential relations to world trade.[9] Middle-level theoretical formulations are more common. Reductions in birth rates, for example, normally provoke reassessments of emotional relationships within the family as individual children become more cherished. Scholars who study traditional workers have defined the "moral economy" concept—the proper relationship between worker and superior and the proper assessment of the amount of work required—which the workers use in reacting to major changes in work routines such as those induced by commercialization or industrialization. Theoretical constructs like these allow diverse data to be organized under more convenient and more interesting headings; they save time; they challenge us to think in ways that mere description cannot necessarily accomplish.[10]

The growth of new theories is one of the fruitful results of increased interactions among humanists and social scientists from several disciplines, including sociology and anthropology. The focus on theory correspondingly constitutes the most creative means of presenting interdisciplinary findings—far preferable to the sterile memorization lists that were once a staple of the social studies.

The new studies of literature are particularly theoretical in a formal sense, arguing that real understanding of cultural products is impossible without playing them off against more general formulations. Some literary theorizing is too abstract or obscurely phrased for widespread use, and some, as noted above, departs too fully from any mooring in literature. Some focused theory, however, has become absolutely essential in getting beyond plot summaries and implicit assumptions about what constitutes a "great" novel or play. One new-style teacher of literature writes about teaching Flaubert's *Madame Bovary* by emphasizing theoretical work on the relationship of representations to desire in order to understand how Flaubert addresses these issues in the novel and also to deal with the involvement of the reader's desire in representations like the novel itself. The theoretical problem of how people link their desires to representations is put first, with the novel used to explore the issue. Culture, in one formulation, produces objects of desire; if the apple were not represented as desirable by the fact of its being forbidden, would anybody ever have desired it? The question ultimately leads to a discussion of the relationship between basic human drives like desire and the cultural formulations that direct and possibly even produce them. Students (and the instructor) find the novel much easier to remember when a theoretical framework enlivens it, and they are also able to link the book's content to contemporary issues of representation and desire in advertising. They enhance their ability to reflect critically on their own desirous investments in the written word and on how such relationships were treated in the past (not necessarily in the same fashion as in a consumer society, with its distinctive definition of economic success). This set of theoretical issues can later be linked not only to other reading, but to other problems in theory such as the role of gender in defining a culture's definitions of pleasure and desire.[11]

Sheer memorization, in the sense of recalling plots, obviously takes a back seat in these formulations, becoming the by-product of a theoretical approach to literature that is designed to advance our understanding of culture and to teach students how to argue about important cultural issues. Under the impulse of theory, students move away also from simply stating their opinions and begin to distinguish between statements of belief and the much more important ability to debate the validity or reasonableness of beliefs when there is conflict over the beliefs themselves. In the new approach to studying literature, these aptitudes far outweigh any conventional ability to recall the facts of great books.

The appropriate use of literary theory—including "new historical" approaches that relate works of literature to interactions between authors and audiences in the larger context of cultural conditions when the works appeared—need not entirely distract us from aesthetics. Some students have always demonstrated an aesthetic appreciation of literature, and the reaction deserves every encouragement. In fact, the presentation of literature within theoretical contexts that do not oblige agreement on any single standard of literary greatness may promote more spontaneous aesthetic engagement than now occurs. Aesthetic standards themselves can be directly discussed; one part of cultural study involves understanding why certain contemporary or subsequent readers decided that a particular work was a classic. The varying aesthetic standards of two different cultures or of two different groups within the same culture can be fruitfully compared as part of the same approach. Literary theories can help students assess their own reactions to a work without insisting that one particular set of reactions is the only correct aesthetic response. By guiding students to an understanding of a variety of meanings in literature and related media, theory can sustain multiple aesthetic responses.

In literature, the arts, and history, theory far more than topical content increasingly drives humanistic research, and this fact must be conveyed in basic curricula. Humanistic theory remains different from theory in the sciences and the most scientific (real or self-proclaimed) of the social sciences. This differentiation persists even as the theoretical sophistication expands. Humanistic theory rarely, if ever, advances propositions meant to hold true for all people in all cultures; any theory so widely applicable is likely to entail little more than common sense, on the order of noting that all hierarchical societies attempt to justify the wielding of power. The level of humanistic generalization cannot match the sweep of some of the laws of physical matter. It is also true that humanistic theories are more subjective than much scientific theory. They cannot be fully proved and often cannot be fully disproved, because they deal with behaviors that cannot be exactly replicated. One society's moral economy, for example, differs from another's, leading to important debates over whether enough common content exists to make the overarching label viable. Students can learn that theories in the humanities are useful in raising important questions and helping to link data, even when they are widely criticized and clearly are partially wrong—though they must also learn that some theories are so deficient as to be obstructive (like the theory cited previously that presumes a historical law dictating the westward movement of civilization). Dealing with theory in the humanities ultimately helps students learn both to distinguish and to forge connections between forms of knowing in these disciplines and the dominant modes of scientific analysis.

The characteristic features of humanistic theory can and should be frankly presented and discussed. When widely disputed theories like modernization are presented in history courses, they can be defined (initially a matter of memorization) and then tested both against theoretical counterattacks and against data from various societies. Students can learn, for example, that a claim that modernization leads to increased formal education is more empirically accurate than a claim that modernization is accompanied by growing political democracy or the increasing empowerment of women—the latter claim being true in some cases of "modernization," but definitely not in all. These students can then decide whether the valid facets of the theory are useful enough to warrant its use, despite the risk of misleading extensions or the imposition of Western-derived standards of progress on societies whose own evaluations differ from ours. They will at least understand the nature of the argument.

With experience, they can begin to apply similar tests to other theoretical claims regarding social or cultural data that they encounter in the future. *Newsweek*'s art reviews, when commenting on abstract styles or complex film plots, routinely refer to the "madness of modern society," implying a link between nonrepresentational culture and the nature of modern life. *Newsweek* may be wrong, but it is clearly advancing a theoretical position worth evaluation—and open to evaluation in classes dealing with contemporary culture. Another recent theory, which is currently discussed among political scientists and is beginning to draw popular attention, relates to the claim that democracies never go to war against other democracies—a theory advanced, obviously, to read hopeful signs into the current spread of democracy and designed in principle to shape our own foreign policy. Is the theory right? What kinds of data are required to assess it? People who emerge from a solid general education in the humanities—including programs that may have been designed before this particular notion was advanced but that were conceived with a strong theoretical flavor—should be able to evaluate formulations of this sort, not on the basis of memorized examples about American or British or Athenian foreign policy, but through familiarity with the kinds of assessments (including adducing factual evidence from established repositories as well as from memory) necessary to handle theoretical claims in an intelligent manner.

Theory is an inescapable part of the way knowledge is managed. The humanities have distinctive kinds of theories, different from those of pure science and requiring special training, but vital in their ability to give facts meaning and to provide connections and short-cuts among various resources. Use of theory is an important part of teaching students to analyze social and cultural issues and helping them to develop capabilities that will extend beyond the school years. Along with new topics—and, indeed, closely related to the assessment of such topics as the impact of emotional cultures or the construction of gender—the introduction of theoretical components into humanities programs and their use in organizing factual coverage constitutes another essential step in moving such programs toward their basic educational goals.

The Need for Organizing Questions

A set of conceptual problems, when properly presented in relation to the exploration of various topics and often in conjunction with applied theory, can give primary structure to humanities training. There is no need to generate an exclusive list of such problem sets, just as there is no need to define a single pattern of factual coverage. Specific organizing issues will vary and change. For, once the coverage rules are stripped away, humanities education becomes in large part a series of case studies, which are designed to encourage particular kinds of analysis but are not themselves fixed in stone—other case studies might work just as well.

Yet the general injunction to advance students' analytical capacities must be fleshed out, however flexible we may ultimately be in implementing that goal. It is essential to include several kinds of analytical experiences in a good humanities program that develops its students through high school and collegiate general education, and some of these follow a clearly sequential order, building on simpler prior achievements. Some capacities are already being taught, at least in better programs; others may require more explicit prompting.

The first charge is the most general, and ultimately the most important. Every course in the humanities, at least by the high school level, should address some basic interpretive problems, and these problems should recur in different segments of the course. In this they would differ fundamentally from the questions teachers diligently prepare for each class's requisite lesson plans—usually excessive in number, often requiring little but factual recall, and rarely linked to questions that might be addressed a week later.

Take a course dealing with developments in the United States in the nineteenth and twentieth centuries. A host of topics spring to mind, and it is easy enough to generate questions for each. What was the New Deal? Why did Roosevelt's court-packing scheme fail? Or, for a slightly more venturesome question: What was the relationship between the principles of New Deal reform and the earlier Progressive reform tradition? And so on, from one class day to the next.

But let us step back a bit: What finite number of more fundamental questions should organize a course of this sort if we wish to address analytical issues and not simply move from one set of facts (old or new) to the next? The basic formulation of American exceptionalism might provide one analytical category. Has the United States been largely distinctive in its historical evolution over the past two centuries, or should it be seen as part of a larger Western civilization? Here is a basic interpretive issue that translates into a host of specific but coherently linked questions. Was the New Deal fundamentally different from Popular Front reforms in 1930s France, and if so, why? Has the twentieth-century American family been uniquely unstable, and if so, why?

Other organizing questions can be added, but in a manageably limited number so that the course is not chopped up into a series of low-level interpretive exercises. My own favorite additional three are as follows:

What were the ramifications, in domestic developments and outlook as well as in foreign policy per se, of the growing importance of the United States in the world from about 1870 onward? This is the least interesting of my three additional questions, in that it risks calling forth largely factual statements about isolationism followed by the shift to new militarism and alliances. The theme is vital, however, because it links U.S. history to developments elsewhere— and not just as a occasional note, peripheral to the main, internal political topics. It builds a real curricular bridge between U.S. and world history. It embraces unexpected vignettes, such as the early dependence of American arms manufacturers on sales abroad, a significant theme since the end of the Civil War. It investigates new strands of immigration and the complex interactions among immigrants, their cultures of origin, and their circumstances in the United States. The assessment of international impact also brings up several less familiar issues, such as the development of American manufacturing (a frequent technological and capital borrower) and farming in relation to the international economy. Finally, the mutual interactions between our international position and the larger cultures of key groups in American society raise an important set of questions about our successive orientations toward the world—not only isolationism but the subsequent preoccupation with an evil adversary in World War II and then the cold war—on terms more encompassing than foreign policy alone.

How did the United States combine an exceptionally early and pervasive political and social democratization with the development of exceptionally hierarchical and domineering organizational structures, particularly in the manufacturing sector but also in aspects of policing and punishment? The nation's precocious democracy made it the only country in the world to extend political opportunities to lower-class men before the upheavals of industrialization, which in turn helps account for such national peculiarities as the absence of significant socialism. The democratic social tone, extending to the informal position of women and children in the family, was noted by a variety of international visitors from the early nineteenth century onward. The democratic theme, in sum, raises important questions about political and social behavior over a two-century span and is analytically interesting in itself. At the same time, however, the United States also pioneered in creating modern organizational forms such as scientific management and its progeny, the assembly line, which had exceptionally undemocratic implications for economic life. This country also has been unusually fascinated with, and addicted to, prisons as a form of punishment. The complex combination raises important questions that run throughout our history from at least the mid-nineteenth century to the present; these questions can help juxtapose developments in aspects of our national experience that are usually kept separate.

What was the process and extent of cultural integration in the United States, and what were the effects of this integration on national life and on the identity and coherence of major subgroups? This question, again, picks up distinctive or partially distinctive national themes—not only the familiar if vital topic of the United States as a nation of immigrants but also the national ability, with the important exception of the Civil War, to avoid persistent, rooted strife among various cultures despite our pluralistic social composition. The question invites student inquiry into processes of assimilation and their impact; into the attitude of dominant groups toward groups judged culturally distinctive (and inferior); into a comparison of differences in relationships to mainstream culture among significant subgroups such as African Americans and white "ethnics" (with African Americans at some points particularly well attuned to mainstream values—this theme has some subtle historical ramifications); and into institutions, like the schools, that performed culturally integrative tasks. This theme also runs through major stretches of American history up to the present day and has the capacity to generate but also to link a host of subtopics (some fairly familiar in survey course work, others less so), providing a genuine analytical challenge.

Courses in American history could be organized around other leading questions, and obviously other history courses as well as courses in literature and the media would require different kinds of analytical themes altogether. My point is to encourage the development of such themes, not to exhaust all the possibilities here. Humanities courses need central organizing questions—real questions that require grappling with analysis and argument, not just coverage stipulations. (Each of the questions above, for example, could be dealt with by using a number of different subject areas as examples; none prescribes a set survey.) The only further "rules" for the guiding questions are that they not become impossibly numerous, that they occupy large segments of a course and not simply a single week or two, that they touch on varied factual subject matter, and that they require thought.

Addressing fundamental analytical themes in a course does not preclude the preparation of more conventional lesson plans, but these themes should genuinely underlie the daily plans and should not be consumed in the latter's detail. Many teachers, when called upon to generate lesson plans related to general themes, either ignore the themes in practice or convert them into sets of facts to be memorized. The movement toward analytical substructures will require real conceptual retooling in many cases at both school and college survey levels.

The Analytical Categories

Developing underlying analytical schema for humanities courses, which could be embellished by relating the questions from one course to those of the next, offers one means of addressing the analytical goals that a humanities program should serve. The second approach, not contradictory, involves sketching at least a partial list of the kinds of more general analytical abilities such a program should progressively strive to teach.

1. *Ability to interpret and combine source materials.* This is the one analytical capacity humanities programs most commonly acknowledge already.[12] English students read entire works of literature, not simply textbook summaries, and some history courses require extensive work with documents. We could pay still more attention to this area, particularly in history segments that so often lean overmuch on textbooks, and preferably we should begin the process of learning to use primary data (and not simply summary) in argument much earlier in humanities education than is often now the case. In addition, the range of source materials could be improved. Too many history courses shy away from statistical materials, thus confirming student belief that mathematics can be left on the humanities' doorstep. A few courses work with material artifacts, but more attention could be paid to such sources. The ability to combine different kinds of sources (literary, artistic, and quantitative) needs specific nurturing. It is striking how many good college students do not know the difference between an original source and a secondary interpretation—even at this most basic level, there is work to be done. Properly carried out, the identification and interpretation of texts and other primary information and the ability to use them in analysis are capacities directly transferable to the arenas of work and citizenship after formal schooling has ended.

Extensive experience in handling various kinds of sources, learning how to make sense of them and to use them in larger arguments, and gaining some ability to recognize characteristic problems of bias and distortion (current cultural theory adds some important ingredients in this area) all constitute the kind of transferable skills that the humanities should be seeking to inculcate. A planned series of humanities courses can deliberately build on prior exercises in working with sources to develop more complex skills and a greater range of applicability for skills already acquired.

At the same time, it is important to keep the interest in working with sources in perspective. A number of high school teachers currently show commendable enthusiasm and imagination in introducing new sources to spice up and qualify the standard textbook history coverage. Some, however, seem to imagine that analytical training is incompatible with these exercises. In fact, the two are inseparable. Original sources give us insight into a culture at a single point in time; by themselves, they may actually discourage attention to change. A wider approach to analytical training is essential simply to enable students to handle sources properly. A recent study compared able Advanced Placement students with graduate students and professional historians in handling sources. The high school students often tested higher in identifying specific factual data. But their approach was largely regurgitative; they could accurately describe a source, but they shied away from asking the kinds of probing, interpretive questions—about anachronism or bias, for example—that trained historians, even those ignorant of the field involved, routinely asked. Of course, even an ambitious analytical agenda will not convert high school students into professionals. But the above study provides a salutary warning that a richer mix should be presented even when the sophisticated use of sources is a primary goal.[13]

2. *Ability to deal with diverse interpretations of issues concerning society and culture.* This capacity figured more prominently in humanities agendas in the past than it now does, though some revival is underway. The ability to manage interpretive dispute is fundamental to humanities analysis and obviously applies to ongoing consideration of social, political, and cultural trends. Beginning in the 1970s, students were widely held to have become less capable of dealing with interpretive diversity than their predecessors. They wanted a single truth—"What are we supposed to know about this?"—and no nonsense. A steady diet of textbook reading in which interpretation—much less dispute—rarely figured in contributed to this mindset. Some students frankly preferred the apparent certainties of science to the inherent debate essential in dealing with society and culture; their expressed preference does not mean, of course, that they should not have been pushed to learn (though not necessarily to privilege) the humanities mode. "Debate" books in college history courses, which had flourished in the 1950s as a

means of varying the textbook diet and exposing students directly to the problems of selecting and combining interpretations from a disputatious array, went out of print for want of teacher interest and student tolerance.

Renewed attention to interpretation is an essential ingredient in inculcating the humanities analytical style and preparing students for the kinds of signals they will receive from experts, frauds, and gurus throughout a lifelong effort to understand what is going on in society and culture. As one historian puts it, "Interpretation is the name of the game in the humanities. . . . Meanings are always contested, reworked, revoked, and redefined."[14] Handling interpretive differences is not a skill gained overnight. It must be balanced against a need to discourage total relativism. Specifically, it must be developed within a context in which students also are given the chance to learn that some interpretations, even if theoretically interesting, are demonstrably—and this means empirically—wrong.

At the same time, confrontation with some diversity in interpretation is a fundamental corollary of learning to handle theory in the humanities, to test its utilities and weaknesses. The confrontation can also provide some of the organizing issues necessary to inject an analytical framework into a larger segment of the curriculum. A teacher in a California community college regularly introduces his students to the ongoing debate between the consensus and radical approaches to American history.[15] The debate, the essentials of which are presented early in the course, raises issues of differential emphasis. It encourages the students to become engaged and to sort out their own frameworks for examining American society. And it gives them experience in evaluating not just specific interpretive disputes, but larger orientations—again, a habit of mind that can be transferred to other situations in which discussions of social and cultural issues force an assessment of divergent viewpoints.

3. *Ability to mount arguments directed at analytical questions in the humanities area.* This capacity responds to the overall goals of humanities education and relates closely to handling both source materials and interpretive diversity. It has received some encouragement from a growing interest in the schools, over the past decade, in critical thinking exercises. The ability too often remains truncated, however, either because no argument is required or because argument without supporting data is allowed. Too many school assignments require merely factual research. A classic case in point involves the frequent appearance, in history classes, of family histo-

ry projects. Students are requested to assemble information about their own families, and as a preliminary exercise this is fine. Rarely, however, do such assignments ask students to assemble the material into an analytical presentation or to relate their family pattern to existing generalizations about family behavior in the relevant time periods. The effort, in sum, fails to go beyond the recording of facts. Correspondingly, college students frequently mistake factual descriptions—data dumps—for argument (though very good ones rarely do), an error that reflects inadequate training. At the other extreme, students also may confuse enunciation of their views with argument, a confusion encouraged by school exercises that, to engage the students' interest, simply ask what their opinions are instead of demanding that those opinions be converted into arguments that use data and grapple with other analytical possibilities. "I think" substitutes for "Here's how I can defend what I think."

The analytical thrust of cultural studies in English (and in some instances, modern languages beyond the basic level) is directed particularly toward this attention to argument. The newer sort of literary analysis promotes the identification of argument in various media and encourages students not only to frame arguments of their own but also to recognize (but not necessarily to abandon) the cultural assumptions they employ in this process. Training in argument, in sum, lies close to the heart of new-style humanities goals.

The ability to argue also forms the crucial juncture between larger analytical goals, including the use of theory, and the necessary exposure to facts in the humanities. Argument requires the use of facts, not their passive retention. It forces students to sort through their data (whether memorized or researched) to answer questions, rather than presenting that data, undigested, in purely descriptive summaries. It serves as the means by which diverse interpretations can be probed, and the means as well by which source materials can be employed to deal with issues. It is the quintessential basic skill in the humanities and related social sciences, and it does not come easily.

4. *The capacity to test models applied to social and cultural phenomena.* This item essentially applies the need to grapple with theory to the arena of explicit analytical training. It is also closely related to the ability to handle analytical disputes. Students need deliberate practice in encountering formulas that purport to apply to broad areas of human behavior—like the idea that democracies do not declare war on other democracies—and then figuring out how

to evaluate and test those propositions. Such exercises not only require analytical strengths, but also the ability to amass relevant data to deal with a problem rather than simply a factual assignment.

5. *Ability to assess causation and the impact of historical change.* One of the most important analytical assignments in historical training must be the identification of points of significant change and the demonstration of some ability to distinguish between minor oscillations and more fundamental shifts. The categorization of change into roughly coherent segments is what distinguishes an analytical approach to the factor of time—what historians call *periodization*—from the memorized dates of a mindless chronology. This assignment applies both to behaviors and institutions within a society and to whole societies. We live in a culture that glorifies change and often exaggerates its nature; we constantly encounter—or are told we're encountering, by means of advertising or in less explicitly commercial evaluations—revolutionary new developments. Using the laboratory of history to practice assessing the magnitude of change provides vital experience not only in dealing with periodization in the past—for time periods essentially are demarcated by points of significant change at either end—but also in interpreting ongoing social and cultural developments.

Increasingly, critical work in literature also assesses change, because it relates literary products to readers as well as authors and both to social context. Dealing with change, including its literary representations and facets, has provided a growing link among humanities scholars in different disciplines, and it can relate discrete humanities courses as well. It challenges and focuses the ability to use sources as more than static windows on a single point in time, and it requires tests of interpretation and often of theoretical models.

Once students have acquired the ability to identify and categorize change, the next analytical step is to erect a range of probable causation for change—and, in turn, to evaluate the impact of that change. Causation in the humanities differs in crucial ways from causation in the sciences, and students should be acquainted with the differences in analysis. Causation in science involves laboratory testing to determine which variables predictably produce which results. Causation for changes in cultural styles and outlooks or for shifts in social structure cannot be proved in this fashion; but the causes can be probed.

One of the kinds of interpretation that students should be called upon to evaluate results from the common penchant for monocausation or determinism. Our culture, for example, frequently thinks in terms of technological determinism; the future is characteristically described in terms of new technologies, on the assumption that these will shape other aspects of life. There are also important examples of technological determinism applied to the past that allow students to use history to test this kind of analysis. Conventional historical surveys, by contrast, imply a political determinism: what really counts is how the state is organized. Few Americans really think this way, but political determinism involves assumptions about causation that are usefully considered in regard to the present as well as the past. Tests of determinism must be juxtaposed with hands-on experience in sorting out multiple causation, determining combinations of significant factors without, on the one hand, tossing in every imaginable development or, on the other hand, claiming final certainties. Causation exercises, like the management of conflicting interpretations, must remind students of the open-ended qualities of humanistic inquiries. Nevertheless, there are specific, teachable skills involved. Students should be able to identify and assess the causation arguments of others in a series of graduated exercises, and they should develop the ability to mount their own arguments about primary causation factors and their combinations.

6. *Capacity to assess the impact of cultural factors in shaping human institutions and behaviors.* This item is really a subset of the more general assessment of causation, but its central role in the humanities and in linking various humanities disciplines makes it deserving of special attention. Most humanistic disciplines depend to some degree on arguments that human beliefs, representations, and deeply held assumptions cause and shape a good bit of "objective" social reality. Culture, in other words, influences the makeup of societies even outside strictly cultural areas. Cultural construction accounts, or helps to account, for gender characteristics, emotional behavior, political priorities, even foreign policy orientations, and for changes in these areas. It is also central to "multicultural" settings in which diverse cultures jockey for position, as in the United States today but also as in earlier periods—useful for comparison—both in this country and elsewhere.

Analysis in the humanities does not depend on cultural determinism, though this is one of the common statements of causation that deserves evaluation in specific contexts. Cultural changes, and the initial establishment of cultures, may as easily depend on economic relationships or even geography. An overall ability to discuss causation will involve weighing culture against such other ingredients. The common interest of cultural anthropologists, social historians, and the new literary scholars in the importance of cultural constructions nevertheless legitimates recurrent attention to the widely held assumptions that show up in phenomena ranging from underlying values in literature and other media (American advertising, for example has been profitably studied from precisely this vantage point)[16] to the ways that wives judge their husbands and even to the family decisions that affect changes in birth rates.

A complete assessment of cultural constructions also entails the ability to deal with cultural relationships between dominant and subordinate groups—to grapple with different historical periods and different kinds of societies in terms of this inevitable complication in cultural analysis. Established cases can permit us to explore wide cultural gaps between the elites and the masses and to assess the changing, and usually mutual, nature of cultural assimilation. Familiarity with past cases, furthermore, can form the basis for some evaluation of cultural relationships, the framework for cultural constructions, in our own society. The subject is still the impact of culture, but that subject can now be understood in terms of realistic complexity, not as the simple triumph of a single set of values. Exposure to this kind of interpretation—one that recognizes the tensions within culture itself and the determining power of the culture—and the ability to argue on its terms is one of the most distinctive humanistic contributions to explanations of social patterns and social change.

7. *Ability to compare societies and cultures in order to enhance understanding.* Any treatment of a society or a literary tradition invites implicit comparisons by encouraging some sense of distinctiveness. Properly developed, explicit comparison enables analysts in the humanities to organize and make sense of varied data that may otherwise lack full meaning. Certainly this is true in teaching. Students who are taught about beliefs in American institutions and values also need experience in comparing those beliefs with ones in some other societies. Students exposed to other societies or to past periods in our own societies will, if they think at all, inevitably compare what they learn: Is this feature better in Japan? How much did we gain when a traditional aspect of American society like community solidarity and intrusiveness shifted toward greater individualism and privacy juxtaposed with bureaucratic controls? How dif-

ferent from our experience is that of the Chinese? How remote are we from the characteristics of a period two hundred years in the past?

Comparison is a basic analytical impulse, but it is too rarely cultivated in courses that present cultures or time periods as discrete segments without confronting probable similarities and differences and the reasons for them. In addition to allowing analytical linkage between different societies and different time periods, comparison may facilitate the selection of cases to be examined. In world history, for example, the impulse to consider every major civilization in an attempt at complete coverage may be tempered by the need to select types of societies that are particularly useful for comparative purposes. Comparison pulls together many of the other desired analytical skills. It obviously calls for an ability to handle diverse interpretations, for serious comparison establishes issues to be considered, not universal agreements. It requires consideration of causation—differences and similarities must be attributed and the role of cultural constructs assessed. It compels argument, because students are urged not merely to lay two cases side by side but to actively compare them. Above all, comparison forces students to remove themselves from their own analytical frameworks, to think about assumptions and behaviors different from their own and, in the process, to gain perspective.

One scholar has argued, quite simply, that the purpose of the humanities is to teach "otherness."[17] I find that formulation only partially correct. Comparison exposes us to otherness; it also encourages analyses of why different patterns develop and what functions they serve; and it helps students to see the "other" in relation to their own institutions and values, illuminating both in the process. In these respects, comparative analysis, which ultimately embraces the fundamental patterns in contemporary society, vividly fulfills the basic purposes of the analytical approach to the humanities.

Seven analytical categories—some of which are already being addressed, at least to an extent, and many of which overlap—do not constitute an impossibly ambitious agenda. All can be introduced in secondary school courses. Each permits sequential development. Source materials, initially approached singly, can with experience be combined and diversified. Conflicts of interpretation can move from sharp polarities to more subtle gradations. Assessment of cultural constructions can focus initially on generalized categories such as gender and move later (particularly at the college level) to the complexities of diverse interactions with mainstream values.

The reorientation of humanities courses to incorporate these analytical categories, thereby overriding the more common coverage definitions, is an ambitious yet an essential task. It requires teachers to challenge themselves and to engage students in active rather than passive learning. It assumes the need for renewed experiments in selecting basic exercises and determining suitable case studies—and some of the experiments will doubtless fall short of full success. Recasting the teaching of humanities toward analysis assumes a certain level of student ability, rejecting the often self-fulfilling negativism generated by needlessly low expectations. It works to infuse the classroom with some of the excitement that now informs current research and analysis in humanistic scholarship, not by converting students into specialists but by admitting them to the kind of thinking that has advanced our understanding of how societies operate. It displays a confidence in the relevance and stimulation of humanistic endeavor, thus transforming humanities curricula from guardians of national treasures into active participants in the quest to understand.

Issues of Assessment

The conversion to a more analytical agenda requires attention to the kinds of testing employed in humanities courses. This requirement is particularly relevant to current discussions about defining national standards, but it applies to the recurrent exercises in individual classrooms as well. Many standard testing devices can and should be reconsidered.

The analytical goals themselves define the principal criteria for assessment. Students should be given examinations and essay assignments that will demonstrate and develop their ability to argue or to test an analytical model. College freshmen in a world history course can probe the strengths and weaknesses of the world economy theory, for example, by comparing two societies in the seventeenth and eighteenth centuries—the task is not at all beyond them. High school students, to expand their capacity to deal with source materials, need exercises that help them move from simple description to more subtle interpretation and active use of resources.

Specific strategies are necessary to focus on the analytical task, for injunctions to evaluate in a more analytic way are not mere abstractions. Comparative and theory-testing exercises can be made more manageable by distributing in advance a finite list of comparative questions from which the essay segments of an examination will be drawn. This will challenge the more conscientious students to sketch out arguments and amass data on more issues than can be covered in a single examination, but it will also provide a framework for students, conscientious or not, who are just moving into comparative or theoretical analysis.

Other exercises can help students move from one skill level to another. A Philadelphia teacher guides her students toward increasingly sophisticated interpretations of material artifacts from West Africa. Initial tests simply establish basic abilities in relation to what is known about a single period in West African history. But subsequent tests probe transferability: Presented with artifacts from a later period in West Africa, can the students ask intelligent questions about them? And can they combine what they know of the earlier period with an anticipation of change by asking what seems to be different in the subsequent century? The goal is not to elicit "right" answers, for the students have not yet acquired data about the later time, but to encourage imaginative yet solidly based hypotheses, which will then be probed as part of the focus of the next chronological unit. Students are given the opportunity to show not only that they know examples and methods from the classroom exercises, but that they can extend both into valid hypotheses about new information; this in turn lays the groundwork for exploring a second time period in class.

Abilities to analyze causation can also be assessed without jumping immediately into risky, open-ended exercises. Students might work through a particular causation exercise in class—either a staple like the causes of World War I or a more novel challenge such as the reasons for the decline in the British birth rate during the late nineteenth century. Once they had covered the subject, they might then be presented, in an essay assignment, with another situation including some necessary data—for example, causes of World War II or the reasons for the decline in the Japanese birth rate in the 1950s. The task would be to deal with the causation of this unfamiliar phenomenon in light of the materials presented, while also demonstrating the ability to apply what was learned about causation in the earlier classroom exercise. The assignment would test the knowledge acquired in the previous exercise, but also the capacity to apply larger skills to new data. The second causation problem should be discussed briefly after the essay or test is completed, in order to round out the analysis.

Innovation in assessment strategies is crucial for tests that measure factual knowledge of the more conventional sort, where the risks of mindless memorization (or failure to submit to mindlessness) are particularly great. Some teachers now experiment with a dual scoring method—one for students who accurately present data, the other for students who demonstrate analytical imagination, with the highest scores going to the group that manages both. The idea has merit in that it moves away from the prosaic fact tests without abandoning the need to encourage usable knowledge. The goal is, increasingly, to figure out how to determine what students can "do" in the humanities, not just what they have memorized.

The obvious point is that testing should link essential factual knowledge to the broader analytical goals. A personal example may help. When I began teaching a large freshman world history course, the need for occasional homework checks seemed apparent, which in turn meant periodic quizzes. Some teachers on the staff quickly adopted multiple-choice schemes, which could be both speedy and comprehensive but which also had a punitive cast. The implication was, let's see what level of detail produces general demonstrations of ignorance. The message being sent to students was obvious: This is a memorization course, whether or not you choose to cooperate. In fact, memorization was not the course's main purpose, and with a modest amount of thought we found that the goals of establishing some essential factual competence without being distractingly punitive could be met. Most of the staff now use short-answer questions that compare two institutions or two ideas, either from two different societies or from two different time periods. The result establishes a student's ability (or inability) to define two significant items —and emphasis must be placed on significance—while also, in a sentence or two, showing some preliminary ability to use these definitions to answer a more important question.

Other approaches to fact-testing may work equally well. Providing a factual checklist—what one high school teacher calls "scaffolding"—will, as noted above, be appropriate at points in working toward essay examinations. Such a list may even facilitate factual retention, because it identifies the main memorization tasks without diluting attention through a bewildering maze of detail and because it encourages the active use of data. Intelligent tests should teach as well as assess. Where factual knowledge is to be elicited directly, the goals should be appropriately focused; for example, factual questions should emphasize essentials rather than confusing the trivial details (such as precise dates instead of approximately accurate points in time) with what really should be retained. A question about the results of medieval European contact with the Arab world thus could include a reminder about the dates of the first Crusades. A question about the impact of the Enlightenment on Western culture could remind students of the approximate dates involved; they will know no less about the phenomenon for being saved from some disconcerting chronological groping.

Teachers will continue to be concerned about factual knowledge, but they can move toward new ways of manifesting this concern in tests by preferring larger analytical contexts over deadening, rote identifications. Student laziness is not encouraged by probing memory through its application to meaning. Certainly no assessment scheme should be based primarily on fact testing. Even grade school is not too early a point at which to introduce students into the essential habits of using data rather than simply parroting it, in reading courses and social studies ventures alike. The ultimate goal is not a fact-free environment but one in which facts have functions.

The most important advance will reflect no single testing strategy, but rather fuller teacher conversion to the new internal guidelines. When teachers can demonstrate that their tests and essays achieve one or more of the basic analytical goals, probing facts only as required to reach these goals, they can be assured that they are moving in the right direction. They can even share their goals with their students once "because it's there" disappears as an implicit rationale for a factual exercise.

Tests drive curricula. The reconsideration of many hoary examination strategies is a fundamental part of the conversion to new teaching methods in the humanities. Admittedly, this is both obvious and challenging. The good news is that practical strategies are available. The plea for wider change builds on existing efforts as imaginative teachers in the humanities reconsider what they really want their students to be able to do.

The Issue of Coherence

Redefinitions of humanities programs through openness to new topics and new topical combinations, attention to theory, and commitment to definable analytical goals, all tied to appropriate assessment strategies, complete the outline of the basic educational task. One other issue, a vexing one, requires attention in our rethinking of basic curricular organization: How coherent should the various humanities components be?

Humanities programs are hardly models of coherence at present, though they sometimes seem closely structured because of their sheer familiarity. American history courses rarely connect with earlier world history segments, on the twin assumptions that students will not remember what they learned last year (a fatal and unnecessary concession, by the way) and that the United States stands alone in any event. They often fail to acknowledge students' concomitant work in American literature. Boards of education spell out K-through-12 programs mainly in terms of different levels of coverage, but this hardly assures much real coherence and often builds in some boring repetition. New curricula like that of California, which deliberately links several different grade levels in world history by avoiding repetition but encouraging recapitulation, point to more imaginative connections, but the results are not yet in.

Yet some of the goals of the new, analytical approach to the humanities may seem to disrupt a seamless web of the sort the canonists like to spin; they may seem to endanger an implicit coherence based on agreements about what facets of society and culture are really worth our attention. The new approach urges the study of historical and literary cases, designed to serve analytical development, over pure surveys. It talks of cultural complexity, rather than tidily uniform portraits. It courts conflicting interpretations, eschewing textbook monochrome. With this approach, will students gain any connected picture of cultural studies? Should we be concerned if they do not? Some new humanist scholars recommend that we simply not worry about incoherence. Literary experts who espouse deconstructionist or post-structuralist theory stress the radical incoherence and fragmentation in contemporary culture and knowledge; by extension, coherence in school programs, at least on the humanities side, could be positively misleading. Some of this thinking has also crept into discussions of history in the form of new emphasis on the impossibility of capturing objective reality and a frank proclamation of the value of subjective statements. Some new-style humanists argue that the only values we ought to try to pass on are those found in the conflict of values.[18]

These are important issues. They should be presented openly in college-level humanities work, as elements of the theoretical debates in which students themselves should be engaged. But they should not, in my judgment, be pressed so far that delight in whimsy comes to dominate the humanities curricula. Granted, humanities programs will always lack the tidy sequences of mathematics that build so neatly from one skill to the next; nevertheless, they can and should be based on some sense of overall structure. Indeed, the analytically grounded approach to the humanities permits new attention to interrelationships that should take us beyond the routine "if it's junior year, it must be American history" thinking that currently passes for planning.

Some sense of coherence is essential for frankly tactical reasons. The need for change is so great that we risk being overloaded by random additions that will jeopardize the more manageable reforms. We are unlikely, for example, ever to do away entirely with an American history segment, no matter how innovative the overall approach. We will need, then, some basis for conceiving the American survey in coherent fashion and for relating it, again coherently, to other segments.

Incoherence, however charming to current radical chic, does not work for students. Some of the structures offered to them will frankly seem more certain, more objectively real, than they are. Most historical periods, for example, are in some measure heuristic; they can always be debated. Did the nineteenth-century Industrial Revolution introduce a fundamental transformation in West European history, or was it really a further statement of changes that had been brewing for at least two previous centuries? Good cases can be made for both arguments. By the college level, students should be able to handle some debates about periodization as part of their training in diverse interpretations and the ability to test models; this capacity will be essential to their evaluation of their own society in terms of its relationship to the immediate past. But at the high school level, such uncertainty risks making the whole enterprise too unmanageable for most students. We must therefore decide how the Industrial Revolution is to be presented, with some allowance for debate where possible.

In my judgment, society and culture are not in fact entirely incoherent, which means that it is neither mendacious nor pandering to portray some basic structures. Middle Eastern culture is, and has been for centuries, generally shaped through the values of Islam. One hastens to add that Islam itself is diverse, that different groups receive even a single version diversely, and that there are important minority religions and, by the twentieth century, secular values systems operating in the region as well. Nevertheless, Islam is a fact, and in approaching the Middle East it provides an obvious beginning point for analysis. If students come away from some coursework on the Middle East with a slightly exaggerated sense of Islam's coherence (and it should not be too exaggerated—even basic presentations must quickly note some ongoing examples of internal diversities), they will nevertheless have a more valid understanding than if the Middle East had not been presented as a cultural entity at all, or had been offered up only in random slices.

Coherence is not, of course, a constant, which is one point that students should learn as part of their basic analytical framework. Some societies cohere more closely than others; the differences suggest a valid and useful comparative issue. In some periods, earlier coherences will diminish because of new cultural disputes between elites and masses, for example; it has been argued that this happened in Western Europe in the seventeenth century, and some exciting conceptual debates have resulted. It may be true in our own day.

On the whole, however, at least two kinds of coherence do apply to most societies in most periods of time, and these can be used without falsification as the bases for some programmatic structure in the humanities. What is called for is intelligent synthesis of the sort currently developing in the maturing field of social history. Synthesis also conveniently cuts through some of the otherwise divisive and sterile debate between proponents of education as an introduction to group identity and their stick-to-the-mainstream opponents.

Coherence number one: Most societies, save in rare periods of great turmoil, have a reasonably identifiable power structure. This encompasses not only political power, but also the power manifested through economic, social, and cultural hierarchies. Power wielders do not operate alone; they must be analyzed in relation to other segments of society. It is not even valid to see basic social change as emanating from the power structure, with other social segments simply reacting to impulses from above, for social historians have demonstrated that change is almost always interactive to some degree—even in slaveholding societies.[19] Power, in other words, is complex, and its complexity drives some of the analytical questions that should be framed for specific courses—for example, the basic analytical themes suggested above for American history, which translated power issues into some specific themes that permeated much of the nineteenth and twentieth centuries.

Coherence number two: Societies in most periods have some common culture—through shared religions, for example, or (as in traditional China) shared values that underlie diverse religions, or through such shared secular values as belief in science or nationalism. This common culture can and should be traced. It is not just an elite product. As with power, we know from the new cultural and social history that cultures result from interactions between elites and others; they are never purely imposed. Common culture is not the whole culture, and subcultures that depart from or modify the common culture must also be traced. Common culture, finally, is not monolithic; what a given religion means to rural folk may differ considerably from what it means to their urban counterparts. All of these complexities warrant attention, but they should not preclude the fact that some shared ingredients do exist—usually, of course, in relation to power structures. Ignoring common culture and power hierarchies would misrepresent social reality to precisely those groups who must learn what their society consists of if they are to have any chance of winning change. Merely celebrating diverse strands of culture would mislead students as well as generating educational unmanageability.[20]

Beyond these themes, though, coherence in humanities education rests on twin bases. The first obviously grows out of the need to teach students how some societies work as combinations of coherent cultures and power structures in interaction with diverse interests and beliefs. This first charge is not the same as a validation of routine survey methods that merely narrate political developments. It focuses on interaction and raises questions about how mainstream institutions and ideas operate amid diversity and conflict, and about how these same institutions and ideas affect some (but not necessarily all—time limitations will preclude a full canvas, which is, in any event, not analytically necessary) diverse/subordinate groups. The principal idea is to introduce analytical questions and to develop capacities that will allow students to sort out the relationships between core institutions and values and groups that operate at some distance. Students should be able to apply this analytical framework to groups not specifically covered in their humanities course; indeed, some of the omissions might suggest a project in a senior high school course that would invite students to research one of their own identity groups in relation to power structures and common culture, past and present. Questions about coherence (instead of a blithe neglect of coherence) can form a common element in the analytical agendas of courses in literature as well as history, and in course segments that deal with the American experience but also the experiences of other societies.

The second basis for coherence in humanities education comes from the major analytical goals themselves, somewhat independent of specific subject matter. Some goals must be explored before others. The ability to test models, for example, depends on prior exercises in researching and interpreting source materials, handling diverse explanations, and developing arguments. Experience with models, in turn, is necessary for certain kinds of discussions of causation and comparison. Establishing an analytical sequence is a vital way of relating one humanities course to the next and exploring linkages among different disciplines within the humanities.

Ultimately, both bases for coherence require that we shape humanities courses around the central problem of exploring what makes societies tick. Questions about power and shared culture constitute recurrent and fundamental themes in this exploration, to be asked in a variety of contexts and using a variety of examples. Analytical goals, though somewhat hierarchical, are driven by the need to give students experience in dealing with the kinds of questions that will help them determine what a cultural representation means, in terms of its social bases and effects, or how a change in political alignments or social structure is to be understood. Teachers need to review and re-review their curricula and their testing strategies with an eye toward these fundamental goals. They should ask themselves—and be prepared to tell their students—how any course segment relates to these goals. "So what?" is a legitimate watch cry. It *can* be answered, precisely because the humanities provide vital conceptual insights into the interpretation of society, but the answers do not cover some of the items that pass for humanistic learning in survey courses today. It *should* be answered as part of the task of focusing and maintaining analytical humanities curricula, and as a way of drawing students into their own engagement with active intellectual exercise.

The idea of organizing humanities programs on the basis of underlying questions and of coordinating them in terms of analytical exposure deliberately counters the common impulse to rely on subject-matter coverage. History surveys may continue to exist in such a recast program, but only if transformed, with memorization peeled back in favor of dealing with interpretive questions. English courses will doubtless still teach Shakespeare along with other literary and media forms, but in a reoriented context. Instead of informing students that Shakespeare provided a beautiful representation of the world (a conclusion they may or may not reach on their own after reading Shakespeare, just as is now the case), courses will examine the nature of beauty and representation and will ask, in relation to Western cultural history, why and to what effect various groups have claimed Shakespeare as an aesthetic standard setter. The level of questioning will change from summary and aesthetic obiter dicta to interpretation. The linkage between past and present, between older and current media, will change too as students study examples and learn methods that apply to their management of information about their own society and culture.

The world we now live in is radically different from the one most teachers of the humanities inhabited as they (we) obtained their early education. Changes in the political climate and the ethnic composition of American classrooms are partly responsible for this transformation. Growing racial diversity has surpassed the educational impact of early twentieth-century immigration, while shifts in the political climate, even amid a period of national conservatism, have probably rendered impossible the outright educational discrimination that constituted the 1920s response. Our more intense engagement with the wider world is another innovation with clear educational impact. The most important shift, however, as far as humanities education is concerned, is in the humanities themselves, where the fundamental contours of scholarship have changed for a variety of reasons. Answering questions, not a bare-bones effort to describe names, dates, and stories or to summarize what a given book says, has become the point of the endeavor. Leopold von Ranke's "how it actually happened" has been outranked, or at least his definition has been reoriented toward the analytical.[21] "What is the meaning of what happened?" is now the operative issue.

Conceptualization takes its place alongside the uncovering of facts, and without it, mere factual recording has no meaning. This is the transformation that must be written into the classroom in order to produce students who are better able to analyze and to argue, students who not only have beliefs (in fact, they have plenty) but also are argumentatively aware of their beliefs, and students more capable of applying humanistic analysis to new settings, including their own ongoing interactions with society and culture. As with most features of education, conceptual ability in the humanities comes easiest to the very bright. But it can be taught far more widely and will ultimately nourish itself as students discover not only new subject matter with which they can identify, but reasons to use humanities materials to answer challenging questions.

SEVEN

Rethinking

Actual Curricula:

The Conversion

to Analysis

The goals of humanities teaching require a radical rethinking of many existing offerings at both high school and college levels. Survey courses must in many cases be overhauled: traditional coverage must be cut back to make room for new topics and appropriate theory; standard textbook fare must be modified with different kinds of materials and case studies; and a variety of analytical exercises must accompany the presentation of topics. Mere tinkering will not suffice. We also need some outright experimentation with types of courses that do not currently exist. Precisely because the humanities have a hallowed quality that encourages limited response to new needs, it is time to combine substantial revisions of humanities staples with some new departures. This chapter suggests logical and feasible innovations that would translate humanities goals into curricular action. It does not advocate a total restructuring or a single curriculum pattern. Survey elements, reconfigured in terms of essential goals and brought into dynamic relationship with other kinds of courses or segments, will still be appropriate. But we must force ourselves to gain some new ground. The results we should expect from humanities teaching may accrue from a real commitment to recasting the content of the courses now commonly taught, including the assessment strategies attached. Yet the prospects are surer if we incorporate additional segments as well. Humanities teachers and planners should give themselves room to dare.

A community college teacher in Ohio begins her U.S. history survey course with an exercise that evolved from inevitable student queries about how many names and dates they would have to learn. Her purpose in teaching is to educe meaning, not memorization, but she confronts a cohort stubbornly convinced that American history consists of regurgitating the names and terms of office of the presidents. Mere explanation that this will not be the emphasis, either topically or in terms of learning style, falls on deaf ears. Hence the current exercise, in which students are provided with a single-page photo of all the presidents and are then asked, after considering this evidence carefully, to write down five to ten things about the history of the country at the base of the photo. This instructor's purpose is teach her students that history does not rely on memorization, but rather involves the ability to select information from the available evidence, organize it, and draw meaningful conclusions from it. The goal is to analyze information in the context of historical evidence and issues—to "think historically" about changes and continuities over time.[1]

Translating the real educational goals of the humanities into courses and programs is no easy task. It requires imagination as well as daring. From teachers accustomed to more conventional ways of doing things, it demands almost a conversion experience in which fundamental purposes are reconsidered and established routines— whether they are simply familiar time fillers or cherished narratives —are reviewed, reconfigured, and not infrequently jettisoned outright. Students, by and large, will need less converting if they are introduced to analytical programs early enough, although, as the Ohio example suggests, by the time they escape from high school in its current form, they too will have developed rooted stereotypes about history and literature that must be grappled with. Conversion then becomes an issue with them, too.

I was trained as a European historian, moved to become a college history major by the content of a persuasively taught Western civilization course and later assigned, as a fledgling instructor, to a Western civilization core course that in most regards worked pretty well. Numerous issues in conventional Western civ courses still engage me and, if the newer social history content is added in, positively enthrall me. Once I was persuaded, however, that the need to convey some understanding of international context—some genuine world history, in short—had come to outrank Western civ as an educational priority in required history programs, I had to do two things. The first, obviously, was to learn enough world history to make my new commitment manageable for myself and my students, a task that involved not only tackling new factual data but exploring what turned out to be exciting new analytical constructs. The second task, almost as hard, was to abandon some of the issues and details of Western history most dear to me and to streamline other aspects of Western coverage into a more efficient and more comparatively relevant educational package. In other words, I needed to convert, not in the sense (visible among some world historians) of wanting to use world history to downgrade the Western experience, but in the sense of almost entirely recasting my own training and earlier ventures in survey course teaching. Compromise and patchwork would not suffice. Nor would a simple translation of Western history approaches to the world arena. A Western civ course can afford to linger over individual nations and particular monarchical reigns, though it need not do so. A world history course that tries to take this approach to a global level becomes hopelessly enmeshed in detail—one reason for the mammoth texts that appear when presentation patterns are extended without adequate review.

At all teaching levels, there is a great need for renewed imagination, guided by a sense of the basic analytical goals to be achieved in the humanities and by an awareness of the new resources, both factual and theoretical, available through recent humanities research. Imagination can lead to a shake-up exercise at the beginning of a particular course, as in the Ohio community college. It can invigorate topic selection and certainly the kinds of exercises used as the basis for grades and evaluations. It will show up in the teacher's own commitment to grappling with issues.

Imagination and *pedagogical conversion* are words that flow easily enough from the pen (or, in this case, drop readily enough from the "mouse"). General guidelines in the previous chapter offered some specifics on how to reorient planning. Nevertheless, some further suggestions about linking goals with actual curricula are necessary to avoid undue abstraction and, above all, to further the process of revivifying the actual classroom experience of the humanities. I do not pretend to spell out all possible curricular manifestations; again, I will use some examples rather than offering comprehensive formulas, while insisting as well that a wide variety of detailed translations can meet the necessary basic guidelines. Several specifics have already been suggested, as in my discussion of assessment strategies. This chapter, adding some other illustrations for existing or potential classroom experiences, focuses primarily on the major curricular segments derived from the more general goals. What might be a feasible set of courses that, in combination with some more familiar segments, would translate humanities analysis into regular classroom routines at both high school and college levels?

Most of the initiatives and readjustments so far suggested as ways of moving innovation further into the curriculum have involved cutting into existing survey approaches and conventional coverage; at the same time, some items have been selected deliberately for a case study approach designed to probe certain types of cultural and historical issues and advance fundamental analytical capacities without overloading the boat. These points have already been raised in principle, in relationship to basic goals. They operationalize the injunction, which I borrow from a world-historian colleague, of daring to omit. They raise specific questions about survey segments and criteria for inclusion and omission, however, that must be addressed after the more positive changes are sketched in.

The Humanities Workshop

One of the most exciting ways of cutting into the survey routine and directly addressing analytical training at the high school level involves the introduction of humanities workshops as regular, evaluated features of the student experience. History courses, for example, could offer three or four workshop sessions over each two-week cycle; the subjects would be related to regular classroom coverage but the tenor and products would be conceived quite differently. Humanities workshops would differ greatly from their laboratory counterparts in science, but they would have the same basic purpose of introducing students to fundamental methods, data management, and generalization in the relevant disciplines.

Humanities workshops would focus specifically on the principal analytical skills that structure the new curricula—skills subsequently to be brought into regular classroom use. During the freshman and sophomore years of high school, they would begin to engage students in dealing coherently with primary evidence of various sorts, from documents to statistics, and around various problems and periods. Exercises would start simply by building arguments from one or two sources, then move to more diverse source collections and ask that a documentary argument be focused on a preset analytical question. (This last is an exercise introduced in the College Board Advanced Placement program under the heading "document-based question.") The workshops could then move, in conjunction with regular classroom activities, to confront diverse interpretations and the structure of argument. By junior year (particularly if the regular class sessions focus on American history), some specific comparative problem sets might be introduced to wean students away from oversimple assumptions about single cultures. Some exercises in causation assessment would also be relevant at this point. Essays and oral reports would be the normal products of each major workshop segment throughout the high school sequence.

Humanities workshops would directly translate graded analytical goals into student experience, providing clear alternatives to maximization of coverage. They would require access to some types of resource materials not currently readily available at the high school level. Document collections and other data sources, examples of interpretive diversity, and comparative models, followed by materials facilitating student-generated comparisons, would be essential ingredients of the workshop manuals. Many of these materials could be assembled without too much trouble, demanding only some experimentation with student reaction and determination of appropriate (though never unambitious) levels of difficulty. Other case study segments would require more thought and might even call for additional scholarly synthesis. Appropriate comparative models, for example, are far rarer than we might wish. In social history, comparative analysis of slavery has so far demonstrated the greatest sophistication, joined more recently by related comparisons of slave and serf emancipation. The sturdy comparative perennial designed to explain why the United States, by comparison with Europe, produced so little socialism is another existing case study candidate, and comparative religious analysis also has a respectable pedigree.[2] A surprising number of topics lack more than a casual comparative structure, however; this is an area in which scholarship and teaching needs might coalesce, despite the separate presentation requirements of each.[3]

Materials are also needed that focus student attention on issues of change and causation, wherein case studies can explore established patterns and then move toward more open-ended inquiry. Workshop segments designed to help students understand how arguments are structured, as the basis for assessing interpretation and identifying the ingredients of their own argument, call for some innovative planning as part of a broadly construed English program or a course in philosophy.[4] The revival of rhetoric programs in several collegiate English departments promotes more formal student work on argument and interpretation, starting with summaries of arguments and moving toward a more formal ability to recognize the ways in which authors argue issues. Through such exercises, students can come to see their own writing as dependent both on intelligent critical reading and on the need to produce good argumentation.

A sequence of workshops, seriously introduced as part of a high school humanities program, would challenge teachers at various levels to participate in the design of manageable goals, encourage training in how to conduct the classes, and demand the production of appropriate materials linked in some cases to genuinely imaginative, integrative scholarship that has been boiled down, but not dessicated, for high school use. College programs might also introduce the workshop mode, at least as a temporary measure until adequate high school preparation preempts the need; college use of this approach could help generate both useful teacher training and some of the new materials necessary for analytical exercises. Ultimately, of course, college-level humanities courses should build such exercises directly into regular coursework, reducing the need for separate hands-on sessions aside from the methods courses designed for humanities majors. At any level, a laboratory or workshop program requires serious commitment from the teaching staff. It may also encourage student teamwork to produce collaborative results and to assist in mutual evaluation. Assessment of the major workshop exercises must form a noticeable and regular component of overall grading. In return, a workshop program provides an exciting mechanism with which to engage students in active learning and to build their experience in identifying and resolving some of the issues raised by humanistic approaches to the understanding of society and culture.

The Contemporary Problems Course

The second major innovation desirable in high school humanities programs is the creation of a senior-year set of contemporary issues courses. In the area of history or social studies, this would be a course on recent history and contemporary social and political problems in lieu of the current ill-defined and often redundant civics offering. In literature, it would be a course, ideally one deliberately related to the history offering, on current cultural trends, including modern media.

These courses would be the capstones of the humanities sequence in the schools. They would inevitably include some factual acquisition, simply to make sure, for example, that students would have some outline knowledge of major historical developments since 1945 (not only political developments but also demographic, economic, and cultural trends; here it is especially important to avoid overreliance on conventional topics). No more should history courses run out of gas by the mid-twentieth century, leaving the ensuing period, in some ways the least accessible to students (falling as it does between the periods covered by conventional history courses and their own memories), in empirical limbo. Factual coverage should however be kept manageable, which means confining the survey approach to real highlights; students do not need a passing acquaintance with each forgettable president of the 1960s and 1970s, however dear or vivid their memories to us older folks.

Contemporary issues courses must also meet three other related criteria designed to differentiate them clearly from mere current events exercises. They must blend disciplinary approaches without necessarily drilling into students exactly where sociology ends and political science begins. They must continue the workshop approach, applying data management, interpretation and argument skills, comparison, and causation analysis to contemporary themes and materials. Some exercises will be made more complicated, compared with previous work, by the heat of partisanship, and unquestionably some tactful management will be required; but experience in handling partisan arguments is a desirable extension of the ability to manage interpretive dispute and to identify the structure of arguments, and it should be courted, not avoided.

Finally, the contemporary issues courses must deliberately cross-reference previous coursework in the humanities. One of the basic points of these courses is to promote active understanding of how the exploration of contemporary issues is linked not only with previously acquired analytical habits but also with knowledge gained in earlier surveys and case studies. Analogies can explicitly be drawn: Does a past period that one studied as a junior or sophomore shed light on an apparently novel contemporary situation? Theoretical constructs come into play as students who have learned to apply some critical theory to literature must now turn to an assessment of more recent cultural products. The ability to conceptualize both historical change and continuity plays a vital role: What late twentieth-century trends are really new, and what causes plausibly explain their novelty? As a cultural context, how greatly and in what significant ways does a diet of television and music video—the primary cultural artifacts that students should be able to analyze in their own lives—differ from the reading and listening diet of pretelevision generations?

Analysis must not be sacrificed in these contemporary issues courses, but rather it must be explicitly utilized and applied. The twin purposes of the courses are to gain analytical knowledge about recent developments and to evaluate this knowledge in genuine historical and cultural perspective. Some new skills come into play, to be sure. The contemporary issues courses do not just provide new doses of partisanship. They should also encourage exercises specifically designed to teach students how to find the data necessary to construct or test an argument rather than relying primarily on prepackaged case study material.

Just as the humanities workshops answer a need to train students more explicitly in analytical techniques, so the contemporary issues courses translate the imperative to link humanistic training to social and cultural analyses in current context. Both of these goals are novel ones in the high school curriculum, at least when they are formally introduced as serious endeavors rather than as occasional diversions from the survey formula. Both subtract from conventional coverage time. Both require imaginative methods of evaluation that move decisively away from primary reliance on the machine-graded memorization test. Both, however, greatly improve the usability, transferability, and, in many instances, the excitement of humanistic study. They merit innovative experimentation, and they merit the creativity that undeniably will be required to reduce and compress the conventional materials to be sacrificed.

The workshop program and the senior contemporary issues courses constitute the most formal of the changes recommended for high school humanities. They must be combined, however, with some of the more general shifts already underway to improve the classroom climate and the training and updating of teachers, or to remove or relocate consumer education units and other diversions. They must be accompanied also by a rethinking of conventional course segments, not just to free up time for the new endeavors, but also to introduce some mix of new and old topics even outside the workshop setting and to generate an analytical superstructure as the basis of an explicit conceptualization in each course. The junior American history course, in this scheme, would have to get through its standard materials in fewer class days than are presently allotted in order to allow for regular workshops, and the condensation would require a combination of selectivity and streamlining. The course would have to deal in a realistic but coherent way with women and at least some minority groups and with central topics such as major shifts in demographic patterns, along with covering the leading political developments. It should explicitly begin the process of relating past to current patterns by establishing recurrent linkages with contemporary society. And it must move toward some guiding questions—which will recur as frameworks for more specific interpretive issues—in order to develop an appropriate analytical tone and to link otherwise potentially unrelated segments and topics. The junior American history course must, this all goes to say, itself be reconfigured well beyond its new relationship to the associated humanities workshop and the ensuing contemporary issues course.

College Programs: Entry-Level Humanities Courses

The determination of general education courses in the humanities at the college level depends, ideally, on what can be expected from the schools. Currently, in history, expectations tend to be limited to some general reading and writing ability and some basic knowledge of American history (which, however, may or may not be called upon specifically in collegiate requirements). Colleges typically require a survey course, most commonly Western civilization at the "better" colleges and, increasingly, world history elsewhere (and this trend is creeping upward). A few programs—as in Texas state colleges and universities, where this is mandated by law—concentrate on another U.S. history survey.

This survey approach, however it is defined, needs rethinking to accommodate analytical goals, even before high schools move substantially toward a more analytical program. The survey format need not be jettisoned entirely, but again factual coverage needs to be trimmed in order to free the students' attention for different kinds of reading and, above all, different kinds of analytical exercises. Similar new thinking must apply with great books courses in literature and philosophy, where simple exposure to the presumed beauties of past writing and thinking should give way, as a primary goal, to more critical tasks (including, in many cases, better linkage with historical context) and to consideration of a greater diversity of cultural products. Colleges owe their students more than conventional coverage. They are better positioned than the schools to relate new humanities research and theory to general education programs without converting these into narrow specialist training grounds. New planning and diverse models that include some outright experimentation, at the collegiate level, will constitute vital elements in the process of overhauling humanities education, because they will communicate new expectations to the schools and offer new, more dynamic kinds of disciplinary training to prospective teachers.

The two fundamental criteria for collegiate reorientation in this area are the decisions to be made about exposure to certain kinds of data that may have been missed in high school and—a more obvious criterion given the primary goals already laid out—commitment to a deliberate process of analytical training. The decision to incorporate data exposure risks being taken as an invitation to conventional coverage, which is not intended. It also risks creating some overlap with school experience; this already exists and indeed is almost inevitable, given the diversity of secondary schools. But a bit of overlap for some students is not really significant if it is embedded in new levels of analysis.

Building on analytical skills can be a straightforward process. If high school students have gained some experience in comparative work, perhaps through a junior-year workshop that offered exercises in identifying similarities and contrasts between selected specific themes in American history (slavery, the frontier, or democracy) and related features in one or two other relevant societies, a college freshman history program can introduce more systematic comparisons (less purely topical) over longer time spans and involving several cases. Students with some prior exposure to diverse interpretations should now be able to cope with higher-powered, more complex theories.

Decisions about data coverage should reflect great selectivity. In history, two goals are particularly relevant. First, high school coverage should not be needlessly replicated, but neither should it be entirely ignored; students should be able to build on some previously acquired facts in their collegiate program. This goal would suggest that some treatment of American history—in its newer as well as its more conventional manifestations—is desirable, as opposed to some college requirements that have moved completely away from the field, leaving any link between high school courses and general education requirements up to the student or up in the air. American history materials can be included in world history or Western civ courses, where the comparative potential is obvious. The second goal demands some serious humanistic treatment of international contexts. This can be achieved through additional comparative work (not all of it focused on the United States), but also through explicit attention to the development, evolution, and current operation of international contacts (commercial and cultural as well as diplomatic and military).

A collegiate general education program in the humanities could thus consist of two to four semester-long core courses, amplified by additional distribution requirements and foreign language work. One course would be world history, defined in terms of focused comparative work and particularly the analysis of international systems, including the timing and causation of such major changes as the West's surge to world power after the previous Arab dominance in the fifteenth-century Asian–Mediterranean–North African world and the partial erosion of Western authority in the twentieth century. Several theories of international systems, combined with an exploration of comparison and causation, could provide the principal analytical targets. A second course in this international program might then move toward systematic comparisons of the American experience, testing hypotheses about American exceptionalism. Students would be positioned to compare not just the United States and Western Europe, but also the United States and other frontier societies or other racially diverse societies, or the United States and Japan as advanced industrial societies in the later twentieth century, or the United States and the Soviet Union as military superpowers. One core package, then, would revolve around international context, comparatively embracing the United States and actively relating historical perspective to general contemporary analysis.[5]

The second core package would focus on cultural analysis, devoting primary attention to cases of cultural change and to general issues, including theoretical issues, in the area of cultural construction. Literature and other cultural media would be joined by some use of history and cultural anthropology as organizing elements in this two-course segment. Students would deliberately test the power and also the limitations of cultural construction in several different societal and chronological settings, including the contemporary era. They would explore the cultural and social meaning of various kinds of cultural expressions, carefully encompassing both popular and elite examples and their interrelationships.

These courses (which could embrace a great diversity of specific works and cases; no set coverage in the conventional sense would be required) would build on previous student experience in identifying authorial argument. Aesthetic objects—novels, plays, cartoons, symphonies, music videos—would be analyzed as constructs that occupy positions in particular cultural contexts and, as they are experienced today, in our own lives; their arguments would be viewed in terms of historical and personal engagement. In other words, they will not be treated merely as cultural consumption objects or passive ingredients of times past. The issue of cultural construction, applied to such social expressions as gender, would be seriously explored in several contexts, including (once perspective is established) our own. The ideas of aesthetic engagement and cultural construction would be applied to students' own prior acculturation, not necessarily to alter it but to subject it to analytical awareness. Instances of significant historical change and comparisons of contemporary cultural diversities would be explored, again using case studies rather than survey-coverage, to determine how much of individual behavior and social institutions can be explained by culture as opposed to other kinds of causation.

Interdisciplinary interaction in both major segments of the humanities core should be considerable. Courses on international context would rely on history as the central ingredient but embrace aspects of cultural anthropology and other social sciences as well. Where student abilities permit, they can also include work in foreign languages. Courses dealing with cultural construction would focus primarily on literature broadly construed but would also include other artistic disciplines, philosophy, history, and cultural anthropology. These courses in cultural analysis should focus shared humanistic interests on the goal of grasping the function and impact of culture, in the process reducing the isolation of particular disciplinary segments. It is time for a reengagement of various humanistic disciplines on the basis of new research and theory, with cultural construction providing the unifying structure and with analytically effective general education as the key target.

Coverage Revisited

The most arduous feature of designing a new curriculum is not the sketching of new courses, combinations, and emendations. Specifics require considerable thought and choice, and experimentation with effectiveness is necessary wherever goals call for ventures not yet widely introduced. In some cases, plans can build on imaginative programs already in use. Some elements of the high school workshop already exist in courses that deal with arguments from documents—the "inquiry method" that has enjoyed a revival in the past decade. Dialogue between scholars of literary culture and of social history is already underway, based on a mutual recognition of new bases for cooperation different from the old, elitist history-and-literature programs that focused on formal intellectual developments and great books alone. Models for world history ventures and for combinations of cultural anthropology and literary author-reader relations also exist, both in scholarship and in the curriculum. More work needs to be done in these areas, and we must strengthen the will to adopt new goals and translate them into curricular development, for such experiments remain the exception rather than the rule. Nevertheless, once the basic goals are recognized, new construction proves an exciting and a feasible task.

Not so easy is surrendering cherished subject coverage. This is a central feature in the canonist appeal, and I have already sketched a response above. Nevertheless, the problem needs one final treatment, in the context of the new curricular options being suggested here. For these options depend on our eliminating or radically reducing a number of great books and familiar historical details that have previously formed part of the standard humanistic canon. New topics and new analyses would be impossible without some severe pruning of this list. In the redesigned high school history classes, time must be found for six or eight workshop days each month, additional analytical discussions in regular class sessions, and some serious attention to new topics, such as basic demographic changes, that are not currently included. It would be desirable as well to free up a bit of time for teacher-preference segments; certainly the new programs should not further constrict opportunities for some teacher initiatives. State-approved or locally mandated syllabi for high school programs already, in principle, dictate what is to be covered for 150 or more days of each school year. To meet the new goals, this dictated content must be rolled back by a third to a half—a radical assignment, without question. Shifts in collegiate programs are less measurable, for some course sequences already include considerable analysis. In these programs too, though, more than casual readjustment of coverage goals is absolutely essential.

Pruning, even the radical pruning now required, does not mean the total elimination of facts. The new humanities goals do not encourage students to sit around exchanging opinions or dreaming up scenarios about the future (the only alternatives some teachers currently can see to straight coverage work). Use of literary theory, it has been argued, will help students remember certain novels better than they now do when asked simply to repeat plot lines. History courses must instill some factual knowledge, though in the context of dealing with interpretive questions, not mindless regurgitation. Students emerging from high school history programs should know some basic facts about the American political structure. They should know something about the scientific revolution and the Enlightenment because of the importance of those movements to recent world as well as Western history. They should know something about the nature and causes of the demographic transition—the reduction of birth and death rates—that occurred in the West beginning in the late eighteenth century and extending into the mid-twentieth century, because of the importance of the phenomenon in our own society (we are still trying to adjust our family goals to the novel experience of having so few children) and because of its implications for demographic patterns worldwide. These are just three examples of factual points that should be learned—two of them common in our present coverage, one more novel—and the list in practice must clearly be longer. This means that some time must be spent on factual explanation, not just on the higher analytical exercises in which the facts will ultimately be used. Clearly, the new humanities require an interpenetration of some factual learning with conceptual goals.

The real question is how to strike the balance, and the difficult decision is what to cut, given the need to make considerable space for new approaches and the fact that the tidiest solution—simply eliminating prescribed factual learning—is neither feasible nor at all desirable. No single formula would be appropriate, for choices of essentials and of illustrations for analytical case studies should vary. I can offer four guidelines, however, to assist in the radical pruning process.

1. The injunction that we help students learn how to look up facts should be taken seriously and pushed well beyond the check-it-in-the-encyclopedia process that too often begins and ends such inquiries at present, at least in the high schools. Encyclopedias can be helpful, but other data compendia must sometimes be consulted; students should become familiar with doing this kind of work, and they should be guided by the need to find facts to answer questions and not simply to repeat descriptive summaries. Students need experience in identifying up-to-date information sources and, of course, in distinguishing between factual materials and interpretive gloss. Many college students, sent to the library and aware that, unlike their experiences in high school, a single encyclopedia article no longer constitutes an adequate research base, often show woeful lack of discrimination in the sources they consult, which means they have not been—and are not being—adequately taught to use available data banks and to distinguish among different types of offerings. As we gain more confidence in our students' ability to find historical or cultural data when they need it, based on more guided student forays, we may be relieved of some of our anxieties about reducing standardized coverage.

2. We must be more explicitly aware that certain kinds of factual data may be selected over others because of their usefulness in case studies, not only because of their intrinsic worth or importance. These choices can be agonizing—and most informed instructors will wish they could cram more in—but they must be made.

In a world history course, for example, it may be necessary to ignore China in favor of India, or vice versa, not because one is historically more important or more interesting than the other, but because establishing one well-integrated, durable Asian civilization for comparative purposes may be all that the available time allows. Too many current guidelines, when they are adjusted to take the world, and not just the West, into account, specify that some attention must be paid to every major area of the world (four weeks on China, three on India, etc.) instead of insisting on a case study method, combined with serious comparative analysis, that might escape the purely Western framework. In a United States survey, if time permits the selection of one turn-of-the-century immigrant group for some special attention, it will not usually make much difference whether Slavic Americans or Italian Americans are picked. There is no time to do justice to all groups. The choice is logically determined by available materials and, sometimes, by the relevant composition of a particular student body. It can be sweetened by varying the selections on occasion—India for one three-year cycle of a world history offering, China for the next—and of course there should be some experimentation as to which study selections prove analytically most effective.

Selection already goes on, because not all parts of the world and not all groups are handled equally. And courses in literature select materials as a matter of course. What I recommend, particularly for coverage-conscious history courses, is an amplification of the principle based on an explicit case study method applied more widely than is now the pattern. But the procedure can be extended to some unfamiliar territory where it can really help the pruning process. Rather than deal with both the Jeffersonian and the Jacksonian eras, for example, American history courses may use just one to illustrate party formation and crucial elections, with the instructors gritting their teeth and leaving out the other option altogether. It is the political process, not every currently familiar presidency, that must be highlighted. As we come to realize that an understanding of certain kinds of historical and cultural patterns, not knowledge of every historical episode, is the goal, we can extend case study principles far more widely than we now do.

3. Even where case study selection cannot clearly be invoked, we must as teachers, or as parental monitors of teachers, figure out how to cut the irreducibles on the basis of redefining what factors have been most influential in shaping a society or in changing the nature of an analytical issue. Sociologist-historian Charles Tilly has described his "big changes" approach in a book entitled *Big Structures, Large Processes, Huge Comparisons*—not very elegant, but conceptually exactly on the mark. Tilly argues, among other things, that there are only two great changes that must be understood in order to grasp the distinction between premodern and modern Europe. Both, in his judgment, took shape in the sixteenth and seventeenth centuries. Change number one, which can be traced through subsidiary modifications to the present day, was the rise of the

nation-state; change number two was the development of a commercial economy and the related shifts in social structure toward basic distinctions between owners and nonowners of property.[6]

I do not intend to overemphasize Tilly's particular conceptualization, which I would argue offers too short a list of big changes and a slightly skewed chronology. The recognition, however, that most societies (including our own) don't undergo fundamental changes very often is a vital key to the kingdom of new selectivity in history and culture courses. We should teach students about the finite number of really big changes that have shaped the modern world. We can use emphasis on these changes to help evaluate some lesser shifts and some additional specific data as time permits, and we should employ case studies that provide additional insight and analytical experiences. Case studies should also permit a fuller sense— short of survey-style completeness—of how the "big changes" operated at a few key junctures and what connections they had with other developments. We most definitely do not, however, have to cover everything else simply because conventional courses once purported to do so.

It is not necessary, in this formulation of humanities courses, to make sure that students can offer some hackneyed description of the Italian Renaissance. The Renaissance is a fascinating period; there is nothing wrong in studying it when possible. Obviously, the Renaissance can be linked to some of the big changes Tilly talks about (though many historians now argue that the Reformation is much more important in that regard). The Renaissance can also be used as a case study of shifts in elite–mass cultural contacts. Or it can be included simply because an instructor feels deeply that it should be—though, as in jury selection, there must be limits on the number of such personal calls. The fact is, however, that the Renaissance by itself does not loom nearly as large in historical analysis of the shaping of Western society as was once the case. It has been dwarfed by the broader process of commercialization and by the later scientific revolution. It can be left out of a course that pares down standard coverage of the West in the interests of developing analysis, comparing the West with other parts of the world, and dealing with some of the newer kinds of topics.

The Renaissance example is deliberately chosen for shock value, though I do seriously contend that a student can adequately grasp the basic features of the Western experience without knowing the Quattrocento, by name or otherwise. Obviously, other instructors will prefer to eliminate quite different subjects from the conventional topic rosters. Other kinds of brush-cleaning are less controversial. It is relatively easy to leave out enlightened despotism or Italian unification, which already are subordinate themes in most coverage efforts. And omission may not be necessary where compression can do the job. The principal impacts of Napoleon, for example, are really quite easy to get across without going through every battle and alliance.

The overall point of this most crucial pruning guideline, however, must be acknowledged: In a context that demands that we seriously cutting back on coverage to get away from sterile, usually transient memorization, the need for new decisions about what really matters, factually, is inescapable. These decisions should be based on the best available scholarship about which episodes have had the greatest impact in shaping a society, culture, or period, and they should be made explicitly. This means that students will not be exposed to some materials that once were coverage staples. They not only won't know these materials, they will not have been asked to know them. Their perceived deficiency will unquestionably produce some anguish among their elders, and it will certainly dismay both the canonists and the routinizers. This guideline is not intended merely to shock, however. It is a response to a real need to reconfigure what we want students to know and, above all, to be able to use in understanding how societies function. Even if we were to discover new rigor in memorization and/or extend the time allotted to certain kinds of humanities programs, we could not fully escape some hard choices. That is why we need to examine the basic motors of society and culture, to make sure that they are conveyed to students, and, at the same time, that they will shape the unavoidable decisions about eliminating or reducing sheer quantities of data. One-damned-thing-after-another, the pattern followed in so many history courses, was never really effective, for it mixed big changes and small in a common mash. It has now become inexcusable because it prevents an analytical focus and distracts our attention from some of the additional topics necessary to grasp the big patterns.

4. We need to be alert to analytical schemas or generalizations that permit more efficient presentation of some essential data. Even flawed theories can be used to good effect not only as part of theory-testing, but also to generate patterns that will help organize more specific factual detail and so reduce the burden of managing data. In world history at the college level, Immanuel Wallerstein's

notion of dividing major societies, from the fifteenth century onward, in terms of their relationship to world trade can serve as a useful example.[7] Wallerstein's world economy distinguishes between societies (initially, parts of Western Europe) that dominated international trade, societies (like early Latin America) dominated in such trade, and societies (like China) long independent of involvement in world trade. Each of these three types of society (there is a fourth in-between type that can be introduced depending on student sophistication) has some generalizable characteristics in terms of political, military and labor-force structure—and the theory can be extended to include some comments about cultural independence or dependence as well.

Wallerstein's theory has been widely attacked for its oversimplification; it rests heavily on economic determinism as a causation structure; and it encounters some problems in dealing with change. Discussion of these flaws is part of theory analysis, and students may ultimately wish to reject the theory's applicability to other major cases (it works badly, for example, for Africa and for the New England and mid-Atlantic colonies of North America in the seventeenth and eighteenth centuries). Nevertheless, presentation and illustration of the theory and the ensuing critical discussion can help to organize a number of basic factual points about most major societies in the world over the past five centuries, and they do so more expeditiously than standard society-by-society coverage. Similarly, use of theory in literature can raise our understanding of literary features far more efficiently than the usual book-by-book summaries. This is not to claim that generalizations will permit retention of coverage goals in new guise; other choices that set priorities and determine case study use remain essential. It is true, however, that in some instances we can induce relevant factual awareness in more stimulating fashion, and in briefer compass, than is now the case through the franker use of theory.

In sum, the sheer amount of coverage must be both reduced and redefined. There is no reason not to be candid, for the changes are necessary counterparts to the twin bases of solid teaching programs in the humanities: recognition that the factual range has itself expanded and commitment to analytical goals above memorization and memorialization. Implementation of the reductions in coverage will be painful. It will involve renewed debates over the canonical tradition. It will also require explanation—for example, to parents who have developed a particular vision of an American survey course as part of their own national consciousness. It will generate useful variety, for although pruning is inescapable, monolithic pruning is not the point. Accomplished intelligently but with some ruthlessness, coverage reduction will produce better, more usable, and indeed better-remembered humanities courses.

Humanities Sequences

Bold decisions on coverage relate to another set of choices about sequencing in humanities programs. In this area, there has been progress in recent years—at least on paper—and that progress needs now to be brought in line with more central analytical functions. The discussion of translating basic goals into practical, innovative curricula has already suggested a possible ordering for some humanities topics, which can serve as starting point for a more explicit orientation toward sequencing.

High school history or social studies should include a course in world history, appropriately selective, relevantly analytical, and including Western and some other civilization themes in comparative context; a course on analytical issues in American history; and the contemporary cultures and societies capstone course.[8] A high school humanities program should also include relevant work in English on literary and cultural analysis, with some linkage to the social studies sequence. Collegiate general education in the humanities would build on this preparatory structure with course sequences on international context and on cultural analysis and cultural construction.

At the high school level, topical emphases can be juggled in various ways. Currently, world history usually precedes American history, on the grounds that the latter, which takes place in a more recent time, will and should be better remembered. This is not flawless reasoning; in terms of graduated complexity, it might be better to put American history first. But the priorities are not worth pitched warfare. What is important is to create interrelationships between one course and the next, so that a junior-year American history course will cross-reference and utilize some of the comparative findings and even some of the periodization themes from its world history predecessors (or vice versa).[9] Interconnections of this sort, as opposed to the splendid isolation of each course in many current programs, are vital to the coordination goals sketched in the previous chapter.

Some coordination between courses can also ease coverage demands, though not to the extent of eliminating the need to implement the pruning guidelines. If world history is addressed in the tenth grade, with some attention to presenting Western civilization in comparative context, and if some of the resulting themes are carried through in subsequent courses—American-European comparisons and United States–international interactions introduced in the eleventh grade and major world issues built into the contemporary cultures capstone—then a fully international focus in college freshman humanities courses may be less jarring to canonical sensitivities. Because humanities offerings are guided by so few explicit decisions about ordering at present, they do generate some needless duplication, the reduction of which, in turn, will permit unexpected if modest compromises between the presently competing coverage demands.

Four other features of the humanities sequence demand comment before we return to the principal criteria involved. First, the sequences I have suggested here are not meant to preclude additional options. The high school social studies program described above could be accomplished in two yearlong and one semester-long course, though obviously it would be helpful to have more time. Students should be able to choose at least one semester elective, to deal with philosophy, psychology, economics, or another relevant specialty course. Even the hoary twelfth-grade civics course, so often boring in its repetitious description of American political institutions and almost invariably unanalytical, might be refurbished and relocated in the ninth grade. Beyond high school, in collegiate general education, exposure to humanities options becomes even more important. Minimal core demands for freshmen and sophomores should certainly be amplified by distribution requirements in the humanities and related social sciences, and these could be patterned in a variety of ways.

Second, the humanities sequence should not begin only with the tenth grade, either in subject coverage or in working toward analytical goals. A number of recent plans, including the Bradley Commission report on history in the schools and the scheme currently being implemented in California or the similar program just approved by the Mississippi Board of Education, call for serious social studies work to begin by the fifth or sixth grades (after even earlier courses that address community studies, state history, map skills, and the like). Most of these schemes see middle school courses as a way of easing later coverage burdens—by introducing students to the initial chronological periods in world history, for example, and leaving the modern five centuries to the tenth-grade course. There are some dangers in this approach, if students learn early that history consists of long factual lists and only later encounter analytical challenge. The same pruning and analytical focus, appropriately adapted to student capacities, should apply to early work as to later, lest opportunities be lost and motivation stunted.

Middle school courses also should not present early chronological segments in isolation; instead, they should help students anticipate how the early experiences will be used to interpret more modern history and even to establish links with contemporary patterns. The point must not be memorization of some slices of early history for its own sake. At the same time, later history segments should not neglect earlier chronological periods for certain analytical purposes—dealing with problems of causation for example. Serious use of the years before tenth grade is essential, and this is one area in which thinking about humanities education is advancing in encouraging ways. A related willingness to link segments signals another gain. The California social studies curriculum deliberately reserves space in the eleventh-grade modern U.S. history course to review and bring back to active usage previous work on the colonial and early national periods. No longer will teachers assume complete vacuums between one year and the next. If these connections are reconfigured in terms less strictly related to coverage, still further gains will accrue. An analytical humanities program can certainly build on these recent initiatives to make the fifth-through-ninth-grade experience a less redundant wasteland than has heretofore been the case. Without going into great detail or venturing some definitive sketch of middle school programs, I can note that the current developments are not only desirable but also readily compatible with the more ambitious goals that must guide the next curriculum formulation.

Third, the humanities sequence at both high school and college levels should make real contact with concomitant work in science. Science education has its own issues and problems, to be sure, and neither space nor my own knowledge will permit extensive analysis here. It is obvious, however, that humanities courses currently pander too much to student interest in keeping science rigorously separate—either preferred or disdained, but separate. Simply as a matter of sensible reinforcement, course segments in history or English that deal with scientific developments should cross-reference with what students are doing in their chemistry or physics classes, at least through high school. Furthermore, an analysis of science as part of modern culture, as well as the role of scientific or pseudoscientific assumptions in popular beliefs and literature and the impact of science on politics, must obviously work into the case studies offered in the humanities sequence, certainly by the junior year of high school and on into college—including, obviously, the segment on contemporary culture and society. It is vital that students understand the often unexamined assumptions about science in their own culture and the extent to which science has itself been culturally constructed. We have argued that humanistic and scientific analytical modes are not the same. This is not, however, a justification for keeping the subjects separate; rather, the very differences invite comparative analysis. Certainly an assessment of scientific discourse and of the causes and impacts of science should loom large in the humanities sequence.

Finally, discussion about core sequences must not prevent our continued attention to humanities skills areas in high school and college alike. The need for improved foreign language training continues despite many reports over the past fifteen years urging prompt action to remedy the situation. American schools begin language training too late and fail to support it vigorously once begun. We waste a lot of time as a result and face too many linguistically ignorant students in college. One result is a tendency to insert basic language requirements into humanities general education programs. Basic language courses do not serve the wider humanistic purposes to which this essay is devoted, though they may convey relevant bits and pieces about foreign culture along the way. They are, however, vital preconditions for the international agenda the new humanities programs are designed to serve. In addition, upper-level courses that use foreign languages, explore language in relation to culture, or probe language analytically do fit directly into the humanities goals described above.

The ideal solution, of course, and demonstrably a feasible one in many other societies, would be to begin basic foreign language training at the grade school level. By high school, or certainly by college, students would be ready for serious cultural and historical study in at least one foreign language (and/or they would be launching initial study of one of the more recondite languages). Language ability would be vastly extended and ultimately blended into the larger analytical agendas of the humanities, with great benefit to the new goals of cultural analysis and comparison. We have every reason to push for a systematic enhancement of the place of foreign language training in our schools and for vast improvements in the timing of its introduction. This campaign is fully compatible with, but not the same as, the analytical humanities agenda described in this chapter. For now, we must continue to hope for at least some upgrading of language offerings, and we must include language segments in the options available at the college level. If this training should not be confused with the analytically essential humanities requirements, the latter should not distract from its necessity.[10]

Geography is another subject that clearly focuses attention on basics while requiring careful distinction between those basics and larger analytical goals. Geographers of late have made much headway in pressing a case for greater emphasis on their subject area. They argue their point mainly by emphasizing the factual ignorance of today's students, which does indeed seem to be abundant. The memorization of locations and place-names, however, is a low-level social studies achievement, and we need to be careful to stipulate how much of this is needed and for what later purposes. Geography basics must be defined and handled mainly in the early school years, then used as ingredients of more active conceptual exercises, including comparative analyses, in subsequent work on history and contemporary society. The current impulse to endlessly repeat memorization tasks even into advanced high school courses, however admirable the intent, confuses the purposes of humanities education. Basics of this sort should be treated as building blocks, not as final goals.

Training in composition is another primary skills staple of the humanities. Basic writing skills must be taught, and when necessary they should be given continued attention at the collegiate level. Like foreign languages and geography, these requirements are somewhat separate from the goals of the core humanities curriculum, and they should not substitute for it. As with the actual use of foreign languages, however, writing, beyond the primary skills level, can and should be part of the analytical education and evaluation central to the principal humanities courses. The relationship to interpretive reading and to the skills of argument make the link between basic composition and the upper-level curriculum particularly dynamic.

Explicit work on identifying and structuring argument dovetails nicely with writing, and most other analytical goals depend on written results.

This book has not focused on primary skills areas, because they are preliminary to the more advanced analytical goals toward which overall humanities programs should strive and because they have received far more public attention than those larger goals. The basic skills are vital, however. They can and should be incorporated into the humanities sequence and, where necessary, must continue to receive explicit attention even at the college level.

The more sophisticated analytical capacities, however, establish the ultimate guidelines for relationships among different segments of the humanities program, within high school and between high school and college. Programs can be arranged to ensure subject coverage while also minimizing time-wasting and redundancy in coverage to a greater extent than has been true in the past. The basic sequence, however, should be based on building conceptualizations, not on decisions about which grade will handle Manifest Destiny. The need to coordinate experience, to encourage the use of previously acquired skills while upgrading them to meet the next analytical level, is fundamental to successful implementation of the humanities program. The old habit of dealing with one course at a time, because of discrete coverage definitions, must yield to deliberate contacts between course levels. The new tendency to avoid revisiting previous courses in factual terms, to obviate the need for repeating materials, must also apply to the analytical experience, defined in terms of a manageable, finite number of steps toward using social and cultural data for understanding.

Majors in the Humanities

Although the primary theme of this book is the role of humanities in general education, there is a clear relationship between that theme and collegiate major programs. As many colleges and disciplinary associations are beginning to discover, the appropriate principles for humanities teaching must be applied to concentrations in subjects like history and English. In a few instances, excellent general education reforms have actually preceded reconsideration of the major, leaving the latter very poorly defined. In a similar vein, some humanists have argued in favor of increased course requirements for prospective teachers without asking whether these courses would do much beyond reteaching long-forgotten coverage data.[11]

Humanities majors are sometimes still constructed around distribution requirements. History students thus select courses from three different time periods—and that's it. Distribution criteria are not entirely unreasonable—in fact, it is more important than ever that we require some work in non-Western areas—but they are inadequate. They reflect a coverage approach, modified only by the recognition that students cannot cover everything.

It is essential to provide humanities majors with appropriately scaled analytical tasks, including the acquisition of some research skills. The same criteria that define general collegiate courses must be translated into a suitable array of exercises in disciplinary concentrations. A history major thus provides, or should provide, opportunities for more sophisticated training in gathering and sorting information and developing arguments. It should generate additional frameworks for comparative and for causal analysis. It should deal with issues of conceptualization, so that students understand basic interpretive structures of major works in history and have some sense of how to project structures for topics of their own. Along with some classics in the field, the major should certainly deal with examples of new work, so that the expansion of knowledge in the humanities is concretely illustrated. It also should develop connections with kindred disciplines, promoting eclectic methodologies for investigating certain kinds of social and cultural issues. The open-ended qualities of the principal humanities fields and their ability to expand the understanding of how societies and cultures function have an obvious place in the disciplinary concentrations for undergraduates.

College graduates in the humanities will, of course, continue to enter a variety of fields, including business and government. The experiences imparted by an updated major will help generate the research and analytical skills desirable in these fields, along with a more general sense of inquiry. Revision of the majors, though desirable as a general goal, is particularly vital where the training of future schoolteachers is concerned. Many potential teachers take too few courses in their substantive disciplines, despite current pressures for expansion in that area. The introduction of more serious humanities work into grade schools and middle schools will increase the need for better training in those categories. The fact is that some humanities majors or segments from which future teachers will spring are themselves inadequately conceived and promote a sense that the humanities consist only of blocks of coverage (literary genres or historical periods to be devoured one by one); the analytical challenge does not come through.

Fortunately, the structure and purposes of college majors is under discussion, with a view toward integrating not just new topics but also new vantage points. The goals are clear enough: to enhance the analytical experiences central to the humanities and, in the process, to provide appropriate basic training for people who may teach those subjects. But the need for continued review and constructive experimentation remains pressing.

Envoi: What Drives Curricular Change

A humanities curriculum that translates new topics, greater theoretical power, and basic analytical goals into a high school/collegiate general education program with appropriate extensions into the disciplinary majors is not impossibly complex. It is, however, different from what we have. This chapter, in addition to sketching a framework for relevant curricular planning, has argued two points. First, to get the curriculum we need, we must transform our thinking about what the humanities are meant to convey; in many ways we must start anew rather than simply rearranging existing ingredients or seeking to return to some idealized canonical vision from the past. Second, achieving the curriculum we need is a feasible goal. It requires daring and imagination, but it does not exceed what we can do. Dramatic innovation and feasibility are, admittedly, tense bedfellows in a field like education, which has trouble changing its stripes and tends to argue that major shifts demand impossibly much of students, teachers, community support, whatever. We have already noted that efforts at reform during the past few decades have not weaned most programs away from routine, except where they have imposed greater reliance on mechanical testing. The track record is not encouraging, which is why the conversion and feasibility themes must sound jointly, and loudly. We—the *we* being the various players in the educational game, from policy makers through scholars and teachers to parents and concerned educational consumers—need to demonstrate a new desire for reconsidering humanities goals and for implementing the results.

Educators often debate what it is that drives serious curricular change. Tests and texts often come in for primary scrutiny—this is clearly one factor in the current enthusiasm for national testing as a means of cutting through otherwise impenetrable bureaucratic routine. Curricular changes of the sort outlined here—and again, no single set of details need be insisted upon—certainly require imaginative attention to tests and texts, but they ask more besides.

Solid humanities programs require evaluations that focus on skills in analysis and argument, not on primary-level skills that can be machine-tested, and certainly not on memorized coverage. Many existing testing programs, particularly those at the precollege level, are not only irrelevant but positively harmful. They enforce routine memorization (if they successfully enforce anything at all). They confuse analytical skills with preliminary fundamentals like reading or basic foreign language vocabulary. Most tests from the early high school level onward either neglect the humanities in favor of additional basic performance testing in math and reading comprehension, or they probe factual retention. This is true even of programs issuing from the College Board, despite that agency's involvement in some admirable discussions of goals. Not surprisingly, given these general signals in addition to the daily burdens of teaching life, most high school teachers, in developing tests for their own courses, follow suit and emphasize easily graded memorization exercises.

We can note several more hopeful straws in the wind. Some moves have been made to develop different kinds of standardized high school tests that would focus on critical thinking and on argument based on interpretive skills. Some discussions of national assessment methods have included similar emphases. Many individual teachers offer imaginative essay assignments and other evaluation procedures that significantly modify or even reverse the single-minded focus on sheer coverage. Some teachers have also experimented quite fruitfully with student-aided grading, which can reduce the burden on teachers of managing essay assignments without diluting the analytical demands on students or the evaluation and resultant feedback.

But the fact remains that the installation of appropriate humanities curricula will depend heavily on a much more sweeping revision of evaluation procedures than is currently underway. Existing experiments in more manageable essay grading and more imaginative assignments need much greater publicity and far more extensive implementation. These changes require new ways of thinking, and they admittedly have funding implications. As I noted earlier in the book, analytical evaluations cost more money than the multiple-choice formats we use now. We may be able to find some valid shortcuts, but there is no question that we will be demanding more of teachers, both those who handle assignments only for their own classes and those responsible for any systemwide assessments. Even at the college level, given the recent tendency to increase the size of required courses in the humanities without proportionately increasing staffing, some funding reconsiderations will be imperative if the signals given by tests are to match the goals that should guide the humanities curricula. We must manifest a new commitment if we are to get the results from humanities programs that we can obtain and should demand.

Textbooks, the second general ingredient in humanities programs, must also change, though here the cost implications are actually rather benign. I have taken textbooks severely to task in previous chapters of this book, agreeing in that respect with some of the complaints from the canonists. Textbooks are almost uniformly too long (and therefore needlessly expensive); their principal benefit for students who faithfully lug them back and forth is cardiovascular, though even at that they fail to compensate for TV and pizza. Major publishers clone each others' works too faithfully, and too few are willing to break away to a smaller, more supple, more innovative product.

Introducing change into the textbook field, particularly at the high school level, will not be easy. Textbook publishers feel locked into customer expectations and such expensive marketing procedures that major innovation is risky. They have evolved slightly: several collegiate products impressively integrate new with conventional subject coverage. This evolution is encouraging, but it must be more widely developed, particularly in the analytical categories, and it must be accelerated. Factual coverage has changed, though too often it has merely added bulk rather than generating the kind of rethinking that would reduce old materials while integrating new ones. Innovative analytical sections are also creeping in. Clearly, however, more substantial change is vital. Teachers in the high schools, and in some college freshman courses, need more flexible instruments.

At the same time, if innovative goals are accepted, the opportunities for new and widely used publications are extensive. Some existing textbooks may, without undue alteration (though admittedly with reduced sales) be converted into reference works that are more directly related to coursework than general offerings like encyclopedias and are widely available as factual compendia, though they may not be in students' hands on a daily basis. New products that offer shorter presentations, including case study materials, more analytical guidance, and in some instances more extensive source compilations, can address the altered humanities menu in a more useful way. Books containing comparative exercises, for example, will become essential components of history courses and the new workshop segments. The responsible, imaginative publisher can contribute immensely to the task of restructuring.

Tests and texts do not stand alone, obviously. Humanities scholars need to pay more attention to issues concerning the curriculum and curricular materials, not only in their own courses but in collegiate and even high school programs. There has been too little initiative. Although some fruitful proposals regarding teacher education have already been issued, we can do more to improve teacher training in humanities disciplines and to encourage greater awareness and usable understanding of what the humanities now consist of. Toward this end, we need to recruit teachers from institutions that have kept pace with curricular developments and to revise laggard programs. Too few major universities, to take one final case, provide relevant offerings in world history at a time when (even aside from radical reform ideas) teachers are widely called upon to deal with a variety of civilizations, not just with the West alone. In teacher training, as with tests and texts, rethinking and a new level of commitment are vital preconditions to more effective education in the humanities.

Retraining of existing teachers will be harder than ensuring appropriate training in the first place. We have moved too far away from incentives for ongoing or recurrent education through pay scales that largely reward seniority. Summer workshops are not clearly effective, as only a minority of teachers regularly visit them, and some of these hop from one session to another without clear purpose or clear intent to apply the results to the next year's teaching. Better incentives and more imaginative use of televised continuing education programs or other means of reaching more teachers on a more effective basis are urgently needed. The desired results will require not only imagination but some new funding.

With all the tasks involved in translating basic goals and feasible curricular approaches into classroom reality, no one implementation path will suffice. Testing may be a key, if properly managed, but it will not stand alone. Change in all major components of the educational process is essential, and shortcuts will be difficult. Textbooks, for example, will not change until teacher demands change, and these will not change until more teachers are better trained and until curriculum committees adopt the goals they even now should be insisting upon. Conversion requires urgent, sustained effort on a broad basis, which is precisely why we need to shake off some current distractions and begin educating a number of factions in our society about what the humanities require.

The challenge is daunting. The goals are essential, the curricular framework is feasible; but getting to both will clearly be difficult. Yet, aside from the importance of the task, there are two reasons not to give up: the availability of many vigorous teachers and scholars willing to guide a restructuring effort; and the political momentum for change.

We have already made significant strides in some areas, and widely discussed changes can be put to good effect. Any time one discusses the textbook situation with high school teachers, the audience for new and more supple products is obvious. Some teachers, to be sure, have not thought much about the basic nature of the blockbuster text, but many have, and they would welcome alternatives. Even without retraining or other supplements, vital support for one key type of change already exists—though obviously it has not yet proved adequate to the task, because of the gap between real teachers and actual textbook selection committees. As new humanities approaches mature, a growing number of scholars are becoming interested in making contributions to teaching beyond their own classes and beyond specific research projects; they too are an existing resource that can be exploited more extensively. Brewing changes include not only the ideas about national assessment of high school students already discussed, but also plans for more discipline-based testing of teachers for licensing purposes. As with other assessment methods, these schemes could go awry if teachers are led by the nature of these imposed tests to believe that only recondite memorization will establish their competence in their fields. If, however, the tests include demonstrations of analytical competence and mastery of the kinds of interpretations, theories, comparisons, and conceptualizations that translate this competence into the classroom, important signals for constructive change will be transmitted.

The momentum of other curricular reform movements can also be tapped. If we approach the curriculum in the humanities and related social sciences as a total package closely related to innovative scholarship, we can build on current impulses while recasting some of the often emotional debate surrounding them. In an earlier chapter I downplayed the lures of simple compromise in favor of a more thoroughgoing examination of goals. This reexamination, however, when combined with constructive bridge-building efforts emanating from the spate of recent statewide commissions on cultural emphases and the social studies in the schools, can significantly advance the larger enterprise.

A 1991 report by a New York State task force on social studies serves as an important example.[12] The task force majority recommended greater attention to minority cultures and instances of oppression in American history (along with some related comments on world coverage in other than Eurocentric terms). A minority of historians dissented, arguing the need for primary concentration on mainstream democratic values. The majority recognized the importance of national institutions, as the report's title suggests, but they wanted the schools to serve as crucibles for an appreciation of diverse ethnic cultures. The idea of some interplay between conventional and more novel coverage is obviously sensible; this report is not an extremist diatribe. The insistence on instilling in students an appreciation for diverse interpretations and the ability to take a critical stand toward generalizations about society constitutes an even more important move in the right direction, suggesting that attention to analysis can supplement debates on coverage. The task force report did not spell out specific implementations of its general goals in terms of day-to-day class plans, which is where much of the battle must be fought. Nevertheless, its blend of older and newer materials in social studies points in the right directions.

But the full transition to the newer principles of humanities education was not made, and this would have helped immensely. The task force did not offer guidance in selectivity; the new goals were not accompanied by suggestions for pruning existing staples or choosing how many diverse groups would be studied. The report continued to stress coverage; it asked for attention to ethnic cultures more to establish identity than for analytical purposes. It also focused so heavily on minority cultural issues that other analytical questions were essentially neglected. Links with the newer scholarship were implicit rather than explicit. Discussion centered on the political and cultural demands of key groups in contemporary American society more than on the ways history has changed to incorporate new issues of cultural and political interaction and new kinds of causation beyond those inspired by identifiable elites. More attention to translating scholarship into classrooms would have moved more clearly toward goals of social understanding, away from the tugs of constituency politics and toward potential syntheses in the presentation of key historical issues.

Above all, an awareness of unifying analytical questions did not adequately emerge from the New York effort. The alternative vision of American history as a procession of discrete ethnic and cultural groups is an improvement over the misleading melting pot framework. But a real synthesis sees American history as a process of interaction between such groups and influential institutions and cultural statements, and this framework was not acknowledged. The difference is considerable. The report left the way open for critics to discover incoherence and unmanageability in its proposals (without, of course, presenting any analytical alternative on their part). In attacking existing curricula and urging major additions but not fully reformulating the overall structure, the report did not quite make the transition to conversion.

The relationship between the political base for change—found in the altered racial composition of the American student population and the associated demands for new coverage—and the needed reforms in humanities curricula is unquestionably tense. Several participants in the New York task force, including scholars who agreed with the results, emerged with wry comments about the completely political nature of curriculum determination and the naïveté of any thought that scholarly criteria could enter in.[13] If their pessimistic view is correct, the humanities may either continue to be a battleground or may change (probably diversely) toward redefinitions of coverage and nothing more.

Yet there is hope for a more fruitful coalition. Advocates of multicultural curricula can demonstrably win out in some individual school districts, but they face formidable opposition in the educational system as a whole. They will fare better if they join forces with relevant scholarship in the same areas to urge a wider restructuring that includes new kinds of coverage but also a more fundamental and more coherent analytical agenda.[14] Multicultural partisans would have to cede some ground in such a coalition. They could not push so exclusively for identity-validating coverage and heroic formulations (sometimes factually questionable) about a group past. However, they would find serious scholarly allies in the quest to reconsider the narrowness of existing canonism and to develop new conceptual issues in humanities fare. Without pretending that scholarship blends easily or automatically with multicultural political goals, it is not fanciful to point to a new alliance. Too many political advocates in the educational arena ignore the innovative research in humanities fields that can undergird and expand their appeal. Too many provoke needless controversy as a result. Too many risk shortchanging their own educational constituents by encouraging narrow, feel-good boosterism that does not provide a basis for analyzing real social issues. Politics is an unruly horse, in education as in other fields, but it might just be harnessable for a larger agenda.

This is the next, impending step. Debates over additional coverage are fruitful to a point, besides being currently unavoidable. Insistence on greater exposure to conflicting interpretations is a still more promising move forward. These steps point convincingly, if not inevitably, to a fuller analytical recasting that will use large questions (questions, not canned answers) to link new materials with old and to coordinate courses dealing with society and culture through analytical steps. This recasting, finally, may help to reduce the polarization between the more intelligent advocates of mainstream emphasis and the proponents of diversity by pointing to conceptual issues that merge many of their concerns. This is where the current momentum for change can pay off, producing something more than a new curricular patchwork as the basis for planning in the humanities.

We should change the present direction of humanities education. We can change it. Realistic history (which is one of the things we should be teaching) suggests that we may not, but perhaps our faith in education of the educators and the education-supporting public need not prove totally misplaced. Because humanities goals and opportunities have not been well presented heretofore amid the distractions of a more narrowly political debate, an attempt to launch a different and more imaginative discussion is worth a shot. If the discussion builds on existing strengths and reform opportunities, if it begins to reformulate some of the ingredients on which curricular change depends, the process may begin to perpetuate itself. The crucial goal is to get better materials into student hands and more relevant concepts into student heads. When we begin to meet this challenge, we will see results that will sustain the difficult process of change.

CONCLUSION

Educating for

Democracy

Refocusing humanities education, though eminently feasible, will be no easy task. It calls for rethinking at various levels and even (though this is not the primary prerequisite) for some new funding, particularly for more appropriate teacher training and more expensive forms of evaluation. Amid all the other tasks on the educational agenda—including dealing with the growing impact of social inequality, controlling disorder in the schools, upgrading mastery of basic skills, and trying to close the heralded international science gap—it clearly would be simpler to leave higher-level training in the humanities alone, or at most to make some gestures toward the greater traditional rigor urged by the canonists. Precisely because so much in our society is changing, and because other aspects of our educational system demand change as well, it is tempting to seek in the humanities program not only the ease of a benign neglect, but also refuge. Many societies have used literature, philosophy, and history as bastions of stability and guardians of past values, buffers against whatever new winds might buffet them in other respects. Clearly, some observers wish us to do the same.[1]

This book has argued strongly that either maintaining the status quo or instituting a more rigorous but traditionalist approach in the humanities would severely shortchange our students and reduce our capacity for intelligent social adaptation and cultural engagement. The types of humanities that were suited to a more agricultural society, in which change was not valued and the challenge of new knowledge was rarely acute, and in which memory itself needed careful nurturance given low literacy rates and limited access to data sources, simply no longer apply. New areas of research, though promulgating some faddish themes and some disconcerting jargon that need not be swallowed whole, present a real alternative in teaching. We have learned more about how society and culture tick, and we can now turn to the task of conveying this new learning in the classroom.

Any argument for sweeping innovation, calling for a radical conversion in subject matter and approach on the part of many of the practitioners already laboring in the educational vineyards, probably neglects the complexity of those changes and ignores the values served by the system it seeks to unseat. Without backpedaling, this chapter seeks to deal with several important issues raised by the basic argument but not yet fully explored, focusing ultimately on the question of the humanities' role in educating for a democracy, where in my judgment the vindication of the new, analytical approach shines through clearly.

Several of the remaining issues that will engage this last stage of the argument are admittedly evoked only briefly, because they are adequately covered elsewhere. The prospect of building on some new signs of flexibility, particularly among practicing teachers but also on the part of some canonists, though touched on in chapter 5, needs to be emphasized again in an appeal calling for further movements in this direction from both of the current political camps. The problem of the student audience also cannot be ignored. And the focal issue—the relationship of the new humanities programs to democratic goals—calls for some final remarks about the inevitability of politics.

Clearing Some Initial Brush: Countering Charges of Arrogance and Idiosyncrasy

The argument for innovation, first of all, risks an accusation of brashness. This book is not the product of long, painstaking committee deliberations about how the humanities should be plotted out. In some areas I think we are too much driven by committee work in education, particularly in the designing of characterless high school textbooks that would benefit from some individualistic analytical flair and even some outright whimsy. Obviously, however, any classroom translation of the goals of the new humanities must involve collaborative efforts, which in turn will adapt the goals themselves and produce a variety of specific formulas for their implementation in the curriculum. The opportunities for varied choices about case study elements, about underlying analytical frameworks for specific courses, even about aspects of sequencing (though ideally not about greater commitment to sequencing itself) invites give-and-take from the planners and teachers who will actually be responsible for carrying these programs into the classrooms.

Although this book pontificates about goals and feasibilities on the strength of individual authorship, its arguments are drawn from a variety of trends or partial trends that point encouragingly in similar directions. There are severe problems of training and morale among many humanities teachers, particularly in the schools, and I have attempted to note (joining with some of the criticisms emanating from other quarters) some real deficiencies that need attention, from the primacy of coaching tasks among many social studies teachers—a clear sign of the low value placed on the product, regardless of the personal qualities of the individual involved—to the difficulties encountered by previous efforts at updating knowledge and approach.

Without retreating from my position, I should also emphasize that many teachers provide examples not only of enthusiasm and devotion, but of specific experiments in curriculum design and evaluation that can serve as building blocks for the larger effort to come. Talented secondary school teachers have led the way in making some tenth-grade world history courses relevant and meaningful; they often eclipse their college-level colleagues in identifying needed programs and making them work. Teachers who want more freedom from the burdens of mechanical testing and overlong texts in order to introduce more analytical meaning need a stronger voice, and we should find new ways to hear them. We can strive to help teachers lead each other. Heightened collaboration, including regular channels of communication between humanities teachers at the collegiate and at school levels (already sketched in some Advanced Placement programs), constitutes another growing current that can be fruitfully enlarged.

Programs and proposals that move in the right direction have frequently been noted, though usually with some warnings about potential pitfalls. In this, too, I by no means stand alone. The College Board offers guidance in history programs that embrace more social and world history and more emphasis on conceptualization—though it has not yet found ways to make its more influential testing programs match its good advice. Attempts to rationalize social studies sequences from late grade school through high school, to assume (but also to foster) some year-to-year retention, and to avoid wasteful and boring repetition are exciting innovations, intelligently proposed and now under implementation as several states upgrade their social studies efforts. Discussion of new testing directions may carry the analytical agenda forward. Even textbook publishers demonstrate more openness toward world history—compared with the situation a decade ago, for example, fewer world history texts today are simply relabeled Western civilization—and toward some of the essential new topics of social history. In this arena, too, there are bases for further, more sweeping reform, and not simply carping attack.

Changes in the canonists' tone from the starkly reactionary pitch of the mid-eighties also carry a hopeful message, though the inconsistencies and limitations are still troubling. I have already noted some concessions to world history by humanities gurus like Lynne Cheney, though a Western emphasis still predominates in the sequence endorsed by the National Endowment for the Humanities. Diane Ravitch, a powerful critic of routine treatments of American history and more recently a defender of the canon, now approves changes in presentation toward franker recognition of cultural pluralism. She notes that the old melting-pot idea, which suggested erasure of group differences, has yielded to the idea of variety as a national strength. Students now learn that "cultural pluralism is a national resource rather than a problem to be solved"; "the unique feature of the United States is that its common culture has been formed by the interaction of its subsidiary cultures." These concessions are real but incomplete. Ravitch still thinks in terms of a unique national culture without bothering to defend it comparatively, and her pluralism is carefully harmonious. What she calls particularist cultures, those that seek to challenge mainstream values and general harmonious commingling, are out of bounds in the curriculum; this ban particularly applies to some of the more vigorous assertions of an Afrocentric identity.[2] With this approach, as with Lynne Cheney's, canonism has stopped trying for a full return to its older staunch conservatism, and although its hesitations still preclude the necessary full rethinking, they do open the way for further discussion. Cautiously engaged, so that minor concessions are not accepted as adequate, these discussions may provide another building block for the genuine recasting that must be sought. At the very least, all-out war has yielded to more complex negotiations, which may clear the air.

This is a time of great excitement in humanities teaching. Not all the excitement is productive, but it is clear that, as a society, we know we need a better understanding of cultural issues. That recognition is an invitation to better presentation in the classroom.

Above all, the prospect of a new thrust in humanities education builds on the innovative scholarship in history and cultural studies that has so dramatically expanded the knowledge base and so dramatically altered elements of the theoretical approach in the constituent disciplines. It is important to remember that although many specific proposals for curricular change are novel, they all work toward the very simple goal of reorienting teaching on the basis of well-established research—the same combination we properly accept in the sciences or in economics. The idea of updating humanities teaching in light of new research—beyond tinkering with this or that biographical datum in response to the most recent work—is oddly radical only because we are so accustomed to regarding the field as a kind of classroom-based museum. The new scholarship itself, however, is not an individual invention. It may be translated into teaching in diverse ways, to be sure: claiming derivation from the new work is no assurance of adequacy. I have indeed quarreled with some impulses emanating from the new scholarship—where they are too heavily politicized, for example, or defiantly extended to challenge coherence in the curriculum. Debate and further refinement are inevitable. The alternative to making a basic connection between the scholarly trends of the past generation, as they continue to evolve, and the education of the future is sterility and lost opportunity. In pointing out a new range of possible connections, this book essentially if belatedly belabors the obvious.[3] It is worth recalling that the process of establishing links was launched a decade ago by a variety of scholar-teachers, only to be shunted aside by the strident counterclaims of the more reactionary canonists. It is now possible to revive but also to generalize and more fully implement the necessary effort.

The new directions in humanities education, as sketched in the preceding chapters, do invite teachers, scholars, and students to collaborate in constructing a program that has no full precedent. The vision requires innovation. The directions it takes, however, are not whimsical, as they follow a variety of current trends and above all seek a fruitful union of education with the essentials of the dynamic research achievement. As the new program is elaborated, it can call upon growing strengths in numerous facets of the humanities and related social sciences disciplines and from committed teaching personnel at various levels in what must be a widely collaborative effort.

The Student Clay

Can the essential goals of a revised curriculum be realized with an American student clientele? After dealing with accusations of brashness, the second challenge for the new humanities program is to justify its ambition where students are concerned. Student response is the rock on which earlier, less sweeping reform efforts foundered when many teachers assumed that student limitations would preclude serious experimentation, and when many experiments seemed to fail because they asked too much of their clientele. Proposals to convert history teaching to a widespread use of documents—the inquiry method—collapsed two decades ago amid teacher skepticism that students could build understanding from primary materials, and also amid some evidence that students really did flail about helplessly in the absence of textbook-level structure. My proposals for the new humanities curriculum do not insist on such a full transition of sources in high school social studies, though this technique is now in fact gaining ground a generation after its doom was proclaimed. The proposals do insist on regular and early workshop exercises to establish the analytical skills of this sort; and they ask for other, potentially more demanding analytical training as well.

Two facets of youth and studenthood require comment, the second more important than the first. One clear appeal of Allan Bloom and other popular canonists has been their service to many Americans who believe that traditional authority structures, which once kept young people in line, are crumbling. Bloom argues that less domineering curricula contribute to this problem. I have already suggested that one of the extracurricular motivations for canonism is a widespread sense, on the part of adults, that their school humanities experience was stupid and incoherent, but that they endured it dutifully and emerged the better for their respectful docility. Their children's obedience to the same routines would be usefully chastening.

This book has argued that the curriculum has not fundamentally changed since any relevant good old days and therefore should not be singled out to blame for real or imagined adolescent defiance—

which, in some measurable respects, has in any event declined since about 1973. I agree that the curriculum has to some extent been watered down by grade inflation (which began before or during the time most current adults were students—so most of them benefited from it, too) and by Mickey Mouse disruptions, and so in that regard I join the canonists in urging greater rigor and more time spent on substance. The new humanities curriculum may relate to student skepticism about some aspects of tradition and authority by teaching them how to translate that skepticism into intelligent, critical questions about the way societies function. It is not, however, designed to pander to the deterioration of youth (real or imagined), because it works to make them more socially and culturally aware, more rather than less involved with pressing issues.

Can youth (whether deteriorated or not) handle a more analytically demanding regimen? This question brings us to the second, and more significant, of my two points about students. As our discussion of new humanities programs advances, many authorities will argue sincerely that students cannot handle them. Many, less sincere, will use assertions of student incapacity to justify their unwillingness even to experiment with new ingredients.

Arguing against the students-can't-do-it-so-we-won't-try syndrome is not easy, in part because my own credentials are incomplete at best. I am not a learning acquisition expert. I have not taught in high school, or even in a college program that recruits students of average ability. I have participated in the successful analytical upgrading of programs for relatively able (but not uniformly brilliant) college students and have been involved in other fairly successful enhancement efforts such as the burgeoning Advanced Placement program in the high schools (though this is not a fully relevant example, insofar as some AP work moves toward greater coverage rather than more challenging conceptualization). I cannot offer a full defense against the charge that we are asking the impossible, and I have no desire to conceal the dilemma. In contrast to the math and science fields, in which foreign examples are routinely cited, there are no fully updated humanities programs elsewhere for us to invoke. Some European curricula come closer than we now do, in building toward essay evaluations rather than memorization tests, but they do not provide ideal models overall. In short, there is no way to prove at this juncture that students will be capable of performing in the program suggested here—though it is also true that disproving their ability to do so is not possible either. We won't know until we try.

Furthermore, established wisdom about age-specific student learning capacity is itself under challenge. Developmental psychologists have clearly demonstrated that earlier ideas about student abilities—the notion that student of age x definitely cannot understand manner of thinking y—are erroneous. The theories of Jean Piaget, the guru of the lockstep capacity approach, have been disconfirmed by repeated findings that children often demonstrate competencies far greater than assumed normal for their age cohort—yet educational thinking, caught in its own developmental warp, has not adjusted to the resultant new, if also somewhat varied, horizons.[4]

A dilemma remains, for we do not know exactly what students can learn in the humanities, or in what stages; this admitted uncertainty, however, should not preclude careful response—necessarily brief because of its speculative quality. Current humanities education, which is predicated de facto on low-level student abilities, produces widely disappointing results, whether one's vantage point is canonical or analytical. Students do derive some assumptions about the United States, though whether from school or from the wider culture cannot be determined. To a greater extent than canonists will acknowledge, our national culture generates a powerful fund of myth and assumption about the American experience. Characteristic school offerings produce other, usually pejorative, assumptions about studying history and literature. Many students quickly become convinced that humanities subjects are boring as they navigate undemandingly through factual accounts of great books and noteworthy historical episodes. They notoriously forget or never learn much of the specific data thrown their way. They appear in each new course essentially as tabulae rasae; most history instructors assume no specific prior knowledge (though the analytically inclined among them must do battle with some of the more diffuse cultural assumptions that have been acquired along the way). There are, of course, important exceptions: some students learn sequentially; others actually like the humanities or at least appreciate some of the goals involved; some good teachers can make even routine treatments come alive. On balance, however, the current evidence is not encouraging; it indicates that many students do not respond well to the humanities. This lack of student interest saps the morale of many who teach in the field, particularly at the high school level, as they come to expect less and less—often, in my judgment, becoming enmeshed in self-fulfilling prophecies in the process.

The poor average performance current among students can be read two ways. The first way would judge that more ambitious goals are undercut by the fact that we cannot even attain the memorization levels we currently aspire to. The second way would argue that we get poor results in part because we ask too little, and in part because we channel our limited requests toward the wrong achievements. We can hardly do much worse at conveying a perspective on society and culture, so a fresh start offers the only sensible alternative.

We are, in a word, underchallenging. We don't engage students' thoughts sufficiently. We don't use the humanities to cover topics of more assured interest as a means of leading into wider analytical perspectives. The widespread assumption that nothing specific will be remembered from one humanities course to the next is shocking testimony to humdrum goals and low expectations; even in mathematics, where test results are currently disappointing, there is some sequential learning. Were the humanities to offer more coherence, based principally on analytical exercises that build from one year to the next and including specific references to what has gone before, there is no reason not to anticipate greater student response.

The basic goals of the new humanities program, furthermore, do not assume a totally lockstep pattern. There is room for experimentation, and in fact teachers have every reason to use segments like the proposed workshops to develop a better sense of what students can do when they are called upon to treat humanities materials actively rather than receive them passively. Some disappointments are inevitable, and it may be necessary to trim the sails at certain points. Nevertheless, if the analytical approach is undertaken seriously rather than being presented briefly, reluctantly, and blanketed by anticipations of failure, I believe that we can progress farther than we now do, even if we cannot know in advance exactly how far. If average students at the high school level learn something about conflicting interpretations, for example, but are put off by formal exercises in conceptualizing causation, so be it. We will not know until we try, and we may, with intelligently designed programs, surprise ourselves. Recent classroom initiatives already show that reigning taxonomies are off the mark; fifth-grade slow learners in Connecticut, to take one example, can interpret and base enactments on historical sources, achievements well beyond the modest memorization skills commonly attributed to their level.[5] Many students respond stupidly to inadequate challenge, but this is all the more reason to venture boldly.

Analysis can engage students' interest, particularly if it is combined with some topics of concern to youth (as diversity proponents have already suggested). Giving analytical attention to issues in contemporary society need not pander to students—some issues with which students have no direct involvement must also be addressed —but it will help students relate to other aspects of humanities offerings. Historical study of social history topics such as youth and family or of social, ethnic, or gender groups familiar to a particular student constituency, valid in itself as part of an intelligent curriculum, may also introduce students to analytical habits that can then be applied to other, less immediate subject matter. Literary theories that are illustrated through current advertising or other media and then applied to works with which students are less familiar have an impact they might have lacked had the works been approached without preamble. No sweeping pedagogical studies have yet demonstrated this special drawing power of the newer humanities approaches, but experience in specific classrooms suggests that innovation may reduce the difficulties we currently imagine when we ruefully contemplate American youth.[6]

The evidence of greater student involvement with topically interesting and analytically challenging programs is hardly conclusive at a scientific level, but it is strongly indicative. Many high school teachers report student excitement at answering real questions instead of parroting facts. Community college teachers recognize their students' appreciation of history that deals with the "realities and perceptions of ordinary people," as one California student response stated. To be sure, committed teachers who find their students drawn in by materials that cover women or African Americans— topics that deal, in other words, with groups from which the students themselves come—may be serving a special interest, but their experiences point strongly to the possibility of intensifying student involvement by diverging from the canon. In addition, there is some indication that student interest can be increased through analytical challenge as well as topical relevance. Community college students with no prior interest in history can be deeply engaged in debates springing from basic conflicts of interpretation about the course of American history.[7]

My own experience, which is impressionistic at best, certainly confirms these results. A physics major takes a history course to fulfill a distribution requirement, only to find that it does not at all resemble what he learned about the discipline in high school. It covers a wider array of facets of the human experience, and it forces him to think about change and causation. Student after student, some simply delighted to find another interest, others drawn into a more durable commitment to history, reports amazement at what the subject really encompasses. Their excitement leads to a real involvement both with analysis of the past and with connections between past developments and present issues.

Student performances and interest levels will, of course, vary as innovations spread. The new humanities will not be a panacea for all. Some able students may prefer the definite methods of science to the more amorphous interests of the humanities, as is now the case; so long as they learn some basic findings and techniques in the latter area, fine. Some less able students will doubtless continue to find any intellectual effort boring or intimidating, though active exercises, properly designed, may draw many of them in. Humanities programs will also continue to depend on good teaching; it is folly to attempt to devise teacher-proof curricula—a lesson that 1960s reform failures taught us quite vividly. It is true that, when we consider teaching at all, we usually place too much emphasis on classroom performance and not enough on the curriculum conveyed through that performance; but the performance will remain essential, and we must continue to encourage more quality and to offer more incentives in this area.

The three fundamental keys to the kingdom of the humanities program are *ambition, engagement,* and *recognizability.* Students must deal with some topics that grab them; they should learn how to approach these topics analytically and then move on to wider perspectives and less familiar subject matter. The humanities must be defined less in terms of remote cultural treasure chests, and the new scholarship and theory must provide the basis for greater topical relevance. Active involvement with humanities data in learning to answer questions and to structure argument is, of course, fundamental to the whole analytical approach. Less passive students will do better in this environment. Also, an ambitious attitude is crucial to success. We have too long asked too little in the humanities arena, expecting lack of interest and generating it in the process. We must experiment to find realistic achievement levels, but we must plan to spur students on, to expect success rather than plan for failure.

There is no reason, in short, to abandon the overall goals of teaching better means of understanding how societies and cultures function, simply because we do not know exactly what various groups of students can or cannot attain. Happily we have already moved beyond the pervasive effort of the 1970s to oversimplify style and vocabulary in the humanities materials prepared for students, having learned that average students must and can be pushed to master normal reading levels. We must carry the process further, aided by a wider topic selection and by the fact that students' direct intellectual involvement in the various facets of the humanities now begins well before college and extends throughout general education programs at the collegiate level. Negativism about student capacities—reinforced by gloomy reports based on the results of current classroom approaches—is certainly not valid grounds for resisting innovation. Properly interpreted, in fact, such negative views argue that innovation, with some flexibility, has become essential.

Efforts to undermine new curricula by undervaluing student potential come mainly from the routinizers in the humanities, some of them sincerely persuaded after tedious years in the classroom that students can do no better, others groping for arguments that will leave their own capacities untested. The more thoughtful canonists—those not wedded to fact-lists as evidence of humanities education—also reject this effort to sidestep challenge. One final question about the program of innovation, however, revives some of the disputes between canonists and the newer humanities scholars concerning educational goals. How will a program geared to social and cultural analysis affect the values students must acquire to maintain American democracy? This is a valid issue that need not be ducked —an issue that can, in fact, be answered with considerable assurance, as part of an explanation of how recasting the humanities fits in with the larger educational effort.

Humanities Education and American Dreams

Any educational reform proposal must address the implications for American democracy. One test of such implications involves accessibility: many educational reforms, desirable in themselves, drive new wedges between rich and poor school districts because the latter do not have the funds to buy the latest equipment or the most imaginative textbooks. Unequal access to humanities reforms must be taken into account, though cost factors are not as great a concern in this area as they are with computer education or laboratory equipment. Modifying textbooks might make them cheaper, not costlier. Teacher retraining is needed as often in posh school districts as it is in inner cities. It remains true, though, that humanities restructuring may be easier in affluent districts capable of affording workshops and newer materials. This observation does not mean that the reforms should not be attempted elsewhere, but it does suggest the need for careful attention to their dissemination and to providing relevant support where necessary. On the other hand, by challenging students and presenting new critical angles of vision, the revised humanities curricula potentially carry a greatly enhanced meaning for many of the students most disadvantaged in the current humanities array. This claim forces us to explicitly consider the contributions of the new humanities goals to the democratic process.

The humanities have long served, in many people's judgment, as the educational center of efforts to teach American students what democracy is about, both by providing facts about the democratic institutions of the United States and the history of democracy in this country and in the larger Western tradition and by inculcating democratic values. This was one of the adjustments to Renaissance elitism noted earlier. Social studies curriculum plans routinely include a values component, which urges the use of certain materials to teach students the importance of respecting others' rights, the need for cooperation, or the goal of racial harmony. Many canonists vigorously endorse these efforts in general, and many add their characteristic emphasis on the importance of providing a common set of cultural icons, as well as inculcating specifically democratic values, to weld a diverse society together and to create the harmony necessary for a functioning democratic state. Paul Gagnon of the Bradley Commission has been particularly forceful in advocating that we put great stress on Western political history in order to show students how arduous the construction of democratic institutions was, how the West produced some of the greatest challenges to democracy in the form of movements like fascism, and how watchful we must be lest this precious yet vulnerable political tradition erode.[8]

These are powerful arguments. Translated, they can seem to justify a keep-things-as-they-are-or-were approach that would prefer to keep the humanities curriculum focused on the Western political tradition, seen as a gradual movement toward democracy; on great philosophers, who sowed the seeds of this tradition; and on the common culture that has helped people sustain political harmony. Learning facts about Western history and particularly about American institutions would gain renewed sanctity with this approach. Values training, implicit or explicit, would inform the whole enterprise. Larger efforts aimed at topical diversification, at using a world historical and comparative framework, and at freeing up more time for analysis would be rejected or minimized because they distracted students from the main enterprise.

The most fashionable anticanonists of course reject these arguments as ethnocentric, scornful of diversity, and manipulatively elitist. They articulate a greater historical complexity than the canonists will admit, and they remind us that we are not only a democracy (an imperfect one), but also a capitalist society with many social drawbacks attached. They score some telling points, in my judgment, but in proposing a wider-ranging new look at humanities education and not just a multicultural counterattack, it is vital to offer a more systematic response, one that agrees with some of the efforts to instill intelligent respect for democracy while arguing that the curricular implications support rather than undermine the thrust toward innovation.

We begin with two points, one by now familiar. First, current humanities education is much more successful in building patriotism than it is in building understanding of or active participation in democracy. Second, a society does have a right to expect its educational system to sustain its basic values, however annoying this must be to perceptive cultural critics.

Concerning the democratic achievements of the standard humanities fare: We don't do very well in creating an "informed citizenry." Levels of citizen information about basic American governmental institutions have not necessarily deteriorated; it is vital to remember that available evidence suggests that there were impressive gaps even in the "good old days"—whenever these actually were—of the earlier twentieth century. The levels of knowledge are not, however, impressive. Equally important, continued educational emphasis on the building of American democracy, perhaps slightly diluted since the "good old days" but not fundamentally diverted, has not prevented the steady decline of voter participation. Reasonably ardent patriotism has not prevented this decline, either. Perhaps we should recognize that the kind of education we are offering may not be very relevant to involvement in the democratic process, an involvement that in turn may depend primarily on social structure and other variables. This is an interesting analytical issue, but hardly resolvable here.

What is clear is that the stated goals of education relate to active citizenship in complex ways at best. Some may judge that, despite low voter participation and other signs of apathy and ignorance, we are doing all right at present because we aren't experiencing major expressions of disloyalty or social protest. However, many observers—including education-for-democracy adepts in the canonical mode—believe that we are not making the best use of the potential education/democracy relationship at present. With political indifference heavily concentrated among younger voters (senior citizens are twice as likely to vote as their juniors, a fact that has significantly shaped—some would say distorted—our current social policies), the contemporary impact of education becomes particularly problematic.

Some humanist-critics, building on aspects of the new scholarship but also on their own political agendas, seek to use humanities programs to combat indifference by challenging basic American values and institutions. Let students see the relativity of various "truths," the inadequacies of elitist pretenses, the beauties of other cultural traditions, and the true mission of education will be realized. Elements of this argument are valid and appealing, but the argument itself goes too far. No society can be expected to support educational agendas that deliberately war with dominant cultural values. Protest of course is legitimate and sometimes inevitable, and at some juncture we may well see fundamental challenges to the existing order revive. Nonetheless, we cannot realistically demand that socially sponsored education base its programs, in the humanities or any other subject area, on pure dissent, however intelligent. The anticanonists' failure to confront this fact opens the way for distorted conservative claims that academic radicalism is nothing more than an attack on basic American assumptions. Fundamental critiques of American society are important, and they deserve a place in the educational lexicon, but short of revolution they will not erase the primary emphasis on presumably more positive features of the American order.

Furthermore, in my judgment many basic tenets of a democratic political order hold up pretty well. I inject this opinion not because

I have any special claims to competence as a political theorist, but because, in this educational arena, political goals do enter in, and candor may help clarify my own position. I wish our democracy functioned more equitably; I do not approve of its drift over the past decade, as growing social inequality and increased militarism have clouded the democratic prospect. But the fundamental system seems to me to work better, at least in our culture, than any alternatives thus far imagined. My own predilections, as well as a realistic assessment of what societies can be expected to demand of education, support my belief that our school system should help maintain democracy.

In sum, education will, as a matter of hard fact, strive to maintain the basic values of the society that hosts it. Our educational system should help students understand what democracy is and why it works reasonably well (though also what may threaten it and where it has proved inadequate). Current school routines do not necessarily jeopardize our democratic achievements, but they hardly anchor them as securely as we might wish, judging by the attitudes and behaviors of recent graduates.

And one other point: as a society, we have relied heavily in recent decades on attacks on foreign enemies as a means of generating internal support for our political system, perhaps excusing along the way a considerable lack of understanding of this system and how it actually works. We fought for democracy, whatever that meant, against Germany. We defended democracy against communism in the cold war. This posture provided such a clear talisman of loyalty, such a certain knowledge of who the enemy was, such an unquestioning acceptance of the bad/good dichotomy that crowned the United States with an international white hat, that the more reasoned capacity to explain and defend our system itself seemed less central. This ideological framework is now declining, though its lingering attractiveness showed in the recent effort to equate Saddam Hussein with Adolf Hitler and to proclaim as another fight for liberty a war based on our national economic interests in defending nondemocratic but oil-rich regimes in the Middle East. We will again have foreign enemies in the future, but they may not provide the easy moral targets we have enjoyed for half a century. We will need to develop a more subtle understanding of our own system if we wish to argue that Japan's is wrong—recent efforts to brand the Japanese as racist and undemocratic notwithstanding. We almost certainly need to seek new reasons for engagement with our own political system, and the quest returns us to some questions about the role of education.[9]

This updated context is one that many educational authorities would accept, in broad outline. It argues against the mere maintenance of present routines in humanities programs, though it does not necessarily dictate massive reform. We are not doing enough to involve our students in our own political process, and the decline of foreign enemies as easy symbols for inducing political loyalty further impels some rethinking. At the same time, renunciations of any positive education/democracy connection in favor, for example, of simply teaching students to praise other cultures or to ridicule the American elite, are off the mark; they distract us from the political realism that should frame educational debate. Even the discontented should want students to learn where power resides in our society and what arguments the powerful use to persuade or lull the rest of the population.

This is the context within which many canonists advance their views about using history and literature to establish our common culture and an active grasp of the historical process that has generated our political system. They want improvement in the humanities, they want greater rigor, they want closer association of humanities programs with American and democratic values. So once more: Why ask for more radical curricular reform? Why, since we accept a number of assumptions also shared by more enlightened canonists, strike out on such a different and at times hostile path?

The answer to these questions recaps earlier arguments but then branches more widely into education's democratic role and the humanities' place therein. Too great an emphasis on traditional intellectual and political materials and histories, however good the intent, risks confirming routine treatments in fact. The lists of names, dates, and "great books" plots lie close to the canonical surface. Routine, in turn, leads to memorization and rote learning, which do not teach active democratic values, as the political apathy of recent youth cohorts amply demonstrates. However moving the appeals to common culture, the canonists' proposals are too close to what we have now, a system already wanting and likely to become more so as we adjust to the lack of an enemy political system.

Furthermore, emphasis on the canon for the defense of democratic principles evokes misleading distortions of history, and it argues for more direct connections between past processes and current values than even the canonists themselves really intend. Most of the "great" thinkers in the Western tradition before the late seventeenth century were not democrats, and many were explicitly hostile to democratic values. Are we to neglect them and so omit this much of the Western canon? Are we to teach them but explain to students that they were wrong? Here's Plato, kids, a great mind but way off the mark. How much of the past, or of past culture, do we enlist in the democratic defense, and how explicitly? The canonical approach involves too many complicated maneuverings, too much neglect of historical reality, and potentially too much preaching either to represent humanistic analysis adequately or to connect it with the kind of education we want for a democracy.

It is conceivable that, somewhere in the educational skein, there should be a course on socially desirable values that frankly and openly tells students what leaders in our society think they should believe: Democracy is good. Too much authoritarianism is bad. Racial tolerance is good. Religious freedom is good. A course of this sort could be embellished with some examples of the kind of thinking that is approved, including perhaps a segment on the origins of our most valued ideas and another on the values particularly to be shunned. Students would be encouraged to discuss these ideas and to take a preliminary look at the current status of each in American society. They might see a few examples of complexity between ideal and practice. But have done with the preaching; make the stance clear. Then move on to the analysis of the ways societies and cultures function—the analysis that really constitutes the heart of humanities education and ultimately generates the kind of understanding people need to participate intelligently (and sometimes critically) in a democratic society.

Too much current school routine in the humanities, too much of the canonist approach, mixes knowledge goals in with specific values acquisition. Separating the processes would be more candid and no less effective. Whether a specific values course should be taught is debatable, for students might reject its authority as they now reject the preachy qualities of larger school programs—by not voting after years of being told how important citizen participation is, or by disliking minority races after years of hearing pious celebrations of racial harmony and progress. Whether we could, in major school districts, even agree on the values to be inculcated if faced frankly with the prospect is another issue. But some experiments might be worthwhile; one might be inserted, for example, into the freshman year of high school before the resumption of the principal analytical sequence. And the basic point is essential: although humanities courses cannot be value free—no courses can—they should concentrate on the values associated with cultural analysis, not with explicitly instilling "proper" political beliefs.

The relationship between genuine education in the humanities and democratic values needs to be given the same fresh examination we have applied to curricular goals more widely, in order to explain why a recast humanities program will truly serve democracy without preaching and without distorting humanities disciplines as sources of analytical understanding by mixing in morality plays. We have already granted the reasonableness of asking the humanities, along with other segments of the curriculum, about their role in a democratic polity. We now must show not only how the question can be answered, but also how it can be intelligently posed.

The first positive step in this reexamination, in turn, is to improve our grasp of how educational and political systems interrelate, now and under any imaginable reform agenda. It is the whole system, not a specific curriculum segment, that really counts. By viewing them as the only main sources of democratic inspiration, we have overloaded the humanities as well as confusing their particular educational purpose.

Alan Kennedy has suggested that the pedagogical task of defending democracy and Western values be shifted temporarily from the humanities disciplines to programs in biology.[10] The suggestion, although exaggerated, shows more than a glimmer of good sense, though it should not lead to neglect of the humanities' distinctive role in *analyzing* values in various ways, including comparison and assessment of causation and change. It remains true that all aspects of curricula and school programs, and not just humanities and social studies courses, convey a society's values—including its political values. Even nursery school structure can be revealing. Japanese nursery schools emphasize interaction among the children as peers, downgrading the independent power of the teacher. American nursery schools are more hierarchical, suggesting different views of authority and, of course, a lower valuation of peer cohesion. Later features of the system can be equally revealing. France emphasizes a meritocratic hierarchy in its school structure. Japan reinforces distinctive personal discipline by having each teacher assign individual preset goals to students at the beginning of each school year; the goals are posted and each student's progress is recurrently and publicly monitored in their light. The United States has sent powerful signals to students in recent decades by inflating grades and reducing the incidence of flunking as attention to emotional smoothness and avoidance of disruption overtook the more traditional achievement orientation.[11] We also send messages through school discipline systems that are not always harmonious with the values we profess to be teaching concerning freedom of opinion and democracy. And, as we are partially aware, we powerfully suggest values priorities with the unique place of sports in our educational programs.

The point is obvious. No amount of curricular emphasis in one set of school programs can rival the overall implications of school arrangements. Inculcation of democracy through education involves a wide range of considerations, some of which may not have been adequately pondered in the United States. Curricula besides the humanities also affect political outlook. Science classes have strong value content, though they unfortunately mask this with a pretense of complete objectivity. Sciences teach respect for certain kinds of data and methods. They teach an orderly outlook toward nature and, on the whole, a secular outlook as well. They can promote a view of knowledge as being massively subdivided, rather than as operating within a unified framework of assessable fundamental ideas. They can encourage a hierarchical respect for trained experts that may clash both with the more contentious atmosphere of nonscience classes and with some of the democratic values we teach in other respects.

Clearly, the humanities are not the only educational sector, curricular or structural, that warrants evaluation in terms of its contributions to political values. They have some vital special connections—partly through tradition and partly through their analytical concentration on social and cultural factors such as democracy and democratic thought—but they are part of a larger total institution. It is simply not realistic to look at the humanities as the program uniquely charged with values inculcation. If other elements of the educational system do not dovetail with the humanities, the effort will be futile, for students will discern the conflicts between preachment and practice and draw their own conclusions. If the various elements of the system are congruent, preachment from one particular sector will be unnecessary. In either case, it fatally constrains the service of humanities programs to see them as values enshriners rather than bases of inquiry.

Finally, of course, the structure of the humanities program itself may contradict its stated values goals. Students may be taught the importance of citizen participation or individual rights, but if they learn by passively memorizing constitutional passages, they will receive no useful stimulus. If in addition they are not given opportunities to analyze effective limitations on citizen participation—of the sort they readily encounter in life outside the school (and often inside as well)—they will further dissociate the stated message from any personal relevance.

The positive implications for democracy of the humanities program in education lie in its enhancement of the critical analysis of ideas and institutions. This is the major political thrust of the proposed new curriculum, eclipsing more elaborate agendas but effectively contributing to an active citizenry. Canonists may, of course, not only identify but also reject the political implications of humanities reform, which reduces detailed indoctrination and emphasis on the role of authority. Many radicals will fault the failure of the same reforms to fully embrace feminist or other agendas. The new curriculum does exhibit a less detailed political commitment, one tied less completely either to existing systems or to radical alternatives, than the humanities debates have featured of late. I have no intention, however, of denying its political import. The politics concern the goals of promoting individual thinking and argument and of basing group consensus on esteem for this critical process and its social utility.

Critical analysis does not require rejection of the political status quo, though of course that possibility remains open. It does require the ability to subject assumptions to the tests of argument, the capacity to grasp and ultimately to formulate interpretive problems as the basis for understanding and not merely parroting the values generated by our culture and the institutions within which we operate. The asking of intelligent questions is a central feature of some key phases of the Western political and intellectual tradition. The analytical experience imparts to students the essential ingredients of the Socratic method, and this lesson far exceeds the value of memorizing Socrates' name, or of narrating the revival of a critical tradition under Abelard or its enhancement by the early philosophers of the Enlightenment. It exceeds even the ability to recall the major articles of the Bill of Rights that protect rights of criticism through assurances of free speech and press—for these articles can be looked up as needed. Experience in diverse interpretation, the ability to formulate arguments, conceptualizing the relationships between cultural forms and political power—these are the intellectual habits a humanities program should hone; these are the intellectual habits essential to an alert citizenry in a democracy.

But the role of the humanities in democratic education is not limited to its basic analytical mission. Several major foci in the humanities sequences translate social and cultural analysis into fuller understanding of democracy and the issues surrounding it. Clearly applicable here are the basic organizing questions in American history courses. The earlier suggestion of a framework question that relates early political democracy to the equally striking American penchant for hierarchical economic structures offers one example of the integration of democratic concerns with relevant evaluations of ongoing tensions in the national experience. Discussions of the relationship between democratic values and the historical and contemporary patterns of minority groups obviously provide another linkage between analysis and a grasp of warts-and-all democratic functioning. A legal historian, for example, has argued that a study of "constitutional rights consciousness" offers a valuable means of integrating a mainstream political theme—the unusual salience of rights arguments in U.S. history, from the Constitution onward—with the diverse experience and interpretations of key groups who are seeking to use such arguments to their advantage but who are also encountering distinctive limitations given other constraints of American society. In this case, a dominant institution—the Constitutional framework—and social diversity are wedded not through some rosy, simplified paradigm of consensus, but through a coherent set of analytical questions.[12]

The comparative approach offers another set of opportunities. Current humanities programs, supported by the wider culture, often convince students that American democracy is uniquely blessed, a conviction that, interestingly enough, may or may not persuade them that the system is worth much attention from them. A more analytical framework turns this implicit assertion into a question: What distinctive features have marked American democracy, for good and for ill, and with what contemporary results? Or, a more general question from a world history program might be: What conditions permit societies to build and sustain democracies? Why are some cultures particularly resistant to democracy in the modern world? Questions of this sort should not monopolize a comparative list, for other issues less based on American criteria must be applied to the values in other civilizations. The questions must be phrased with enough subtlety that both positive and negative features of nondemocratic traditions can be grasped—which is not the same thing as attacking American democracy through comparative example. Nevertheless, exploring the causes and results of democratic systems and their attendant strengths and vulnerabilities as part of a comparative history agenda provides a legitimate set of analytical questions; it simultaneously sustains the process whereby we acquire an understanding of this crucial political system, as opposed to mere exposure to educational cheerleading or memorization of story lines linked to the building of the system.

New topical range is a third ingredient of the innovative humanities program relevant to education for democracy. Political systems do not function in vacuums. They must be grasped as they interact with key groups in the population and as they relate to a variety of activities. Relationships between authoritarian family structures and political arrangements form one such link. Leisure offerings designed to discipline or distract the population in a political sense form another. In dealing with contemporary culture, attention to the impact of new media on the functioning of politics offers a vital perspective that ties in a number of humanities and social science disciplines. The list need not be exhaustive, and no one course sequence need explore the whole range. The point is that, along with their tendency to stress political facts over thought-provoking concepts, too many education-for-democracy courses now teach the political story in an artificial isolation that further limits analytical potential and effective understanding. An exploration of the ways in which the actual impact of laws and constitutions may differ from their framers' presumed intentions translates the relevance of wider topical case studies into this area directly. Attention to issues in contemporary society that relate to previous patterns is an even more obvious topical extension essential in allowing students to think constructively about political systems.

Finally, the examination of issues in cultural construction furthers the kinds of analysis relevant to democracy. Democracy itself embraces a changing set of cultural constructs. Its meaning varies depending on time, place, and cultural group. The relationship between democracy and other cultural constructions highlights both tensions and consistencies. The example of science has already been evoked; humanities sequences, at least by the college level, should help students understand the cultural assumptions underlying modern science and scientific claims of expertise. Humanities perspectives need not debunk or attack, but they should help problematize beliefs that many students currently are urged to take for granted. The questioning process, in turn, facilitates student understanding of some of the dilemmas involved in simultaneously embracing the science-blessed authority of experts and the political potential of ordinary people. Such dilemmas are not only important in American democracy today but were operative in earlier historical passages such as the Jacksonian combination of democratic agitation and disdain for the professional claims of medical doctors.[13] At an earlier level, students can be exposed to the relationship between nationalism and democracy as two often overlapping but not identical constructs, both of which demand analysis in modern culture.

The strengths of an effective humanities program need not be packaged solely in terms of exploring democracy. They certainly differ from traditional educational aims by urging open-ended analysis over uncritical praise, sheer memorization of factual materials presumably sacred to the democratic tradition, and narrow concentration on political themes alone. Nevertheless, the challenge of relating the appropriate directions of humanities education to the legitimate needs of a democratic society need not be evaded. The goals of the new humanities do not neglect democracy; they do not derive from a subversive attack on its American version, from a commitment to any particular critical vantage point, or from an attempt to overwhelm democratic convictions through immersion in a set of randomly relative values. The new humanities goals do urge us to teach students about the problems as well as the strengths of democracy, about comparative drawbacks as well as advantages, and about cultural claims versus real reception, through case studies and contemporary analysis. They encourage the development of an ability to handle interpretive questions relating to democracy rather than stressing the testable capacity to reproduce facts about a particular set of institutions. They push for real exposure to diverse interpretations, including critical interpretations about democracy and its functioning. They work toward an ability to marshal facts and identify argument, so that democracy gains real meaning as one of the key systems of modern life.

New scholarship in the humanities improves the questions we can ask about how democracy emerges and how it works. Current efforts to rebuild a synthesis between political and social inquiry—to "bring the state back in"—and to deal with relationships among cultural assumptions, including specifically political values, provide a direct backdrop to the recasting of education for democracy in the humanities. These efforts cannot stand alone. Other aspects of the educational system—even the biology program—must remain relevant to the overall political impact of American schooling. But the humanities, in the new scenario, do not bow out; rather, they improve their contributions by focusing on building the capacity for critical understanding.

Will the new orientation provide a sufficiently common culture for democracy to operate? One of the concerns recently raised about the New York State social studies report centers around the need to use schools to disseminate shared beliefs in an otherwise diverse society. "It is politically and intellectually unwise for us to attack the traditions, customs and values which attracted immigrants to these shores in the first place," says historian Kenneth Jackson (somewhat simplifying immigrant history in the process). Arthur Schlesinger, Jr., joins in with objections to magnifying "ethnic and racial themes at the expense of the unifying ideals that precariously hold our highly differentiated society together." Jackson, warming to the task, mutters about the ethnically based collapse of Yugoslavia, a fate that may befall us as well if we fail to highlight mainstream culture. Other critics fear that undue emphasis on conflicting interpretation will so erode belief that, again, our society will fall apart.[14]

These are not petty concerns. Societies do need some connecting beliefs to establish a workable degree of unity; indeed, an interesting and relevant task for humanities curricula involves exploring what kinds of beliefs have held various societies together, including our own past and present societies. Do modern industrial societies require more active "glue" than agricultural civilizations, beyond having new technical means for pounding home preachments of unity? The new humanities curriculum does not encourage blanket relativism as a final goal. Rather, it trains students to understand disagreement without losing the ability to reach conclusions and mount arguments. It can in this sense support, rather than undermine, convictions. It does not argue that no unifying threads have held the peoples of our society together, but instead urges us to assess these unifying threads as a way of linking a grasp of essential diversities and a recognition of a certain amount of national coherence into a manageable analytical package. This aspect of the new humanities goals departs from some of the recent pleas for celebrations of diversity for group identity purposes, though it does not prevent some work in this direction as well. Further, the new curriculum clearly supports certain beliefs in the value of humanistic inquiry, in the importance of critical analysis, and in the vitality of conflicting interpretation. These beliefs have new features that reflect advances in humanities scholarship, but they are not new to the American tradition.

Like the argument for democratic education, then, the pleas for some common educational culture (quite apart from shared programs in science; again, humanities are not the whole show) can be met, albeit in distinctive ways, through the new curricular programs. They need not be evaded, for it would be educationally unsound and politically unwise to do so. The distinctiveness must be delineated; concern for common culture must not override a thorough rethinking of the mainstream emphases that have survived so durably in educational routines to date. Past uses of common culture form valid items for historical and literary analysis, along with larger interpretive frameworks deriving from the consensus tradition. Part of our history is colored by the long-standing effort to use education to promote harmony, and this effort can be studied and debated in itself. Asserted common culture does not tell the whole story, however, even when approached in an analytical rather than hagiographic vein. Too much emphasis on it risks promoting clearly erroneous past beliefs about the United States as a consensus society—and error is not a sound basis for reliable political unity.

Multiculturalism aside, our knowledge of comparative history and contemporary patterns of violence in the United States—along with our record high levels of incarceration—faults the consensus approach except as it represents an interesting effort at myth-making.[15] Portraying the political values and institutions transmitted from England as if they were blithely accepted by all comers, regardless of their own native cultures and their own power positions in the new land, simply gives a false historical picture. It risks disillusioning the most marginal students in our polity, those who can readily see the irrelevance of a humanities program that presumes to portray national values and claims at odds with their own experience. The problems we face as a society do not include a present danger of such intense ethnic polarization that we need to define our educational system in terms of crisis prevention; and if we should reach a Yugoslavian pass, it is unlikely that educational defensiveness would save us.

Political concerns vary, to be sure. In my own view, the current need to reexamine nationalist arrogance is far more compelling than the promotion of a monolithic democratic vision. We err more egregiously when we mistake our position in the world than when we dispute our democratic values at home, at least at the present moment. Others have identified excessive individualism as a politically relevant target for educational attention. The desirability of building capacities for critical analysis overrides particular values agendas, however. It certainly supersedes the scare tactics about group diversities currently rending the national fabric.

Conclusion

We need to be willing to take real risks in our humanities programs, to improve student abilities to analyze social and cultural processes. We must take the risk of experimentation in new testing methods and new approaches to factual data that move away from sterile coverage. We need to prompt students themselves to take risks in dealing with conflicting interpretations without losing the capacity to select, combine, and argue. We need to push them to riskier engagements with conceptual problems that are vital to imposing some meaning on social and cultural developments, rather than viewing the humanities arena as a location for passive acquisition of accepted values and established facts. In advance of the implementation of such a program, it is impossible to prove that the results, by encouraging a more effective grasp of history and a critical approach to cultural issues, will be healthier for our democracy than those generated by current programs. The promise is there, however, as the humanities move toward habits of active inquiry and expanding arenas of knowledge that are as relevant to effective citizenship and intelligently shared values as to successful schooling.

The humanities remain in turmoil. Demands from newly active political constituencies complicate settled routines. Conservative counterattacks claim that we have shortchanged our students by denying them an adequate grasp of the Western classics. It is clearly time for a new approach, at least as demanding but potentially liberating as well, that blends what we teach in the humanities with what the humanities disciplines are helping us learn about society and culture. It is in this respect that our students are too often shortchanged by being deprived of the insights, factual range, and analytical habits that await curricular translation from scholarship to the classroom.

When we watch younger children learn new concepts that explain to them how some previously mysterious aspect of their social environment works, the wonder and excitement of discovery are clearly visible. These qualities cannot be preserved unaltered through the experience of further schooling and the buffetings of puberty. They need not be forever lost, however. Inspiring teachers can elicit them again in high school or college, bringing some students to a social or cultural awareness that genuinely moves them. The challenge is to build curricula to match, making inspirational teaching easier and even more ordinary teaching periodically inspiring to many. Humanistic research, blazing new paths in recent decades, can clear the way by rekindling the joys of discovery. From these discoveries come the new tools, the analytical methods and probing theories, that can reach for greater meaning and renewed enthusiasm in the classroom. The key achievements, and the excitement, are transferable to feasible principles in curriculum design. Our field is the human experience, our task the teaching of some of the central meanings and intriguing issues in this experience.

This is a precious moment in humanities education. The need for greater vitality is obvious; virtually every entrenched camp agrees. The importance of the humanities disciplines, in a moment created by powerful new research and a national confusion of purpose, has won widespread acknowledgment. We have not witnessed a comparable moment since the late 1960s, when a lack of adequate vision and a lack of educational courage aborted most reform attempts.[16] The urgency is greater now, a generation of student apathy later. The opportunities are greater as well, for the domain of humanistic scholarship has expanded and clarified.

Explorations of culture and society do not stand still; fundamental new research directions have been staked out. The demands on humanities teaching change with new social complexities. Student capacities need to be constructively exercised. The context is ripe for a new start on the daily tasks of teaching.

NOTES

Preface

1. Arthur M. Schlesinger, Jr., *The Disuniting of America* (New York, 1992)—a fairly limited compromise statement that largely defends the European heritage; Partisan Review, *The Changing Culture of the University* (Boston, 1991); Paul Berman, ed., *Debating P.C.: The Controversy over Political Correctness on College Campuses* (New York, 1992); Darryl Gless and Barbara H. Smith, eds., *The Politics of Liberal Education* (Durham, N.C., 1991). For an important recent effort to skate between traditionalism and radicalism in English, see David Bromwich, *Politics by Other Means: Higher Education and Group Thinking* (New Haven, Conn., 1992).

2. Arthur M. Melzer, "Tolerance 101: A Truce in the P.C. Wars," *New Republic*, July 1, 1991, pp. 10–12.

Introduction

1. *Newsweek*, December 24, 1990, pp. 48–56. For a fuller exploration, see Dinesh D'Souza, "Illiberal Education," *Atlantic Monthly*, March 1991, pp. 51–79.

2. It is important to note that NEH funding for social history did not disappear, though for collective projects (as opposed to individual research) it dropped considerably. Lynne Cheney has been less fiercely anti-innovation than her predecessor, but the commitment to funding programs that deal with "the canon" and the fascination with classic texts—*texts* being the dominant buzzword for NEH orthodoxy—has largely persisted.

3. Allan Bloom, *The Closing of the American Mind: How Higher Education Has Failed Democracy and Impoverished the Souls of Today's Students* (New York, 1987); E. D. Hirsch, Jr., *Cultural Literacy: What Every American Needs to Know* (Boston, 1987); Roger Kimball, *Tenured Radicals: How Politics Has Corrupted Our Higher Education* (New York, 1990).

4. Gertrude Himmelfarb, *The New History and the Old: Critical Essays and Reappraisals* (Cambridge, Mass., 1987).

5. Michael Frisch, *A Shared Authority: Essays on the Craft and Meaning of Oral and Public History* (Albany, 1990).

6. I deliberately do not worry in these pages about careful use of the term

235

social studies, which is commonly substituted for history and the other social sciences as a generic label for programs in the middle schools and high schools. The social studies movement, launched in the 1930s, does differentiate its goals from the constituent academic disciplines, often stressing additional value components clearly relevant to the present inquiry. Critics of social studies emphases have also raised points germane to this discussion. See Diane Ravitch, "The Decline and Fall of Teaching History," *New York Times Magazine*, November 17, 1985, sec. 6.

Because the social studies–history debate is well established—the Bradley Commission report also takes it up—but also perhaps slightly dated, I thought it best to avoid constant terminological apologies and the resultant complexity in labeling. The fact that I am talking about goals in both schools and colleges—as programs in the humanities and related social sciences link across institutional levels—further excuses some neglect of the social studies tag. The substance of the following discussion, however, is as relevant to social studies programs as it is to work in history, anthropology, literature, and so on. I hope that the substance can be engaged even though diverse terminology is not always given its due.

7. Paul Gagnon and the Bradley Commission on History in Schools, eds., *Historical Literacy: The Case for History in American Education* (New York, 1989).

8. Ibid.

9. For good statements to this end, see Darryl Gless and Barbara H. Smith, eds., *The Politics of Liberal Education* (Durham, N.C., 1990).

10. See the statement by a group of historians headed by Diane Ravitch and Arthur Schlesinger, Jr., *Newsday* (June 29, 1990); Jim Sleeper, *The Closest of Strangers: Liberalism and the Politics of Race in New York* (New York, 1990).

11. John D. and Catherine T. MacArthur Foundation and Pew Charitable Trusts, award for new student assessment systems, December 1990. The emphasis here will be on performance examinations, long-term problem-solving projects, and extended portfolios encompassing a variety of work products. The intention is to move away from single, standardized examinations without sacrificing reliable evaluations of performance.

12. Elizabeth Fox-Genovese, *Feminism Without Illusions: A Critique of Individualism* (Chapel Hill, N.C., 1991) pp. 190–91. See also Peter Seixas, "Parallel Crises: History and the Social Studies Curriculum," paper delivered at the American Educational Research Association meeting, Chicago, 1991; Donna L. Van Raaphorst, "Teaching History: Creating an Educational Environment for All Learners." I am grateful to Seixas and Van Raaphorst for sharing their work-in-progress. On the literature side, see David Bromwich, *Politics by Other Means: Higher Education and Group Thinking* (New Haven, Conn., 1992).

13. On the literacy claim, see Carl F. Kaestle et al., *Literacy in the United States: Readers and Reading since 1880* (New Haven, Conn., 1991). This most recent study, echoing previous findings, suggests a very slight dip in literacy in the early 1970s, but not since. Yet the capital made by claims of literacy decline has been immense, despite its factual inaccuracy. The whole

literacy debate suggests the tendency to idealize past achievements and so wrongly to base arguments about present needs. The same may well be true in humanities beyond the basic skills levels. I point this out not to argue against change now, but only to put forward a more accurate and farsighted definition of the basis for change.

14. Chester E. Finn, Jr., *We Must Take Charge: Our Schools and Our Future* (New York, 1991).

Chapter One

1. Advisory Panel on the Scholastic Aptitude Test Score Decline [Willard Wirtz, chair, et. al.], *On Further Examination: Report of the Advisory Panel on the Scholastic Aptitude Test Score Decline* (New York, 1977); Willard Wirtz, *What Shall We Do about Declining Test Scores?* (Washington, D.C., 1978).

2. Arnold Heidenheimer, "The Politics of Public Education, Health, and Welfare in the U.S.A. and Western Europe: How Growth and Reform Potentials Have Differed," *British Journal of Political Science* 3 (1973): 315–40.

3. Joan W. Scott, "The Campaign against Political Correctness: What's Really at Stake," *Change* 23 (1991): 30–43.

4. See, in this regard, Roger Kimball, *Tenured Radicals: How Politics Has Corrupted Our Higher Education* (New York, 1990); Dinesh D'Souza, "Illiberal Education," *Atlantic Monthly*, March 1991, pp. 51–79.

5. Carolyn J. Mooney, "As Curricular Reform Continues, Its Scope and Effectiveness Are Questioned," *Chronicle of Higher Education*, January 8, 1992, pp. 15, 18. A six-year debate at the University of Miami, for example, yielded an increase in required writing courses—and that's all. A requirement in a non-Western culture was discussed but not adopted. To be sure, other campuses have moved toward greater change, but few, if any, have become unrecognizable by prior humanities standards.

6. Again, note that several widely received claims about deterioration from past levels are probably wrong, as historians have shown. Literacy achievements, for example, may demand attention, but not because they have worsened in the past two decades—for they have not. Standards, however, and perhaps real societal needs, have indeed changed. The same holds for several of the declension models in humanistic subjects. See Carl F. Kaestle et al., *Literacy in the United States: Readers and Reading since 1880* (New Haven, Conn., 1991).

7. This is not necessarily true, despite common belief, for we are also more accustomed to change than our forebears who confronted, say, the initial industrial revolution or the stresses of enslavement or immigration. This is an interesting analytical problem to discuss with students—though not a clearly resolvable one.

8. C. P. Snow, *The Two Cultures; and, A Second Look: An Expanded Version of "The Two Cultures and the Scientific Revolution"* (New York, 1963).

9. I do not pretend to review these possibilities here, but they certainly

carry some potential in advancing less routine kinds of evaluation in the humanities. See Roger Schrank, *Tell Me a Story* (New York, 1990); Ray W. Karras, "A Multidimensional Multiple-Choice Testing," *Perspectives* 23 (February 1984): 3–5, and "Let's Improve the Multiple-Choice Test," *Magazine of History* 6, no. 1 (Summer 1991): 8–9, 43.

10. Daniel P. Resnick, "Educational Policy and the Applied Historian: Testing, Competency, and Standards," *Journal of Social History* 14 (1981): 539–59.

11. See the report on the National History Standards Project, *Education Week*, January 9, 1992, p. 25. Preliminary signals from the project were at best mixed. A solid world history commitment was ventured over the more conventional Western civilization approach; but world history risked being defined in terms of survey knowledge, with standards focusing on memorized content, not analytical understanding. There has been some rethinking of the most literal conservative stance, but the basic goals remain dishearteningly familiar. Historian-consultants almost uniformly urge more fundamental reorientation, but it is not clear that their voices will be heard. By late 1992, the best news about the project was that it was delayed by internal disputes, raising the hope that less detailed but more appropriate guidelines could be considered at last. For another, more chastening, indication, however, see the National Center for History in the Schools, *National History Standards Project: Progress Report and Sample Standards, November 1992* (Los Angeles, 1992). The American history materials presented in this report emphasize detailed factual coverage above all else, including some intricacies from the War of 1812; analysis is low-level and entirely geared to prior memorization. Not, in my judgment, a happy signal.

Chapter Two

1. Compare, for example, the (largely sensible) diagnostic comments in Cheney's *Tyrannical Machines: A Report on Educational Practices Gone Wrong and Our Best Hopes for Setting Them Right* (Washington, D.C., 1990), with her more stilted *50 Hours: A Core Curriculum for College Students* (Washington, D.C., 1989).

2. Susanna Dawson, *Charlotte Temple* (Philadelphia, Pa., 1991); see Carroll Smith-Rosenberg, "Domesticating 'Virtue': Coquettes and Revolutionaries in Young America," in Elaine Scarry, ed., *Literature and the Body: Essays on Population and Persons* (Baltimore, Md., 1988), pp. 160–89.

3. For a useful summary with the additional merit of linking with the concerns of history, see Joseph Kelly and Timothy Kelly, "Searching the Dark Alley: New Historicism and Social History," *Journal of Social History* 25 (1992): 677–94; see also Richard Levin, "Unthinkable Thoughts in the New Historicizing of English Renaissance Drama," *New Literary History* 21 (1990): esp. 443; and Carolyn Porter, "Are We Being Historical Yet?," *South Atlantic Quarterly* 87 (1988): 743–86.

4. James B. Gardner and George Rollie Adams, eds., *Ordinary People and Everyday Life: Perspectives on the New Social History* (Nashville, Tenn., 1983); for a general overview in relation to the conventional disci-

pline, see Peter Novick, *That Noble Dream: The "Objectivity Question" and the American Historical Profession* (New York, 1988). Other useful definitions are found in Peter N. Stearns, ed., *Expanding the Past* (New York, 1988), and Olivier Zunz, ed., *Reliving the Past: The Worlds of Social History* (Chapel Hill, N.C., 1985).

5. See, for example, John Smail, "Manufacturer or Artisan: The Relationship between Economic and Cultural Change in the Early Stages of Eighteenth-Century Industrialization," *Journal of Social History* 25 (1992): 791–814; Peter N. Stearns, *The Industrial Revolution in World History* (Boulder, Colo., 1993).

6. Richard Roberts, "Teaching Non-Western History in the United States," paper presented at the How We Learn History Conference, Chapel Hill, North Carolina, April 1991.

7. For radical critiques of social history, see Elizabeth Fox-Genovese and Eugene D. Genovese, "The Political Uses of Social History: A Marxian Perspective," in Stearns, ed., *Expanding the Past*, pp. 17–34; Tony Judt, "'A Clown in Regal Purple': Social History and the Historian," *History Workshop* (1979): 66–94.

8. Charles Tilly, *Big Structures, Large Processes, Huge Comparisons* (New York, 1984).

9. Theda Skocpol, "Bringing the State Back In," in Peter B. Evans, Dietrick Rueschemeyer, and Theda Skocpol, eds., *Bringing the State Back In* (Cambridge, 1985).

10. Roger Chartier, "Intellectual History or Sociocultural History?: The French Trajectories," in Dominick LaCapra and Steven Kaplan, eds., *Modern European Intellectual History* (Ithaca, N.Y., 1982), pp. 13–46; Robert Darnton, "Intellectual and Cultural History," in Michael Kammen, ed., *The Past Before Us* (Ithaca, N.Y., 1980), pp. 327–54; James A. Henretta, "Social History as Lived and Written," *American Historical Review* 84 (1979): 1293–1333; Patrick H. Hutton, "The History of Mentalities: The New Map of Cultural History," *History and Theory* 20 (1981): 237–59.

11. Mark C. Carnes and Clyde Griffen, eds., *Meanings for Manhood: Construction of Masculinity in Victorian America* (Chicago, 1990).

12. The question of historical narrative, or the story-telling mode in its most explicit "once upon a time" form, has been much debated in the context of the increasing use of different, more explicitly analytical forms of historical presentation. Museum experts have displayed great ingenuity in using stories, not as ends in themselves, but to convey larger messages. The subject is sometimes presented grumpily, as part of a lament about history's sad decline (see Simon Schama, "Clio Has a Problem," *New York Times Magazine*, September 8, 1991). But new uses of narrative also can be constructively discussed by scholars open to diverse modes of prose in the interests of greater historical understanding (see Lawrence Stone, *Past and Present* [London, 1987]). See also Thomas Holt, *Thinking Historically: Narrative, Imagination, and Understanding* (New York, 1990), for one of the most intelligent recent statements. The subject remains open and warrants continued experimentation, even as agreement on analytical goals expands.

Chapter Three

1. Joan W. Scott, "The Campaign against Political Correctness: What's Really at Stake," *Change* 23 (1991): 30–43.

2. James B. Gardner and George Rollie Adams, eds., *Ordinary People and Everyday Life: Perspectives on the New Social History* (Nashville, Tenn., 1983).

3. Solid texts in American history that integrate new historical materials with some familiar landmarks include Gary Nash, Julie Jeffrey, et al., *The American People: Creating a Nation and a Society* (New York, 1986); Mary Beth Norton et al., *A People and a Nation: A History of the United States* (New York, 1987); James K. Martin et al., *America and Its People* (New York, 1989).

The incorporation of social history into standard teaching implements is a development of great promise for the future, even as it solidifies beneath the current fires of debate. Some observers, trying to fuel the debate, have claimed that these innovations have directly contributed to the decline of student learning in the humanities; this is a central contention in Gertrude Himmelfarb, *The New History and the Old: Critical Essays and Reappraisals* (Cambridge, Mass., 1987), and we must take it up subsequently. Improvements in the history texts are far too recent to have had such an impact, and, as I noted earlier, it is not clear that student learning has declined in any event. Problems there may be in the effectiveness of history teaching, but curricular innovation is demonstrably not involved—at least to date.

4. College Entrance Examination Board, *Academic Preparation in Social Studies* (New York, 1986); College Entrance Examination Board, *Academic Preparation for College* (New York, 1983), pp. 25–27.

5. Linda Rosenzweig, "Urban Life and World History: Can Social History Bridge the Gap?," *Social Education* 46 (1982): 186–90.

6. Robert Proctor, *Education's Great Amnesia: Reconsidering the Humanities from Petrarch to Freud* (Bloomington, Ind., 1988).

7. Roger Kimball, *Tenured Radicals: How Politics Has Corrupted Our Higher Education* (New York, 1990).

8. Charles Krauthammer, editorial, *Pittsburgh Post-Gazette*, December 27, 1990.

9. John Searle, "The Storm Over the University," *New York Review of Books*, December 6, 1990, pp. 34–42.

10. New-style historians are beginning to know a lot about this process, too. See Eric Hobsbawm and Terrance Ranger, eds., *The Invention of Tradition* (Cambridge, 1984).

11. Northrop Frye, *Anatomy of Criticism* (Princeton, N.J., 1957).

12. Lynne V. Cheney, *Tyrannical Machines: A Report on Educational Practices Gone Wrong and Our Best Hopes for Setting Them Right* (Washington, D.C., 1990).

13. There are, to be sure, real differences between great books courses and Western civilization offerings in that the latter offer a wider variety of vantagepoints. However, the tendency in the Western civ lexicon to emphasize standard intellectual history and a sense of ongoing political traditions

links these courses, if both loosely and critically, to a more narrowly canon-ical tradition. The specific links between great books endeavors and a hal-lowed Western civ course at the University of Chicago, stemming from the Hutchins era, point in the same direction.

14. Lawrence Levine, *High Brow, Low Brow: The Emergence of Cultur-al Hierarchy in America* (Cambridge, Mass., 1988).

15. Searle, "Storm," pp. 41–42.

16. Lynne V. Cheney, *50 Hours: A Core Curriculum for College Students* (Washington, D.C., 1989).

17. On the American penchant for seeking and using tests, not just to evaluate students, but as quality-control devices, see Daniel P. Resnick, "Ed-ucational Policy and the Applied Historian: Testing, Competency, and Stan-dards," *Journal of Social History* 14 (1981): 539–59.

18. Diane Ravitch and Chester E. Finn, *What Do Our 17-Year-Olds Know?: A Report on the First National Assessment of History and Litera-ture* (New York, 1987).

19. Dinesh D'Souza, "Illiberal Education," *Atlantic Monthly*, March 1991, pp. 51–79.

20. E. D. Hirsch, Jr., *Cultural Literacy: What Every American Needs to Know* (Boston, 1987); John Garraty, *One Thousand and One Things Everyone Should Know about American History* (New York, 1989).

21. For other examples of past ignorance, oddly downplayed by a focus on contemporary miscreance, see Diane Ravitch, "The Decline and Fall of Teaching History," *New York Times Magazine*, November 17, 1985, sec. 6.

Chapter Four

1. Barbara Herrnstein Smith, "Cultural Literacy: Hirsch, Literacy, and the 'National Culture,'" in Darryl L. Gless and Barbara H. Smith, eds., *The Politics of Liberal Education* (Durham, N.C., 1990), pp. 69–88; see also Roger Kimball, *Tenured Radicals: How Politics Has Corrupted Our High-er Education* (New York, 1990).

2. For one of the vigorous Afrocentric statements, see Molefi K. Asante, *Afrocentricity: The Theory of Social Change*, 2d ed. (New York, 1990), and also Asante's essay in Paul Berman, ed., *Debating P.C.: The Controversy over Political Correctness on College Campuses* (New York, 1992). On multiculturalism more generally, see also Carl Grant and Mary L. Gomez, *Campus and Classroom: Making Schooling Multicultural* (Boulder, Colo., 1993).

3. George L. Levine, ed., *Speaking for the Humanities* (New York, 1989).

4. Typical post-structuralist asides can include invocations of such move-ments as "anti-racism, ecological, anti-nuclear, non-heterosexual discours-es"—certainly a handful (see Mark Poster, "Poststructuralism and Histori-cal Literacy," paper presented at the Social Science History Association annual conference, Minneapolis, Minn., October 21, 1990). For a some-what similar deconstructionist tweak that infuriated many social historians who were not themselves canonists, see Elizabeth A. Smith and Ellen Somekawa, "Theorizing the Writing of History: Or, 'I Can't Think Why It

Should Be So Dull, for a Great Deal of It Must Be Invention,'" *Journal of Social History* 22 (1988): 149–61. For a more serious debate over post-structuralism as applied to intellectual history, see John E. Toews, "Intellectual History after the Linguistic Turn: The Autonomy of Meaning and the Irreducibility of Experience," *American Historical Review* 92 (1987): 879–907; and the response by Richard Harvey Brown, "Positivism, Relativism, and Narrative in the Logic of the Historical Sciences," pp. 908–20. See also Dominick LaCapra, *Rethinking Intellectual History: Texts, Contexts, Language* (Ithaca, N.Y., 1983); and Mark Poster, *Foucault, Marxism, and History: Mode of Production versus Mode of Information* (Cambridge, 1984).

5. Bryan D. Palmer, *Descent into Discourse: The Reification of Language and the Writing of Social History* (Philadelphia, Pa., 1990), an "old-fashioned" social history response to deconstructionist history. Another attack, heavily laced with confidence in rationality, is Brigitte Berger's essay, "The Idea of the University," in *Partisan Review* 58 (1991): 315–28.

6. Caleb Nelson, "Harvard's Hollow Core," *Atlantic Monthly*, September 1990, pp. 70–80.

7. The political quality of canonism is vigorously summarized in Joan W. Scott, "The Campaign against Political Correctness: What's Really at Stake," *Change* 23 (1991): 30–43.

8. Nathan Glazer, "In Defense of Multiculturalism," *New Republic*, September 2, 1991, pp. 18–22.

9. Joan W. Scott, *Gender and the Politics of History* (New York, 1988).

10. John Bodner, Roger Simon, and Michael Weber, *Lives of Their Own: Blacks, Italians, and Poles in Pittsburgh, 1900–1960* (Urbana, Ill., 1980); Joe W. Trotter, ed., *The Great Migration in Historical Perspective* (Bloomington, Ind., 1991).

11. Asante, *Afrocentricity*; Martin Bernal, *Black Athena*, 2 vols. (New Brunswick, N.J., 1987–91).

12. Arthur M. Melzer, "Tolerance 101: A Truce in the P.C. Wars," *New Republic*, July 1, 1991, pp. 10–12; for a characteristic, borderline-disingenuous statement on multiculturalism from a canonist, see Diane Ravitch, "Multiculturalism: E Pluribus Plures," *American Scholar* (Summer 1990): 339–47.

Chapter Five

1. Ernest L. Boyer, *Scholarship Reconsidered: Priorities of the Professoriate* (Princeton, N.J., 1990), esp. pp. 18, 23.

2. Lynne V. Cheney, *Tyrannical Machines: A Report on Educational Practices Gone Wrong and Our Best Hopes for Setting Them Right* (Washington, D.C., 1990); Diane Ravitch, *The Troubled Crusade: American Education, 1945–1980* (New York, 1983).

3. David Thelen, "Memory and American History," *Journal of American History* 75 (1989): 1117–29; Michael Frisch, "American History and the Structures of Collective Memory: A Modest Exercise in Empirical Iconog-

raphy," *Journal of American History* 75 (1989): 1130–55. See also William Greider, "Bloom and Doom," *Rolling Stone*, October 8, 1987, pp. 39–40; Jerry Herron, *Universities and the Myth of Cultural Decline* (Detroit, Mich., 1988).

4. Susan Ferraro, "You Must Remember This," *New York Times*, April 9, 1989, Education Life, p. 34.

5. See Introduction, above. On the growing and constructive participation of non-Western specialists, long content with narrow area-studies courses, see Richard Roberts, "Teaching Non-Western History in the United States," paper presented at the How We Learn History Conference, Chapel Hill, North Carolina, April 1991. Roberts describes a new Stanford offering that compares Mexico, Nigeria, and China as historical case studies. Several Africanists are not only raising important questions about the analytical categories suitable for teaching non-Western history, but proposing viable, even exciting, solutions. See also Kevin Reilly, ed., *World History: Selected Course Outlines and Reading Lists* (New York, 1991).

6. I have no intention here of joining a blame-the-teacher campaign. Limited training in substantive subject areas—the fields of history, literary analysis, and so on—helps explain teachers' frequent reliance on routine materials; even with modest recent improvements, many high school history teachers have had at most one or two college-level courses in the subject they teach. Increased class size (a problem in college-level humanities courses as well as the lower schools) and a host of additional demands of discipline contribute as well. These structural limitations must be addressed, as humanist educators of various sorts are urging even now. The purpose of this chapter is not to assign blame for current problems but to encourage an appropriate and imaginative framework for curricular improvements along with—or, if necessary, even aside from—reforms in teacher training, classroom burdens, and the like.

7. In the approach to facts in terms of their use rather than as ends in themselves, due attention must be given to students' learning capacity. Educational theory preaches the distinction between fact learning, based on "concrete operational thinking," and higher-level analytical skills. Students must at some stages simply learn facts, and they must have some facts, initially taught without much additional goad, simply to continue learning—they must have some sense, for example, of what a government is. Obviously, the plea for reorientation must not ignore practical needs and limitations. Even here, however, some caution is essential. Many teachers have been trapped by their marriage to Benjamin S. Bloom's *Taxonomy of Educational Objectives: The Classification of Educational Goals* (New York, 1956); they think that students have more rigidly demarcated abilities than is in fact the case. Even aside from this misperception, initial recognition that the analytical skills of young students will be limited too often leads to a failure to challenge not only these students but older ones as well. The concrete operational mindset hardens—as concrete is wont to do.

8. For examples of work on thinking skills that skirts the boundaries of contentlessness, see Fred M. Newmann, "A Test of Higher-Order Thinking

in Social Studies," *Social Education* 54 (October 1990): 369–73; see also Newmann, "Promoting Higher Order Thinking in Social Studies," *Theory and Research in Social Education* 19 (1991): 324–39.

9. Peter Seixas, "Parallel Crises: History and the Social Studies Curriculum," paper delivered at the American Educational Research Association meeting, Chicago, 1991, p. 11; Alan Singer, "Multicultural Education Is Good Education—but It Can't Perform Miracles," *Perspectives* 29 (December 1990): 14–16; Diane Ravitch and Arthur Schlesinger, Jr., "Statement of the Committee of Scholars in Defense of History," *Perspectives* 29 (October 1990): 15.

10. Bradley Commission on History in the Schools, *Building a History Curriculum* (Westlake, Ohio, 1988).

11. Paul Gagnon, "Multicultural and Civic Education: Can They Live Together?," *Basic Education* 35 (1991): 3–5.

12. As we return to proposals for real rethinking, rather than tinkering, the obvious should be noted: Many scholars and teachers have been working constructively toward precisely this end, clearly talking about effective new curricula rather than formulaic mixtures of new and old. See, for example, Organization of American Historians, *Restoring Women to History*, rev. ed. (Bloomington, Ind., 1990), which discusses the preliminary integration of a vital new subject area into the standard survey course; Mary Kay Thompson Tetreault, ed., "Women, Gender, and the Social Studies," *Social Education* 51, no. 3 (March 1987): 170–80. See also the several survey texts mentioned above in chap. 4, note 3; for Western civ, see Constance Bouchard and Peter N. Stearns, *Life and Society in the West*, 2 vols. (San Diego, Calif., 1988); and, among the many exciting efforts at real integration in world history, see Ross Dunn, "History for a Democratic Society: The Work of All the People," in Paul Gagnon and the Bradley Commission on History in Schools, eds., *Historical Literacy: The Case for History in American Education* (New York, 1989), pp. 216–33.

Chapter Six

1. On teaching methods in relations to facts, see James W. Davidson and Mark H. Lytle, *After the Fact: The Art of Historical Detection*, 2 vols. (New York, 1985).

2. Thomas Holt, *Thinking Historically: Narrative, Imagination, and Understanding* (New York, 1990), p. 13. For further discussion of the woeful lack of analytical awareness in much social studies teaching, see John Goodlad, *School, Curriculum, and the Individual* (Boston, 1966).

3. Suzanne M. Wilson and Samuel S. Wineburg, "Using Performance-Based Exercises to Assess the Knowledge of History Teachers," paper delivered at the American Educational Research Association meeting, Chicago, 1991, p. 42.

4. Stanley Hoffmann, "Fragments Floating in the Here and Now," *Daedalus* 117 (1988): 371–408.

5. Catherine A. Lutz, *Unnatural Emotions: Everyday Sentiments on a*

Micronesian Atoll and Their Challenge to Western Theory (Chicago, 1988); Robert I. Levy, *Tahitians: Mind and Experience in the Society Islands* (Chicago, 1973); Carol Z. Stearns and Peter N. Stearns, eds., *Emotion and Social Change: Toward a New Psychohistory* (New York, 1988); Arlie R. Hochschild, *The Managed Heart: Commercialization of Human Feeling* (Berkeley, Calif., 1989); and Arlie R. Hochschild with Anne Machung, *The Second Shift: Working Parents and the Revolution at Home* (New York, 1989).

6. Colin Campbell, *The Romantic Ethic and the Spirit of Modern Consumerism* (Oxford, 1987); Neil McKendrick, John Brewer, and J. H. Plumb, *The Birth of a Consumer Society: The Commercialization of Eighteenth-Century England* (Bloomington, Ind., 1982).

7. Invocation of gender and use of terms like *patriarchy* continue to be red flags to a few teachers who view their history or literature classrooms as final bastions against the chaos of modern life. In urging that these issues be treated, I do not endorse a single political formula; they can and should be taught as part of an open-ended inquiry, not as obligatory paeans to the women's movement. The fact remains that subjects like patriarchy add a vital analytical perspective on how cultures operate.

8. Paul Gagnon, "Multicultural and Civic Education: Can They Live Together?," *Basic Education* 35 (1991): 5.

9. Immanuel Wallerstein, *The Modern World-System: Capitalist Agriculture and the Origins of the European World-Economy in the Sixteenth Century* (New York, 1974), *The Modern World-System II: Mercantilism and the Consolidation of the European World-Economy, 1600–1750* (New York, 1980), and *The Modern World-System III: The Second Era of Great Expansion of the Capitalist World-Economy, 1730–1840s* (San Diego, Calif., 1989).

10. The most extensive discussions of moral economy as a theoretical structure are in James C. Scott, *The Moral Economy of the Peasant: Rebellion and Subsistence in Southeast Asia* (New Haven, Conn., 1976), and *Weapons of the Weak* (New Haven, Conn., 1987). On modernization, a relevant recent application with abundant references is Gilbert Rozman et al., *The Modernization of China* (New York, 1982).

11. Alan Kennedy, "Memory and Values: Disengaging Cultural Legacies," *Liberal Education* 77 (May/June 1991): 34–39.

12. J. M. Greevy and L. Hyink, *Documentary History Exercise*, Tech. Rep. no. H-1, Teacher Assessment Project, Stanford University, Palo Alto, 1989.

13. Samuel Wineburg, "On the Reading of Historical Texts: Notes on the Breach between School and Academy," *American Educational Research Journal* 28 (1991): 495–519. Wineburg says: "What accounts for the fact that a group of bright high school seniors displayed such a rudimentary sense of how to read a historical text? How could they know so much history, yet have so little sense of how to read it?" (p. 511).

14. Joan W. Scott, "The Campaign against Political Correctness: What's Really at Stake," *Change* 23 (1991): 43.

15. Richard Hofstadter, *Great Issues in American History* (New York, 1969); and Howard Zinn, *A People's History of the United States* (New York, 1990).

16. Roland Marchand, *Advertising the American Dream: Making Way for Modernity, 1920–1940* (Berkeley, Calif., 1985).

17. Chandra T. Mohantry, "On Race and Voice: Challenges for Liberal Education in the 1990s," *Cultural Critique* 14 (1991): 204.

18. Bryan D. Palmer, *Descent into Discourse: The Reification of Language and the Writing of Social History* (Philadelphia, Pa., 1990); Elizabeth A. Smith and Ellen Somekawa, "Theorizing the Writing of History: Or, 'I Can't Think Why It Should Be So Dull, for a Great Deal of It Must Be Invention,'" *Journal of Social History* 22 (1988): 149–61.

For recent and thought-provoking discussion of historians' approach to "objective" reality and of evolution in this approach, see Peter Novick, *That Noble Dream: The "Objectivity Question" and the American Historical Profession* (New York, 1988), and the discussion of Novick's book by J. H. Hexter and others, "The Objectivity Question and the Future of the Historical Profession," *American Historical Review* 96 (1991): 675–708.

19. This is a basic point in Eugene D. Genovese, *Roll, Jordan, Roll: The World the Slaves Made* (New York, 1976).

20. These points are elegantly made with references to feminism and the canonical debates in Elizabeth Fox-Genovese, *Feminism Without Illusions: A Critique of Individualism* (Chapel Hill, N.C., 1991), pp. 191–205.

21. Fields within history that have failed to make the turn to a more conceptual approach, relying instead on purely factual narrative combined with interpretation of events rather than a larger analytical framework, have frankly withered on the vine. Diplomatic history, once a flourishing staple, now barely survives save in the contemporary field, where recording functions still serve good purpose. Some diplomatic history has migrated to political science, where conceptualization is more readily acceptable. The position of the field in history is a serious scholarly challenge, with significance for teaching in this international context as well. It reminds us, however, of how much historical scholarship has changed overall, and of the kind of conversion necessary to keep teaching apace with current trends.

Chapter Seven

1. Donna Van Raaphorst, "The United States History Course: Expectations, Realities, and Recommendations," *Ohio Council for the Social Studies* 26 (1990): 19–23.

2. George Reid Andrews, "Comparing the Comparors: White Supremacy in the United States and South Africa," *Journal of Social History* 20 (1987): 585–99; John W. Cell, *The Highest Stage of White Supremacy: The Origins of Segregation in South Africa and the American South* (Cambridge, 1982); George M. Frederickson, *White Supremacy: A Comparative Study in American and South African History* (New York, 1981); Stanley B. Greenberg, *Race and State in Capitalist Development: Comparative Perspectives* (New Haven, Conn., 1980); David Brion Davis, *Slavery and Human Progress*

(New York, 1984); Peter Kolchin, *Unfree Labor: American Slavery and Russian Serfdom* (Cambridge, Mass., 1987).

3. This is also an area in which, at the college level, we need new reward structures. The division between teaching and research, which I have already discussed in terms of some of its unnecessary dichotomizing, has further tended to confine definitions of teaching to classroom performance, or of research to the inevitable scholarly monograph. Both sets of criteria remain important, but along with rewards for curricular planning we also need to encourage works of scholarship that synthesize information for classroom use. The array of teachable materials available to handle new topics—but particularly new analytical goals and new integrations—is surprisingly scanty in many instances.

4. Alan Kennedy, "Memory and Values: Disengaging Cultural Legacies," *Liberal Education* 77 (May/June 1991): 34–39.

5. The need to view the United States in an international context is a crucial invitation to new kinds of historical synthesis, leading to important organizing questions in both the American and world history fields. The quest to determine whether the United States is a separate (exceptional) civilization provides one angle. Another investigates issues about the United States's impact on the world at large as it gained international influence after about 1870. See Peter N. Stearns, "Point of View: U.S. History Must Be Taught as Part of a Much Broader Historical Panorama," *Chronicle of Higher Education*, January 3, 1990, p. A44. A third angle involves the exploration of international impacts on the United States, including the relationship of global conditions to U.S. culture in its imperialist, isolationist, and cold war phases. The interpretive challenge and its teaching ramifications in these connections are fascinating.

6. Charles Tilly, *Big Structures, Large Processes, Huge Comparisons* (New York, 1984); Olivier Zunz, ed. *Reliving the Past: The Worlds of Social History* (Chapel Hill, N.C., 1985).

7. Immanuel Wallerstein, *The Modern World-System: Capitalist Agriculture and the Origins of the European World-Economy in the Sixteenth Century* (New York, 1974), *The Modern World-System II: Mercantilism and the Consolidation of the European World-Economy, 1600–1750* (New York, 1980), and *The Modern World-System III: The Second Era of Great Expansion of the Capitalist World-Economy, 1730–1840s* (San Diego, Calif., 1989).

8. Without meaning to bury current controversies in the footnotes, I would like to stipulate here that *world history* does not mean simply the substitution of African for Western emphases in high school classes. Neither society was the world, and even in combination they omit some important comparative themes.

9. Stearns, "Point of View."

10. Paul Simon, *The Tongue Tied American: Confronting the Foreign Language Crisis* (New York, 1980); American Council on Education, *What We Can't Say Can Hurt Us: A Call for Foreign Language Competence by the Year 2000* (Washington, D.C., 1989); Commission on Foreign Language and International Study, *Strength through Wisdom: A Critique of*

U.S. Capability. A Report to the President's Commission on Foreign Language and International Studies (Washington, D.C., 1979); Merle Krueger and Frank Ryan, eds., Language and Content (Lexington, Mass., 1992).

11. Assessment of American Colleges, Program Review and Educational Quality in the Major (Washington, D.C., 1992); and Association Task Force, "Liberal Learning and the History Major," American Historical Association Perspectives 28, no. 5 (May 1990): 3–5.

12. The New York State Social Studies Review and Development Committee, One Nation, Many People: A Declaration of Cultural Interdependence (Albany, N.Y., 1991).

13. Nathan Glazer, "In Defense of Multiculturalism," New Republic, September 2, 1991, pp. 18–22.

14. Political realities may soon generate another spur for a serious linkage between constituency demands for multiculturalism in the schools and the scholarly basis for treatment of cultural diversity as a vital theme in American society. The need to incorporate a variety of groups under the multicultural banner risks conflict with a frequent, de facto implementation of multiculturalism as a largely African American preserve. Multiculturalism in theory allows for many groups, but decisions about who gets what treatment may in practice be genuinely difficult, and this is where a larger framework comes in—one that defends multiculturalism but also provides ways to select case studies that illustrate broader points and that link multicultural perspectives to other themes such as the manipulation of political power. Curricular planning that is based on research syntheses exploring relationships among cultural groups and racial issues in U.S. history will facilitate compromises in what might otherwise become blatant turf battles—compromises that maintain the larger excitement of dealing with cultural pluralism while sustaining analytical coherence.

Conclusion

1. For example, in 1992 Pennsylvania issued a new set of educational goals for secondary schools, replacing mere course requirements. They included important criteria in the area of mathematics and science and also in the area of general values, but they left "humanities and the arts" essentially undefined and set no analytical requirements for understanding how societies work. This report was criticized from several angles; among other things, it incorporated no clear sense of the humanities except as repositories of standard cultural forms—save insofar as, in unspecified ways, humanities courses might relate to the tolerant values being sought.

2. Diane Ravitch, "Multiculturalism: E Pluribus Plures," American Scholar (Summer 1990): 339–47; Andrew Barnes, "Blaspheming Like Brute Beasts: Multiculturalism from a Historical Perspective," Contention: Debates on Society, Culture, and Science (Spring 1992): 37–58.

3. An essential part of this argument, offered in earlier chapters, points out the other work that connects solid new scholarship with ambitious yet feasible teaching agendas. Several essays in the Bradley Commission report do this for history, as does Elizabeth Fox-Genovese's discussion of the

application of feminist findings to humanities teaching. See also the curriculum proposals relating to social history and world history alike in Bernard R. Gifford, ed., *History in the Schools: What Shall We Teach?* (New York, 1988), which are based on pre-canonist, pre–political correctness curricular conferences.

4. CHART project sponsored by the Connecticut Humanities Alliance, Annie Fischer School, Hartford Conn., 1991.

5. See chapter 5, note 7. On the new findings about learning, see Robert S. Siegler, "The Other Binet," *Developmental Psychology* 28 (1992): 180–88.

6. Linda Rosenzweig, "Urban Life and World History: Can Social History Bridge the Gap?," *Social Education* 46 (1982): 186–90; Alan Kennedy, "Memory and Values: Disengaging Cultural Legacies," *Liberal Education* 77 (May/June 1991): 34–39.

7. Samuel Wineburg, "On the Reading of Historical Texts: Notes on the Breach between School and Academy," *American Educational Research Journal* 28 (1991): 495–519; teachers' reports at conference, "Teaching Undergraduate History," Los Angeles, Calif., February 29, 1992.

8. Paul Gagnon, "Multicultural and Civic Education: Can They Live Together?," *Basic Education* 35 (1991): 5.

9. Thomas Prangle, *The Ennobling of Democracy: The Challenge of the Postmodern Age* (Baltimore, Md., 1991).

10. Kennedy, "Memory and Values."

11. Carol Z. Stearns and Peter N. Stearns, *Anger: The Struggle for Emotional Control in America's History* (Chicago, 1987); chap. 6 traces this process in relation to wider changes in American values.

12. Hendrik Hartog, "The Constitution of Aspiration and 'The Rights That Belong to Us All,'" *Journal of American History* 74 (1987): 1015, 1033. For a similar though vague suggestion on the theme of tolerance, see Arthur M. Melzer, "Tolerance 101: A Truce in the P.C. Wars," *New Republic*, July 1, 1991, pp. 10–12.

13. Paul Starr, *Social Transformation of American Medicine*, (New York, 1984), pt. 1.

14. Paul Berman, ed., *Debating P.C.: The Controversy over Political Correctness on College Campuses* (New York, 1992); see also Arthur M. Schlesinger, Jr., *The Disuniting of America* (New York, 1992).

15. See, for example, Ted R. Gurr, *Violence in America*, 3d ed., 2 vols. (Beverly Hills, Calif., 1989).

16. However, the belated gains of some 1960s reforms—like the inquiry method, no longer so labeled—are a reminder that the earlier efforts were not entirely in vain.

INDEX

Multiculturalism, 6, 11, 27–28, 61, 100, 104, 108, 128, 203–5, 231, 248

Napoleon, 189
National Association of Scholars, 2
National Endowment for the Humanities (NEH), 2, 13, 15, 27–28, 62, 114, 209
National History Standards project, 143, 238
Nationalism, 76
New historicism, 38, 147
New York, 27, 127, 203–4, 230

Pacesetter project, 11, 116
Patriarchy, 138, 139, 166
Periodization, 57, 157
Philosophy, 5, 36, 72, 137, 176
Piaget, Jean, 213
Plato, 223
Plutarch, 69, 76
Political correctness, 1, 12, 20, 31, 60–61, 96–104, 117, 122
Portfolios, 10, 114, 236
Post-structuralism, 37–38, 97
Power structures, 167–68
Prisons, 151, 231
Psychohistory, 45

Quantification, 41, 58, 62
"Quarrel between ancients and moderns," 71–72

Ranke, Leopold von, 170
Ravitch, Diane, 127–28, 209
Reagan, Ronald, 12, 28
Reformation, 43, 188
Relativism, 100–122, 155, 165, 230
Renaissance, 30, 43, 67–75, 94, 188
Research, 31–32, 35–61, 110, 247
Rhetoric, 39, 177
Romanticism, 72

Sacajawea, 107
Schlesinger, Arthur M., 127, 230

Science, 4–5, 16, 23, 24, 69, 70–71, 73, 113, 132, 137, 147, 148, 157, 193–94, 225, 228
Scientific management, 151
Scientific revolution, 185, 188
Sequence: of humanities courses, 189–92
Sexuality, 138
Shakespeare, William, 38, 72, 74, 76, 70, 94, 170
Slavery, 40, 51, 82, 92, 168, 176
Snow, C. P., 23, 81
Social history, 22, 39–44, 48, 49, 54, 62–63, 124, 128, 167, 215
Socialism, 176
Social studies, 5, 218, 236
Society for State and Local History, 62
Sociology, 4, 21, 35, 58, 137, 145, 178
Socratic tradition, 78, 98, 226
Sources, 153–54, 211
Sports, 225
Stanford University, 30, 95, 112, 142
State and society, 49, 50, 76, 229

Teacher training, 115, 133, 197–98, 201–2
Teaching, 111, 216
Testing, 3, 14, 19, 24–27, 83–84, 87–88, 90, 113–14, 119, 134, 167–74, 199–200, 202
Texas, 62, 87, 180
Textbooks, 3–4, 62–63, 87, 115, 100–102
Thelen, David, 116
Theory, 143–51, 179
Thucydides, 56
Tilly, Charles, 49, 187
Tubman, Harriet, 21, 101

U.S. Department of Defense, 2, 99
U.S. Department of Education, 15, 27

Vietnam, 89
Violence, 231